LETTI

The Fast-Bowling Thre

C000156141

Simon Wilde is a senio
Times. Both *Letting Rip* and his first cricket book, a
biography of the legendary Ranjitsinhji (1990), were
runners-up in the William Hill Sports Book of the
Year. *Ranji* was acclaimed as 'arguably the best
cricket biography of the decade'.

By the same author

RANJI: A GENIUS RICH AND STRANGE (1990)

LETTING RIP

The Fast-Bowling Threat from Lillee to Waqar

SIMON WILDE

GOLLANCZ/WITHERBY

LONDON

To My Father
Who took me to see Fred
beat the Australians

First published in Great Britain
by H. F. & G. Witherby 1994

First Gollancz/Witherby Paperback edition published 1995
by Victor Gollancz
An imprint of the Cassell Group
Wellington House, 125 Strand, London WC2R 0BB

© Simon Wilde 1994

The right of Simon Wilde to be identified as author of
this work has been asserted by him in accordance with
the Copyright, Designs and Patents Act, 1988

Photographs by Patrick Eagar

A catalogue record for this book is
available from the British Library

ISBN 0 85493 244 5

Photoset by Rowland Phototypesetting Ltd
Bury St Edmunds, Suffolk
Printed and bound in Great Britain by
The Guernsey Press Co. Ltd., Guernsey, Channel Islands

Contents

Introduction

This is not intended to be a definitive history of modern fast bowling. There have been so many outstanding exponents of the art over the past twenty years that it would take twenty volumes to do justice to them all. Dennis Lillee, Jeff Thomson, Michael Holding, Andy Roberts, Bob Willis, Joel Garner, Geoff Lawson, Malcolm Marshall, Richard Hadlee, Imran Khan, Craig McDermott, Merv Hughes, Courtney Walsh, Curtly Ambrose, Wasim Akram and Waqar Younis all deserve – if they have not had already – tributes to their skills and extensive achievements. And behind them lie many other excellent performers, bowlers such as Wayne Daniel, Sylvester Clarke, Sarfraz Nawaz, Len Pascoe, Garth le Roux, Patrick Patterson, Winston Davis, Ian Bishop, Allan Donald and Devon Malcolm, some of whom would certainly have gained more recognition in another era and some who may yet go on to greater things. As Imran has said, there were never so many fine fast bowlers playing at one time as there was between 1976 and 1986.

But it is the batsmen for whom I feel the greatest admiration. They have had to withstand this physical and mental onslaught. Many have tried, many have failed, and a glorious few have not only avoided the casualty wards and psychiatrists' chairs but have also managed to score a few runs in the meantime. What on earth makes them want to do it?

This is just one view of one of the most extraordinary and exciting periods in cricket's history, a period in which the game was driven by the money that had flooded in, which drove the all-consuming desire to win, which drove the all-consuming desire for pace, which is the most efficient form of attack yet devised, until it no longer bore any resemblance to the elegant spectacle that it represented to past generations and present romantics.

I'm not saying that the game as it used to be played was any worse for being more sedentary than it is today. It certainly had enough about it to get me hooked as a teenager, when I would race away from school in the direction of Headingley cricket ground to catch the end of Geoffrey Boycott's 24 not out against Gloucestershire. I used to try to hook potential girlfriends by investing in them my enthusiasm. It always failed. 'Uh, cricket!' they used to say. 'I can't stand cricket. It's so *slow*.'

If only they'd stuck around.

Simon Wilde
London, December 1994

I

Nasty, Brutish and Short

As anyone who has ever played the game will know, a cricket ball is a hard object. A sense of trepidation lurks in the mind of any batsman standing at the crease waiting to receive a delivery from someone whose aim is to bowl as fast as he can. The ball may be beguilingly light at slightly over five and a half ounces, but a direct hit can deliver anything from a nasty bruise to an unanticipated death. Anyone familiar with wielding a bat knows that one of its primary functions is to assist self-preservation.

To glimpse a new cricket ball is to glimpse your own mortality. Blood-coloured leather glistens with more than a hint of the life-stuff itself and the delicate stitching of twine that holds together the two lids of leather around the cork centre resembles a surgeon's work on a split eyelid. In the broad, bare hand of a strong fast bowler of a certain disposition, this object constitutes a lethal weapon.

At the root of every cricket match is a primal confrontation. It may be a team game, but each delivery is a contest between batsman and bowler, between hunter and hunted. When a fast bowler is involved, this contest is all the more elemental. One of the most common questions asked of professional batsmen is, 'Who is the fastest bowler you have faced?'; one of the most common questions asked of fast bowlers is, 'Do you set out deliberately to hit batsmen?' What the questioner is really asking is, 'How much do you enjoy the hunt?'

Few fast bowlers attempt to articulate what the pursuit feels like. Frank ('the Typhoon') Tyson talked of revelling in the 'glad animal action' of bowling fast, of the sense of omnipotence it offered. Dennis Lillee may have expressed it best. 'It's the scent of battle that keeps you going. It's a packed crowd chanting "Lil-lee . . . Lil-lee". It's the air of expectancy that holds the ground when you have the new ball in your hand and a fair breeze on your shoulder. It's the sheer "I can fly" exhilaration of being able to bowl really fast. It's seeing that look of apprehension on your quarry's face.'

OK. So like every other Englishman, you think you want to open the batting for your country in a Test match at Lord's? To do so would be a dream come true. All right, let's enter that dream and see what happens. For reasons that will become clear, it is not the here and now but some time in the recent past; say, the early eighties.

Yours is a spectacular rise. You are twenty-two years old and have had three seasons of elegant run-making for your county. You begin the season well and only narrowly miss selection for the first Test match against West Indies, who are the touring team this year. The West Indies are a strong team and they win the first Test match comfortably. By the second Test the selectors feel they can ignore you no longer. You are chosen and are to be given your chance at the top of the order.

Before the match, you practise in the nets at the Nursery End with the rest of the England party. You are pleased with your first net, in which you get your off-drive (your best stroke) going nicely, but during your second net one of the England coaches comes over and insists that you have a session against tennis balls bowled at you from eighteen yards.

The morning of the match dawns bright. About an hour before the start of play the team has a workout on the outfield and half an hour before the start the captains toss. Watching from the balcony, you learn from a signal from Mike Gatting – who happens to be the captain of this imaginary England team – that you are batting first. You retreat into the dressing room to put on your body armour, leaving you no time to spare before you are required to go out to bat.

You are to open the innings with Geoff Boycott, who gets ready much quicker than you and is now preparing to bat by twisting and jumping up and down on his toes in another corner of the room. Gatting, the number three, has his pads on and is buzzing round the room repeatedly banging a ball up and down on his bat. David Gower is doing a crossword, while Allan Lamb is on his mobile phone trying to get a friend to place his bets on the afternoon's races. Ian Botham, a bag of nerves, is smoking incessantly. The five-minute bell sounds, followed shortly by a ripple of applause signalling the emergence on to the field of the umpires. The twelfth man comes in to say that the fielding side are on their way out and before you know it your team-mates are offering you back slaps of good luck and encouragement and you're on your way out of the dressing room and down the stairs. (Because it's a Test match and because there are dangerous fast bowlers on show, all your team-mates will watch at least the first half-hour of play intently from the balcony.) By this point your heart is in your mouth, but you console yourself with the knowledge that at least, as you're opening and going out with an experienced partner, you won't lose your way in the Lord's pavilion (as David Steele did in his first Test match in 1975) and end up in the gentlemen's toilet in the basement.

You get out to the middle and first thing you notice – having overcome the shock of the size and noise of the crowd – is how far back the wicketkeeper and the slips are standing. (In fact, they are not as far away as the Australia cordon were at Sydney in January 1975, when they stood thirty-six metres from the England batsmen for Jeff Thomson.) You assure Boycott that you are happy to take first strike.

Michael Holding is to open the West Indies bowling from the Nursery End. As he runs in for his first ball, you find yourself almost mesmerized by the effortless and rhythmic way he shimmers over the turf towards you. He has a particularly long run because it helps him build up momentum and the way his head rocks gently with each stride is enough in itself to make you forget what you are about. The umpire will barely hear anything until Holding bangs down his left foot in delivery stride. Not for nothing is he known as Whispering Death.

Right. Here it comes. Your first ball in Test cricket. Fortunately, because Holding has such a classic means of delivery you are able to get an early sight of it. It's straight, perhaps slightly on off-stump, and pitches on a fast bowler's normal length. Your eyes send a message to your brain to move your arms, your legs and your hips. You get across, the bat comes down. *Chrrrrist!* The ball isn't there. After pitching it has exploded like a rocket off the seam towards the slips. One thought goes through your head: that is the fastest ball you have ever faced.

In fact, it was no more than a loosener. The next ball is a bouncer, which you are a little slow ducking – Holding's bouncer is about the best in the modern game – and it strikes you a glancing blow on the head. The impact shocks you and you feel like yelling with joy when you remember that you are wearing a helmet and have escaped unhurt. Your appreciation of Holding the athlete evaporates. This guy is like a Hound of Hell. He would rip your ears off with his teeth given half the chance.

Later in the over, Holding gives you another short ball which you shape to hook at before realizing that it is not going to get up sufficiently, and the ball hits you on the arm protector. Your forearm is so badly jarred you wonder whether the bone might be damaged. It could be – Jeremy Coney once had his forearm broken by Joel Garner despite wearing similar protection – but it isn't, and after a couple of minutes the pain is forgotten. You've got other things to think about.

At the end of the over, Boycott comes down the pitch and tells you sternly to give up all ideas of hooking: if you show you are keen to hook, he says, they will feed you the shot and sooner or later you will give a catch. Besides which, he adds, it is very dangerous. Don't you remember what happened to Derek Randall? He once misjudged a hook against Holding, splitting his upper lip and smashing his nose and teeth. Blood spurted everywhere. Or what about the captain himself? Gatting got caught in two minds going to pull a ball from Malcolm Marshall – who is now pacing out his run at the Pavilion End – and had his nose smashed so badly that they found a piece of bone embedded in the ball. Desmond Haynes, who was fielding bat-pad at the time, likened the injury to a shotgun blast. When Gatting later went to blow his nose, blood had gushed out of the top. OK, so you're wearing a face grille on your helmet, but that's no guarantee against injury. People have had the grille dented so badly that they've sustained fractured cheekbones before now.

Marshall is surprisingly small for a fast bowler. He is built like a water biscuit. Botham reportedly refers to him as 'the skinny wimp', although he may not say that to his face. You watch him from the non-striker's end. There seems little that is threatening about his fast-pedalling run-up or fluid delivery, but when you come to face him you find his arm action is so fast it is difficult to sight the ball and when you do it always seems to come skidding through to you at head height. Nor does it always come through at the same speed, for Marshall has some subtle variations in pace. If you don't want to end up like Andy Lloyd, who spent nine days in hospital and reckons he never recovered 30 per cent of his right-eye vision, it's best to keep your eyes on the ball when facing Marshall. Being astute, though, you notice that Marshall does not often bowl at the stumps and you are able to leave alone many of his deliveries. When he strays slightly down the leg side, you tuck him away to fine leg for a single.

You are off the mark but your relief is tempered by the knowledge that you have retained the strike and must face Holding again. He quickly drops you another bouncer. In order to evade it you find yourself leaping off your feet as you coil under the ball – and you discover why Boycott was so keen to do those jumping exercises in the dressing room. This is followed by a devastating yorker – this is a favourite combination of Holding's – and you do well to get half a bat and half a boot to it. It is just as well you are wearing steel toecaps.

Holding is now fully loosened up and really slipping it. Apart from anything else, he is bowling so straight that he is regularly hitting the seam: the ball is flying all over the place. During a competition staged in Australia in January 1979, his bowling was timed at 87.76 miles per hour. Only Thomson was faster: he was measured at 91.86 miles per hour (and he'd had his shoulder injury by then). Just think about it. The ball is being propelled at around 90 miles per hour by a man some nineteen and a half yards from you. It will take, therefore, just 0.44 seconds to reach you, or little more than two-fifths of a second. *Two-fifths of a second!* In which to pick up the flight of the ball from the bowler's hand, judge its speed and length, decide whether or not you are going to play a stroke, if so, which stroke it should be, and then execute that stroke. According to studies carried out in Western Australia twenty years ago, it takes a batsman about 0.3 seconds to react to the ball (that is, see the ball, predict its course and decide on a stroke) and another 0.3 seconds to perform the chosen stroke, a total of 0.6 seconds. If some deliveries take only 0.44 seconds to reach you, the only way to give yourself even a chance of coping with them is by starting to react before the bowler has released the ball, or starting to play your stroke before knowing where the ball will pitch. It may sound bizarre, but this is exactly what the world's best batsmen sometimes have to do. Usually this involves a step back and across, to get themselves into what they expect to be – God preserve them – the line of the oncoming thunderbolt. John Snow meant it when he said, 'Speed defeats reactions.'

Not only do you have to half-anticipate events; if you get the timing of your stroke even fractionally wrong, you are in trouble. You cannot be late on your shot, or indeed early. Being

one-twentieth of a second late could, for example, be the difference between the ball going wide of gully for four runs and
flying into the hands of first slip. If it is the latter, you will have
let down your team-mates and your team's supporters, and you
might contribute to your team's defeat – in which case you will
be vilified in the national press and your place for the next
match will be in jeopardy. Alternatively, one-twentieth of a
second early on, say, a hook shot and probably the next thing
you'll know after the flash-thought, 'Oh God, I've got this one
wrong', will be – in keeping with the time-honoured threat
of all fast bowlers – hospital food. Such things as these are
determined by your actions inside two-fifths of a second. And
when your enemy is two-fifths of a second, there can be no
refuge. It takes more than two-fifths of a second to read this
sentence.

Somehow, you and Boycott survive the next half-dozen overs.
Some of the balls are simply best left alone, others inevitably
hit you, more still you evade by the skin of your teeth. (Boycott,
masterfully, drops two or three throat balls dead at his feet.) A
handful realize runs, mainly through edges square or behind
the wicket, though Boycott pushes one half-volley from Holding
through the covers for two. You, too, receive a half-volley, from
Marshall, but you are so surprised to see it – you had long ago
given up thoughts of scoring runs in favour of those of survival
– that you flash at it stupidly and miss out. Rightly, you curse
yourself, for you realize it will be a while before you see one
of those again. They don't believe in letting you get on to the
front foot in the West Indies. As they like to say out there, if
you want to drive, go and rent a car.

Marshall is not happy. He is nearing the end of his spell, and
decides to go round the wicket. This is bad news. It means that
from that angle he will be directing the ball into your body and,
short of making a rapid retreat towards square leg (a manoeuvre
more common among respected players than you would think,
the young Richard Hadlee among them), you'll just have to
make sure you don't miss the ball with your bat. It is a common

and perfectly legitimate tactic but it is one reason why some people think that Bodyline is not a strategy last seen in the thirties but one that is still alive and kicking off just short of a length on many modern Test match grounds. (Harold Larwood, the principal agent of Bodyline, has recently claimed that the tactic is far more aggressive now than it was sixty years ago. 'I might sometimes have bowled at the batsman's ribs,' he said, 'but never at his head.')

By now, the blood is really starting to pulse in your temples and your heart is pounding like it is the size of a cricket ball. You are living on pure adrenaline. Being confronted by such raw pace is, as Peter Roebuck claims, like being on a drug, 'self-preservation being a powerful force'. It is, as Robin Smith has said, 'unbelievably exhilarating'. You are actually starting to enjoy this.

Several times against Marshall the ball thumps into your chest protector or whistles past your face. You try not to look intimidated but it obviously doesn't work because during one of your mid-wicket conferences Boycott warns you not to shuffle your feet or look anxious because these guys will sense it and you'll be finished. (There is, anyway, something decidedly predatory about Marshall. Whenever he races in, shoulders rocking rhythmically, you can't help but think of the stealthy beat of the *Jaws* music. Dean Jones once likened these guys to sharks: one sniff of blood and they're in for the kill.) Actually, you don't look too bad; certainly not as bad as Gordon Greenidge did against Lillee and Thomson on his first tour of Australia, when he was so terrified he could feel the bat shaking in his hands. Perhaps you should try humming Beethoven; it used to work for Mike Brearley. Then again, maybe it didn't.

There is a bowling change. You have escaped the clutches of Whispering Death. You let out a sigh of relief. Perhaps there will now be an opportunity for you to get the score moving, because so far you've hardly had a chance to get out of the crease. You can take consolation from the fact that Gatting is also predominantly a front-foot batsman and will face similar

frustrations, but not from the fact that it is Boycott's belief –
as he once told Dennis Amiss – that you will never be a Test
batsman off the front foot. Then you notice that the new
bowler is Colin Croft. He is even taller than Holding, and is
arguably the most aggressive man ever to don whites. For
some reason you again find yourself taking first ball from him.
Boycott is up the other end, which they do say is the best
place from which to watch top-quality fast bowling. Are you
sure you still want to go on with this? We could stop now if
you like . . .

Croft does not bother even to start by bowling over the
wicket, but straight away goes round. He comes gangling in,
into an open-chested delivery, his delivery arm almost over his
left ear and his feet splayed and so near to the edge of the
crease that the ball comes at you from the edge of a pavilion
sightscreen. It is a ferocious force coming out of a black hole.
You again have problems picking up the flight. Croft's most
deadly ball is the one that – contrary to everything you'd expect
from his action – darts away off the pitch to take the outside
edge, but this ball is of fairly full length and rips into you off
the seam, rapping you on the inside of your right thigh. It's just
as well you are wearing a pad there. Many players don't bother
but anyone who's heard about the cysts they had to cut from
Bruce Laird's leg after the battering he once took in a Packer
match will not need to be reminded twice. Croft appeals for
leg-before but the umpire turns it down; with Croft's slant and
the Lord's slope the ball would have comfortably missed leg-
stump. The decision inspires a lot of hand clapping and chatter
from Death Row (the slips area) and someone makes some
comment about having seen better bats in a cave. Ignore them.
You're still alive and ducking.

Croft bowls from so wide of the crease that you find yourself
constantly wanting to reach for the ball with your arms away
from your body, so you quickly change your guard from middle
to off-stump, a sensible move. Many of his deliveries also come
through at around chest and head height, which is usual for

him. Many of the injuries he has caused are head wounds –
indeed he once hit Boycott above the eye in a Test match at the
Oval – and his response would have been the same then as it
is now; he just glares down the pitch at you, as though you
shouldn't be allowed to sway out of the way. They say that
nobody ever cared less about hitting a batsman that Croft.
Something makes you check that your box is still in place,
although to be honest these guys are quick enough to knock it
inside out if they catch it right. Ask David Lloyd.

There has been another change of bowling. Joel Garner is
coming on for Marshall (I said this was a strong West Indies
side). Garner is huge. He's 6 foot 8 inches and the ball comes
down at you from about nine feet. You watch him bowl the
first over to Boycott. Each ball looks like it is going to be short
but lands on a full length, only to rear up like a snarling dog.
By the time Garner next bowls, you're on strike. The first three
balls rise into your ribs. Each time you get your bat up in an
attempt to play the ball down, but each time all you get to the
ball is your gloves or bat handle. One of these balls squirts
away wide of the slips and you get two runs but you've been
standing still for so long that your knees are stiff and it feels
strange to run. The ball after that is a yorker, which you do
well to dig out. This is followed by a delivery that rises even
higher than the others. It doesn't climb towards your chest but
towards your face and you jolt your head back only just in
time. You feel the brush of air as the crimson blur brushes past
your nose. It's the perfume ball: smell the leather. You let out
a small gasp of relief at having escaped again, and hope no
one has heard you. Even if they have – which they haven't –
you certainly wouldn't have been the first. Viv Richards,
who is standing at first slip – one arm folded, the other playing delicately with the gold crucifix around his neck, as he
chews gum and stares right through you – has heard many a
top batsman squeal only too audibly as the leather tears past
his face.

Only one more ball of the over to go. By this point you are

so shaken you're not quite sure whether it will be the yorker or another bouncer. It's the ball from hell. You find it again flying at your throat, you're slow reacting and instead of dropping your wrists and swaying out of the way you attempt to play the ball. All you do is get a glove to it and the ball balloons off your thumb towards the slips. No one ever gets a release from Death Row. To whoops of delight and pink-palmed high fives, you're on your way.

You made seven runs and, after eighty minutes of play, the score is 21 for one. Although you did not make many, you return to the pavilion (passed on the steps by Gatting, who for some reason is not trotting out with his characteristic briskness) not completely downhearted. Your arm feels sore from the thump it took from Holding and your thumb is throbbing from that last blow from Garner – you are not even sure that it is not broken – but you are close to a state of elation at having survived out there for so long.

In fact, your self-congratulatory mood is misplaced. You survived fifty balls – which, as it happens, is the average number of deliveries it takes these Four Horsemen of the Apocalypse to claim their Test wickets. As a specialist batsman you should be doing better than this average. And, although even the most successful batsmen only score their runs at around twenty per hour against West Indies, you also made your runs slowly. Carry on like this and your place in the team will soon be in danger. And it is only when you reach the confines of the dressing room that you sit in a corner, reflect on what might have happened to you out there, and start to shake uncontrollably.

Do you know you *died* out there?

That may have been only make-believe, but it is the way professional cricket is played in the modern age. And it isn't just when West Indians are bowling. Most sides, whether they are Test, county or state teams, know the power of pace. Ferocious fast bowling is an accepted, and dominant, part of the game. In recent years, both England and Australia Test captains have frankly admitted that if they could muster as much artillery as West Indies, they would use it, and Pakistan and South Africa are well on their way to building up even more sophisticated pace attacks than West Indies. In any case, one lethal weapon can often be enough. You can get hit only by one shell at a time. West Indies may have more fast bowlers than everybody else, and many of them may be among the better ones, but for every ball Marshall fires in at your ribs from round the wicket there could be one from Merv Hughes, of Australia; for every devastating bouncer-yorker combination from Holding could be one from Waqar Younis, of Pakistan. In this age, the fare – and life in the middle – is often nasty, brutish and short.

  If you can't survive, you can't play, it's as simple as that. They probably don't mind breaking your bones, but it's your nerve they really want to crack. It is, literally, the fast route to victory. When Blair Hartland made his Test debut for New Zealand against Pakistan in January 1993, Wasim Akram and Waqar Younis would have failed in their duty if they had not immediately tested him out with the short ball. This they did, and Hartland was left nursing a cut head and split helmet. Whether Hartland will go on to build himself an international career remains to be seen, but if he does it will be only after coming to terms with the fast men. As Peter Roebuck observed: 'If word gets around that "X is shell-shocked" or "Y doesn't fancy it", as soon as they come in the fast bowler will be summoned. The bush telegraph is very effective in cricket.'

  Unfortunately, the bush telegraph doesn't publish weekly statistics. It would be useful if it did. They would be far more use than the traditional batting averages on display in the newspapers, in which a figure of fifty might disguise a century off an innocuous undergraduate attack in the Parks and a duck against Waqar at the Oval. What the bush telegraph might tell us is that, although there was some nifty footwork against the spinners in the Parks, it was nothing to the footwork going on in the direction of square leg at the Oval.

  A few examples might help illustrate the point. Glenn Turner and Zaheer Abbas both finished with outstanding – and, as it happened, remarkably similar – career records: over 34,000 runs, average of around fifty, over 100 hundreds. The sort of figures only a handful of batsmen achieve. Real all-time-great material. Both, also, were established players by the time the 'rules of engagement' began to change.

Let's take Turner first. His Test record for New Zealand was also good (nearly 3,000 runs, average 44). However, his Test career was effectively over by 1977, before his thirtieth birthday. After that, his only international appearances for New Zealand were based around the 1979 and 1983 limited-overs World Cups. Turner spent potentially his best years as a batsman in dispute with the New Zealand cricket authorities. He had a seemingly endless list of grievances he wanted settled before he would play, most of them involving money. Turner had a strong belief in his own monetary worth, although strangely enough he did not join Packer, who was just the man to help a cricketer fulfil his pecuniary potential. As far as Turner was concerned, if the New Zealand cricket board could not provide, others would. As a result, you had the bizarre situation of New Zealand playing Test matches while their best batsman was in the commentary box giving his opinion on play to television viewers.

Whether money was the only reason for Turner's absence is far from clear, however. Five of the first seven Test series Turner missed were against England, Australia and West Indies and many fine fast bowlers were in their ranks. These matches would have provided Turner with the opportunity to confirm his position as one of the world's leading batsmen. Yet he chose not to play in Tests for his country, seemingly content to forego the chance for further glory. The world was left to speculate on whether or not he was capable of meeting the sternest challenges.

Moreover, Turner was involved in two strange incidents late in his career. The first was for Worcestershire against West Indies in 1980. Against Marshall, Croft and Garner, Turner batted in the most reckless fashion, stepping back and slogging at almost every delivery, and making 45 in 24 balls in the second innings before stepping on his wicket. Some suggested that he had not wanted to play in the match because of a back strain (Roy Booth, the county chairman, later interviewed Turner and issued a statement that the player had no grievance with the club); others, that his approach was linked to criticisms he had made of West Indies' conduct on their recent tour of New Zealand when, even by their standards, they had been bouncer-crazy and fallen out so badly with the umpires that they had almost gone home early.

The second incident was slightly more transparent. It occurred during Turner's last season in county cricket, in 1982. Confronted by the Nottinghamshire pair of Richard Hadlee and Mike Hendrick – both lively bowlers but neither of the highest pace – on a pitch of uneven bounce at Trent Bridge, he again batted perversely, backing away to square leg to guide the ball over the slips and covers or stepping outside off-stump to chip the ball over mid-wicket. He was eventually bowled round his legs for 54. If Turner played this way out of an apprehension of injury, his worst fears were painfully realized in the second innings when he was hit in the ribs by Hendrick and forced to retire hurt. Whatever the precise explanations for these two bizarre performances, Turner was clearly not willing to play fast bowlers in a proper manner.

Zaheer was an artist of an altogether superior strain to Turner. He was a magnificent strokemaker, playing the ball late and – when he was going well – timing it to perfection. His style cast back to the great amateurs of the turn-of-the-century Golden Age, but also gave hints of Viv at his best. The technical margins within which he operated, though, were so fine that he was always vulnerable to losses of form. He scored 5,062 Test runs at an average of 44 (again, a similar figure to Turner's) but his tally was bolstered by eight scores of 168 or more. He was expert at taking his toll of attacks blunted by friendly pitches: all of his twelve Test centuries, and many of his big innings for Gloucestershire, were made on 'belters'. Having said that, he was always a master of spin bowling and in his early years had no undue difficulty with pace, when he fought some brave duels with Dennis Lillee and played a memorable innings of 80 against West Indies in Georgetown in 1977. However, his overall record against Australia and West Indies – the countries who were blessed with the strongest pace attacks during his career – was only modest. He liked to hook but was not particularly good at it, and in his first year with Packer's pace-dominated World Series Cricket he made no impact at all.

Zaheer's ego was reputedly as inflated as many of his shirt-fronted scores, but it was badly punctured during a home series against West Indies in 1980–1, when he was thirty-three. He had shown signs of being suspect against pace in the Caribbean four years earlier. Now, he seemed to be suffering from delayed shell-shock. According to Imran Khan, Zaheer missed the first Test on the pretext of a shoulder injury and when he played in the second 'was in a terrible state against Marshall and Clarke, actually backing away from the fast bowling. I knew that this was the beginning of the end for Zaheer's reputation . . .' In the third Test, Zaheer was hit on the head by a bouncer from Croft, a blow which left a two-inch dent in his helmet. 'He was never the same,' Imran said. Marshall, who felt that Zaheer's reputation must have been made on the comfortable batting surfaces of Bristol, was more blunt: 'He was scared.'

He was certainly never the same. Zaheer promptly surrendered his number three position for Pakistan, dropped down the order to number five and never returned. In October 1985, a month before West Indies were to make their next visit to Pakistan for a series of five one-day games, he announced his retirement from international cricket (this was in the days before legislation was introduced curbing short-pitched bowling in limited-overs games). If this was deliberate it was a smart move by Zaheer, because the series was to be notable for some particularly hostile bowling from Marshall, Holding, Tony Gray and Courtney Walsh. Some would say then that, when it came to bravery, Zed finished up firmly at the end of the alphabet.

In the incidents I have just described, Turner and Zaheer were, of course, lucky to escape serious injury. Turner took a bang on the ribs and Zaheer a crack on the helmet. Big deal. Here's what could have happened; here's the sort of thing they probably feared.

Max Walters was an opening bat for Queensland in the late seventies. Like Zaheer he wore spectacles and like Zaheer was nervous against the short-pitched ball in certain circumstances. In November 1978, Queensland played a fixture against the touring England team on a badly underprepared pitch in Brisbane. The bounce was unreliable and the England bowlers, especially Bob Willis, did not need to drop the ball short for it to spit nastily. Walters was out for a duck in the first innings and clearly had little stomach for the fight by the time he went out to bat a second time. By then, a colleague, David Ogilvie, had been led from the pitch with blood streaming down his neck after he had been hit on the head by a ball from Willis.

Walters looked desperately uneasy, fidgeting and nervous. The situation invited a bouncer. Willis dug one in just short of a length, the ball took off and Walters played back. 'The ball smacked him sickeningly straight between the eyes,' Boycott said. 'There was blood everywhere . . . Mike Brearley began to dash forward from slip and then turned back momentarily to compose himself while Walters doubled up on his knees in the crease. The bridge of his spectacles had been forced into his nose but fortunately the glasses had spun off without breaking.' Walters was helped off the field, took no further part in the game, and never played for Queensland again.

Then there was Roland Butcher. Butcher was a natural stroke-maker. He first played for England in a one-day international in 1980 and began by taking a half-century off Australia in 35 balls. He was then selected for the 1981 tour of the Caribbean, where he struggled in the three Tests he played partly because of an overwillingness to hook the fast bowlers. The way he batted, this was always a problem and during a county match for Middlesex against Leicestershire at Lord's in July 1983 it cost him dear. On an easy-paced pitch, he made 62 in the first innings and had begun batting confidently again in the second when he was early on to a hook shot against a bouncer from George Ferris. Ferris was only eighteen years old but was a bowler of genuine pace.

As usual, Butcher was not wearing a helmet. He just had time to know he had got the shot wrong. He sustained multiple fractures to his left eye-socket and cheekbone and was carried off the field and away to St Mary's Hospital, Paddington. He was in hospital for two weeks. The details of his treatment are not for the squeamish. Although he was in excruciating pain, he could not be given medication for twenty-four hours because he was being monitored for brain damage. The first operation, in which the doctors attempted to wire the smashed bones together, failed; the jaw dropped back down again. The doctors did not seem to know what to do next. After considering putting a steel rim around Butcher's head and pinning the damaged area up from the outside, they opted to re-try the first operation. This time, it worked.

Butcher admitted he had never been so frightened in his life. When his wife, Cheryl, first visited him in hospital she was horrified at his appearance. 'I just wanted to scream. His face looked like someone had forced a cricket ball into his eye and put the skin back over. The left-hand side of his face had caved in.'

Butcher returned the following summer to successfully re-establish himself in the Middlesex side, but it was only after overcoming blurred vision and encountering bouts of depression so extreme that Cheryl considered leaving him. Butcher was told by doctors that if he was hit in the same area again, his playing career would be over. Several years later, it was apparently still possible to feel the wiring under the skin near his left eye.

A similar thing happened to Mark Nicholas, who was said to be never the same batsman against pace after he paid the price for not wearing a helmet against Gladstone Small at Southampton in 1982. He went away with a depressed fracture of the cheekbone.

This is the bottom line for every batsman. They all know that one error of judgement, or even one piece of bad luck, and they could sustain an horrific injury. Not that they can afford to go around thinking like that. As Graham Gooch – one of the best and bravest of batsmen against pace – said: 'If I went out to start an innings thinking about being hit, I could not play the game . . . my entire technique would collapse.' This is, perhaps, what happened to Zaheer.

Some players, like Gooch, have been very good at not thinking about what might happen to them and have won reputations for coolness and tenacity under fire. Some of them have even been specially selected for the toughest assignments and then left out when the circumstances were more relaxed and less suited to their skills.

David Steele was one such man. Called up for the first time at the age of thirty-four to blunt the spears of Lillee and Thomson in 1975, after England had lost five of their previous seven Tests against Australia, he proved a spectacular and unlikely success. Bespectacled and grey-haired, he was dubbed 'the bank clerk who went to war', but thrived on the challenge facing him, one which had recently broken many more naturally talented cricketers than him. Relying on the solid, front-footed defensive technique and powerful concentration that had served him so well in county cricket, Steele accumulated 365 runs in the series, topped the England averages and helped prevent any further losses. Once he had found his way out of the Gents at Lord's, Australia had great difficulty flushing him out.

Steele was retained for England's next series, against West Indies the following summer, when the pace of Holding and Roberts presented similar difficulties. At first, he proved just as obdurate and courageous, scoring a century in the first Test at

Trent Bridge, before West Indies uncovered a weakness in his execution of the hook shot. He nevertheless finished the series as England's leading run-scorer. However, come the winter tour of India, he was unceremoniously omitted because of doubts about his ability to play spin and never played for his country again.

Peter Willey was more obviously suited to the role of street-fighter. A natural back-foot player and immensely powerful, he demonstrated on his first Test appearance – when he took the attack to the West Indies pacemen at Headingley in 1976 and scored 36 and 45 – that fear was not a word in his vocabulary. Fifteen of his 26 Tests were against West Indies sides packed with top-class fast bowling and his record against them (757 runs at an average of 31.54) was noticeably better than it was against other countries (427 runs at 21.35). England won none of these fifteen matches but innings of 62 not out, 100 not out, 102 not out and 67 from Willey played substantial parts in them earning four of their six draws. Willey must be the only man to have square-cut Croft for six in a Test match (at Antigua in 1981: 'I can't remember seeing the ball') and his bravery won him the admiration of colleagues and opponents alike. 'I wouldn't say Willey had a good technique, but he is a very difficult player to dislodge and he doesn't seem afraid,' Holding once said. 'He's always getting across.' Botham reckoned only Gooch was as good a player of West Indies fast bowling as Willey.

So, who are the better batsmen, who the more valuable players? Whose reputations are the least tarnished? The records of Turner and Zaheer ensure that they are players who will be remembered as long as the game is played. Will history remember Steele and Willey, whose career batting averages are no higher than the low 30s but who could be relied on in any test of temperament and courage?

These days, when international cricket is played in such a fierce cauldron of competitiveness, there is no room for those who cannot stand the heat. Chris Smith's England career came to an end for what was no more than a perceived weakness against fast bowling. A couple of catches given to short leg off rising balls and – bang! – he's gone.

It's like that now. It's been like that for over twenty years.

2

The Bowler From Hell

How did we get into this state of affairs? How come the game swung over into the fast lane and stayed there, its foot jammed hard down on the accelerator? What was the inspiration for this obsession with speed? We could spend a long time going down an awful lot of avenues, taking many tracks off the beaten path, seeking out the answers. Should we examine Caribbean cricket's historical preoccupation with pace, dating back at least to Constantine, Martindale and Griffith? Dissect the West Indian fear of defeat and humiliation? Or look at the age-old desire of the horny-handed son of the Ocker soil to come in from the outback and use his muscular advantage to put one over on the Townies? Perhaps we should touch on Australia's need to avenge the injustices of Bodyline, or England's failure to find a fast bowler who could put the fear of God into the Aussies in the way only Larwood, Tyson, Snow and Willis have done this century. All these subjects might be worthy of study. However, I doubt if there would have been any need to do so had there not arrived on the scene a tornado called Thomson.

Jeff Thomson didn't exactly walk in from the outback, but he was an outdoor boy from the outskirts of Sydney who loved the land, the sea and the sky, and felt he was overdressed unless he was barefoot and there was sea salt in his hair. He was at one with nature; indeed, as a sportsman, he was a force of nature himself. There was even something primeval about the way he bowled the ball; that slingshot action of his made him look like he was chucking a spear, made him look like he was a hunter. In his playing days, he was a magnificent athlete, with a superb throwing arm. He was not only powerful, but so supple he could put his feet behind his head. When he bowled, he had an unexpectedly slow run-up to the wicket (it was nearly half the speed of Lillee's approach): he jogged in, mane flopping casually, as though he knew he had his prey within striking distance and was just lining up the killer blow. You bet he was.

Thomson's delivery action was the root of most of the unusual problems he presented batsmen with, aside from the obvious one of the terrific pace he generated. Pulling back his right shoulder two strides out in order to get into position for a long swing of his arm, he showed the batsman only the studs of his left boot and a large area of his back during delivery, and hardly anything of the ball, which spent most of the last seconds before release down by his right thigh and thus concealed by his body. It has been calculated that during the final supercharged sweep of Thomson's right arm above his pivotal left leg, the batsman was allowed a view of the ball for only 0.04 of a second before it left the hand at a speed of 90-odd miles per hour. Picking up the ball's line was therefore a serious problem, especially as Thomson's direction was always liable to be erratic. The other problem was that, because Thomson used his height to the full, the ball would often explode from almost a full length, threatening the chest, neck and head of even the tallest batsmen. In other words, most of his deliveries were very fast bouncers. Greg Chappell described Thomson's throat ball as coming up at you 'like a snake out of the grass'.

Thomson's difficulty was that because of his side-on action he couldn't move the ball the way more chest-on bowlers could. He had to use his wrist to apply the swing rather than the rotation of his body, and he never learned to vary his methods in the way that, say, Lillee did. On pitches with any life in them this was not a problem, as his speed was usually sufficient to account for most batsmen, but on dead, slow pitches, such as those he encountered in Pakistan and occasionally in England, the threats he posed were greatly reduced.

Greg Chappell played a central role in Thomson's meteoric rise to fame. As an established batsman in the Australia side and brother of the national captain, he was in a position to do so. It did not happen immediately. Thomson had played one Test match for Australia, at Melbourne in December 1972 against Pakistan, at the age of twenty-two after displaying in just five state matches for New South Wales his hostility and speed (he had spent the previous five years, in his own words, 'getting wickets and breaking bones and scaring Christ out of everyone that ever walked on to our field'). He was awful, returning figures of 19−1−110−0. The following season Thomson could not even get into the New South Wales side until the final Sheffield Shield match of the season. This proved to be the turning point. The opposition happened to be Queensland, who were in their first season under Greg Chappell's leadership and for whom a win would almost certainly secure them the Shield for the first time after fifty years of trying. On a lively Sydney pitch, Chappell's and Queensland's hopes were destroyed by the devastating speed of Thomson, who claimed nine wickets in 30.5 overs in the match. That he conceded 125 runs, more than four runs an over, was immaterial. At the end of the season, Queensland, saying they'd guarantee him a game, signed Thomson up. He proved his worth immediately. In his first match for the state, in October 1974, he helped Queensland take swift revenge over New South Wales with a nine-wicket win in Brisbane. Thomson had his former team-mates hopping about the crease during 17 fearsome overs which cost 72 runs but reaped six wickets. Chappell later recalled that Thomson bowled as quickly in this match as anyone he had ever seen: 'Absolutely lethal.' At the time, while others thought Thomson too erratic, Chappell advocated his selection for the forthcoming Test series with England. 'He will terrify them out,' he said. 'They'll be running scared.' A month later, they were.

Chappell was, I think, secretly appalled by Thomson's speed. One of the world's best batsmen, he nevertheless admitted in his autobiography that Thomson's bowling in the match in which he denied Queensland the Shield was 'too quick'. (Most batsmen, as we shall see, aren't in the habit of admitting bowlers are 'too quick', even from the safety of retirement.) There was the suspicion that Chappell's eagerness to get Thomson to Queensland was at least partly motivated by a desire on his own part never to face his bowling again (which he never did, although Thomson more than once fractured his fingers when Chappell was obliged to attempt to take screaming catches off his bowling at slip).

England were almost literally caught on the hop in Australia in 1974–5. They had not anticipated being confronted by bowling of extreme pace and had themselves left at home their most hostile and experienced pace man, John Snow, despite the fact that he had played the leading role in England winning the Ashes on their previous tour four years earlier. Snow, though thirty-three years of age, would have been an uncomfortable proposition on the bouncy pitches in Australia. He bowled persistently just short of a length – it was a meanness, Dennis Lillee claimed, to match his spirit – and most of his deliveries rose sharply into the batsman's ribs and chest so that it was hardly necessary for him to bowl an out-and-out bouncer. The problems he would have posed would have been similar, in fact, to those presented by Thomson.

England may not have anticipated coming up against one bowler of extreme pace: what they actually got was two. They did not envisage facing Thomson; nor did they envisage facing the man who shared the new ball with him in the first Test match at Brisbane, Dennis Lillee. It was not that they hadn't heard of Lillee before. They knew his Machiavellian-moustached face only too well after his emergence during their previous tour and his outstanding performances in England in 1972, when perhaps his crowning achievement was putting a yorker through the barely formed defences of Boycott,

England's most technically accomplished batsman, during a one-day match at Lord's. He bowled a fuller length than Thomson but his trademark was a lifting ball on off-stump that was quite deadly. He never let a batsman rest, constantly probing for a breakthrough. Keith Fletcher said that he would expose every area of your technique; Lillee described himself as like a bull terrier who would not let a batsman go if he had him by the throat. However, although Lillee was a fine athlete and had a classical side-on technique, a heavy schedule had taken its toll in the Caribbean eighteen months earlier when he broke down with a stress fracture of the back, an injury so serious that virtually his whole torso was encased in plaster during his recuperation. When he missed the 1973–4 season, most people – England's cricketers among them – gave him little chance of making a full recovery. When he did re-emerge at Brisbane, he bowled well within himself, but as the series progressed he gained in pace as he gained confidence in his strengthening back. In normal conditions, his bowling was only some eight miles an hour slower than Thomson's, which meant Marsh, the Chappell brothers, Mallett and Co in Death Row still standing over thirty metres from the bat, but Lillee undoubtedly found it difficult working himself back to top speed in this series when there was such a tornado blowing at the other end.

England failed to anticipate not only the barrage of bouncers but also a barrage of bad-mouthing. Australia had not beaten England in a Test series for over ten years and Ian Chappell, their captain, who said after the first Test that Lillee and Thomson were the quickest combination he had ever come across, was not slow to make the most of his discovery. His captaincy had always been forthright; now he backed up Lillee and Thomson with an intimidating number of close-in fielders who displayed their ruthless desire for victory not only through brilliant catching but through the verbal liberties they took of their proximity to opposing batsmen. They even had nicknames for each other, the like of which you mightn't call your worst enemy. Lillee, for example, was 'Fot', which was OK until you knew it stood for Fucking Old Tart, and Thomson 'Two-up', because, well, he couldn't give a stuff. Chappell's leadership attracted much criticism, perhaps most graphically from Mike Brearley, who would one day accuse him of having 'nudged cricket in the direction of gang warfare', although few captains with fast bowlers at their disposal have escaped the censure that comes with being seen standing at first slip supervising the systematic scything down of the opposition (and Brearley was certainly not one of them). What has to be said in Chappell's defence is that he himself would never have shirked the challenge of facing his own side's bowling. He was a superb player of pace, not afraid to get in line with the ball and an expert hooker whose attitude to a bouncer was that if you were playing well it was worth four runs.

Most disturbing, though, was the demeanour of Lillee and Thomson themselves. Neither seemed to care a jot whether they hit a batsman or not. In fact, both went on record during the series with England as saying, more or less, that they *wanted* to hit batsmen. In his book *Back to the Mark*, published shortly before the series, Lillee was quoted as saying: 'I bowl bouncers for one reason, and that is to hit the batsman and thus intimidate him . . . I try to hit a batsman in the rib-cage when I bowl a purposeful bouncer and I want it to hurt, so that the batsman doesn't want to face me any more.' Despite arousing much controversy with these remarks, Lillee reiterated them on several occasions, including on television during the Brisbane Test and in *The Art of Fast Bowling*, published three years later, when he wrote that every fast bowler would admit to these sentiments if he were being honest. At least in the latter book Lillee was also honest enough to admit that the bouncer 'should only be used against those batsmen who appear to be capable of handling it'. Unfortunately, Lillee's judgement as to who was, and who was not, capable of handling it often let him down when he got into the middle.

Thomson said some even more bloodthirsty things. Shortly before he left New South Wales, he was quoted in a magazine article as saying that he enjoyed hitting a batsman more than getting him out and it didn't worry him to see a batsman 'rolling around screaming and blood on the pitch'. At the time, it created more publicity for him than anything he had ever done on the cricket field, which was no doubt a factor in what he said, although he was to say plenty of similar things. This is what he said about having smashed someone straight in the eye during a grade match: 'It was frightening to see this bloke just screaming and shaking, and the pitch was splattered with blood as it poured through his fingers. He was in the intensive care unit of the hospital for a week . . . I never let this sort of thing put me off.' (What did make him pause for thought, Thomson said, was the death in December 1975 of his flat-mate Martin Bedkober, who was killed when he was hit in the chest by a fast bowler in a Brisbane club match. He collapsed at the wicket and died two hours later in hospital. *In the chest*. Who said the game's safe now that there are helmets?)

The Australian crowds caught the mood of this underworld language, which the media had not been slow to exploit. As eager for victory as their team, they turned up in huge numbers to watch the Tests with England and roar on the executioners at work. The fact that the pitches on which the Tests were played were – surprise, surprise – fast and uneven ('No one could have played Lillee and Thomson on those pitches,' Fletcher said) served only to whet the appetites of the onlookers. They may or may not have used the words 'kill, kill,' but that was their sentiment. (Gordon Greenidge, of West Indies, recalls that in the Melbourne Test a year later the crowds used exactly those words.) At Sydney, the chants from the crowded Hill of 'Lil-lee . . . Lil-lee' marched in time with the bowler's thirty-yard walk back to his mark and the first half of his run before a ghastly, expectant hush fell as he neared the bowling crease. This wasn't Australia versus England, it was Lions versus Christians, and it wasn't long before the Christians threw down their shields, turned and ran.

England were rather slow on the uptake. They went into the

Brisbane Test suspecting little. They had come across Thomson
in their final warm-up match but he seemed curiously uninspired
(probably because Greg Chappell was deliberately 'hiding' him)
except for his first ball to Dennis Amiss, England's leading batsman, which reared up and struck Amiss a shuddering blow on
the Adam's apple. And when Australia batted first in the Test,
England's innocence was exposed by their liberal use of the
bouncer, with which they claimed five wickets, every one of
which they would gladly hand back by the time the match was
over.

Then the mayhem began. In England's first innings, Amiss
had his thumb broken by perhaps Thomson's deadliest delivery,
an inswinging bouncer bowled from wide of the crease; the ball,
having crunched Amiss's thumb against his bat handle, flew to
gulley where it was caught by Jenner, the first of 38 catches
held by the Australia slip and gulley fielders during the series.
In the second innings, Edrich's right hand was broken by a ball
from Lillee. In the second Test at Perth, it took Thomson only
five balls to inflict his first injury: Luckhurst hit on the top
hand. Although Luckhurst was able to bat on, his hand swelled
overnight so that he was unable to field and had to bat at
number seven in the second innings, x-rays having revealed
broken bones. Later in the same match, Thomson hit David
Lloyd in the groin, denting his box and forcing him to retire
hurt. In the fourth Test at Sydney, Edrich was injured again,
his first ball in the second innings, a skidder from Lillee, fractur-
ing two of his ribs. It was, *Wisden* would report, the 'greatest
battering in the history of the game'.

At first, there was some brave resistance. Edrich toughed it
out for three and a quarter hours before his injury in the first
Test, stemming the tide after an early collapse, and Lloyd self-
sacrificingly offered to take Lillee's bowling when Cowdrey
joined him at the crease in Perth. Cowdrey, aged forty-one and
a proven player of fast bowling, had been flown out to
strengthen the party following the injuries to Amiss and Edrich
in Brisbane. Cowdrey himself got into line well, tirelessly

moving across his stumps (so far that he was once bowled behind his legs), and was the first England batsman to hook Thomson.

It was not long, though, before the teetering walls of resistance fell. Amiss said the England morale started to go as early as the fourth day at Brisbane, when he and Luckhurst had to endure a heated period before stumps. 'It was the most awe-inspiring spell of fast bowling I'd ever faced,' he recalled. 'Lillee and Thomson bowled like men possessed . . . Thomson was warned for sending three whistling past my chin in failing light. He didn't take a blind bit of notice and made no attempt to pitch the ball up – if anything the next four flew even faster past my face.' None of the other players had experienced anything like it either. Even Cowdrey, who had toured Australia five times before, had never seen a bowler extract the sort of lift Thomson did. By the time of the second Test, the England camp was clearly a shambles. Cowdrey, who had only recently arrived, noticed that the match was 'not discussed much among the team' and found himself being asked shortly before the match by the captain, Mike Denness, to bat number three. Denness became completely fazed by the whole affair. Once, when Lloyd returned to the dressing room after batting in the third Test at Melbourne, Denness was shocked to notice Lloyd's whole body quivering. 'His neck and the top half of his body, in particular, were shaking,' Denness said. 'He was shell-shocked, suffering from the effects of never having to move around so quickly in his life.' Denness had to go out and bat shortly after this. He failed for the second time in the match and then, though captain, dropped himself for the next Test. His technique had been exposed. Faced with the highest pace, his first movement had been to step back towards square leg, from which position he would play his only attacking shot, the cut. Seven times in eight innings, he was caught behind or in the slips/gulley region. Most of the England players simply did not have the stomach for the fight. On being joined by Fletcher and asked, 'How's it going?', Edrich – as battled-hardened and experienced as

Cowdrey – had laconically replied: 'One tour too many, Fletch, one tour too many.'

Fletcher, it has to be said, overdid the bravado. By Sydney, most of the players knew which way the wind was blowing, but there was Fletcher encouraging Greig, who had just hit Lillee on the arm with a short ball, to let him 'have it'. Compared to Australian sledging, this was mouse-like in its timidity, but it was like kicking a bull terrier in the street. Lillee alarmed Fletcher by vowing revenge, both at the time and, shortly afterwards, on a national television chat show. When Fletcher's turn to bat came, on the way out he passed Lillee, who growled, 'Good luck, Fletch, you're going to need it.' It was Thomson who provided the *coup de grâce*. He gave him the inswinging bouncer, a delivery of such red-hot virulence that it smashed into Fletcher's cap via his flailing glove – mercifully the glove took the worst of the impact – with such force that the ball bounced out into the covers where it was almost caught by Ross Edwards. Fletcher, hardly surprisingly, was out two balls later. He did not sledge Lillee again.

Long before the series ended, the England players had had enough. They even had a joke that the chair in which sat the next man was the 'condemned cell'. For no one was this more appropriate than Amiss, whose run-scoring abilities had singled him out for special attention from Lillee and Thomson. 'Several times I walked to the middle beaten before I started. The bat in my hand seemed superfluous against those two . . . batting was a complete misery.' Lillee in particular psyched him out, dismissing him for nought in each of his last three innings of the series and getting him cheaply three more times when the sides met in England the following summer. Nought is not many when the previous year you had scored nearly 1,400 runs in 13 Tests. Luckhurst's appetite for the game was dealt an even more severe blow. The Perth Test in which he was injured was the last he ever played and he retired from the first-class game shortly after having his right index finger broken by Sarfraz Nawaz in a county match in June 1976.

Those for whom you felt sorriest were the tailenders, whose batting skills were simply not equal to the terrifying ordeal to which they were subjected. The first ball Underwood ever faced from Thomson nearly took his ear off and Willis frankly admitted that he did not see many of the balls bowled him by Thomson (the whole tour, he admits, was 'quite terrifying'). Arnold, for his part, was lucky to escape serious injury in Sydney, where Lillee gave him one of his infamous off-stump lifters. Arnold, unbelievably, stood stock still, as though transfixed by the brutally hard object hurtling towards him, only for it mercifully to miss him, seeming to brush the contour of his face as it passed (the ball carried on over the head of Marsh, the wicketkeeper, and flew first bounce into the sightscreen). What would have happened had the ball hit Arnold, goodness only knows, but not many people can have come so close to dying on a cricket field. Even Lillee looked relieved.

The only man who responded to the challenge was Tony Greig, the Great Showman himself. Most of Greig's team-mates thought him mad. Here he was, up against the two most fearsome bowlers in the world, and what did he do? Play dice with the Devil, that's all. When he bowled, though he was of only medium pace, he used the bouncer like it was going out of fashion (which it most assuredly was not). He would point dismissed batsmen to the pavilion. When he batted, he used his great height to impudently steer wide, short balls over the slips for four. Having hit Lillee for four, he would go down on one knee and signal a boundary with an exaggerated flourish of his long arm. If Lillee bounced him, he clownishly pretended to try to head the ball away. Signal his own fours? Head the ball? This wasn't kicking the bull terrier, this was taking him by the throat and tickling his tummy.

Surely Greig had got the message at the start, hadn't he? The first ball Lillee had bowled to him at Brisbane had been a bouncer, and after he had bowled it he came down the pitch, fixed Greig's gaze and made a mark on his own forehead with his finger. *He was after him*. It was not that Greig wasn't scared

– before first facing Lillee on his Test debut at Old Trafford in 1972, he had been so nervous he had chain-smoked his way through an entire packet of cigarettes – it was just that he had learned to leave his fear behind in the dressing room. Greig's competitive instincts were on a par with those of his opponents. He loved to rile Lillee, thought it worked to his advantage. On England's previous tour, to the Caribbean, when he had been vice-captain, Greig had adopted similar tactics, orchestrating a campaign of abuse in the belief that he could cajole West Indies into getting out to angry shots, a tactic that had often, admittedly, worked in the past.

Greig also seemed to love the crowds, and the atmosphere. It was like the Colosseum out there, but it inspired Greig. To him it was the equivalent of a billion volts: he described Brisbane, where he scored a century, as 'absolutely electric'. Greig may have had technical flaws – Thomson in particular exploited a weakness to the fast yorker, or 'sandshoe crusher' as he christened it – but he was undoubtedly the batting success of the tour. Most bizarre of all was his eagerness after the close of play to have a few beers and a laugh with Lillee. The man had spent the day trying to terrorize him half to death and there was Greig, playing hail-fellow-well-met with him.

Only Alan Knott, England's wicketkeeper-batsman, was inspired by Greig's example. Knott was a good foot shorter than Greig (who used to be known as five foot nineteen inches) but thanks to a hawkish eye and brilliant use of the upper-cut he was no less adept at slicing boundaries over the slips. Knott was the only other England batsman apart from Greig to score over 350 runs in the series and the only other England batsman apart from Greig to score a century in the five Tests in which Lillee and Thomson played. Knott was by nature more circumspect than Greig – when he struck Thomson for six in the Leeds Test the following summer, he instantly thought of the consequences and wished he hadn't done it, the sort of thought that would never have crossed Greig's mind – but there would

come a time in the not-too-distant future when it was Knott
who had to remind Greig where his courage lay.

Australia, of course, took the series comfortably. They won
four of the first five Tests easily and then, strangely, England
won the sixth and last match by an innings. The ironies of that
last match. With Thomson out of the series having injured his
shoulder playing tennis on the rest day of the previous Test at
Adelaide (when he needed only four more wickets to break
Mailey's record of 36 for an Ashes series) and Lillee breaking
down early in the match after taking his twenty-fifth wicket of
the rubber, England's battered batsmen were allowed to make
hay. None did so more than the hapless Denness, who more
than doubled his run aggregate by scoring 188, an innings that
had a good deal to do with his retaining the captaincy into the
home series with Australia the following summer and perhaps
to the revival that that series witnessed for England's batsmen.
(Although not before England's batsmen had persuaded
Denness to field first in the opening Test at Edgbaston and
thereby delay their reacquaintance with the gruesome twosome,
a decision which cost England the match and Denness his tenu-
ous grip on the leadership.) The irony, too, on the first morning,
of seeing Peter Lever, who could be decidedly sharp on his day,
putting one on the chin of Greg Chappell, who promptly lost
his taste for the battle and was out shortly afterwards. Chappell,
the man who had acted as zephyr to Thomson's tornado, *visibly
squirming*. And then the final, and bitterest irony, that after all
that had happened it should be an England bowler who came
nearest on the tour to actually killing a man. Ewen Chatfield,
the New Zealand number eleven, deflected a bouncer from
Lever into his left temple during a Test match in Auckland.
Chatfield swallowed his tongue, his heart stopped beating and
he was saved only by the quick thinking of Bernard Thomas,
the touring team's physiotherapist, who gave him heart massage
and the kiss of life.

Thomson's shoulder injury in Adelaide was a serious business. It dramatically affected the way he bowled and he added

to the damage when he collided with Alan Turner going for a catch during a Test with Pakistan in the same city two years later. His greatest days were then behind him. Like a comet in the cricket heavens, they had come and gone, leaving a brilliant memory, trailed by a gasp of wonder. 'It was a tragedy he got injured,' Alan Knott said. 'I thought for four Tests he was a genius. After that he never bowled the same and was never as hostile. After his second injury he had a longer run and follow-through. In those first four Tests he had a short run and had completed his follow-through within a pace. And when he threw his bowling arm back for delivery, he used to nearly stroke the ground. For a big man, he was like a bit of rubber.' Willis, too, was full of admiration and feels that others could benefit from emulating Thomson's singular methods. 'He was a brilliant physical specimen. Quite an economical action, although it has never really been repeated. It's perhaps a more natural way to bowl than Dennis Lillee or Fred Trueman. The first shoulder injury certainly diminished both his speed and his control but he still went on to get 200 Test wickets.'

If England thought they were scared, they should have seen West Indies. West Indies toured Australia a year after England, and the hype even out-hyped the hype of twelve months earlier. If England couldn't give the Aussies a good game then this lot – the team that beat Australia in the final of the inaugural limited-overs World Cup in June 1975, Lillee, Thomson and all – certainly would. (Few people paid much attention to the fact that West Indies only just avoided collapse against Lillee and Thomson in that Lord's final thanks to a brilliant and far-from-repeatable century from Clive Lloyd.) This was going to be the world championship of cricket. What really got the antipodean saliva going was that West Indies had their own demon bowler, one half of their own Lillee-and-Thomson: Andy Roberts.

Roberts was fully up to the billing. Not only was he frighteningly quick – during the tour his bowling speed was timed at somewhere between that of Thomson and Lillee – he was also a frightening character. He had a physique like steel set in concrete, possessed tremendous stamina, thought a great deal about how to get batsmen out, and had an intimidating stare that put Lillee's glare to shame. It was a look of curious menace, the sort that said: 'You're not thinking of hanging around, are you?' He may not have gone around saying he liked to hit batsmen, but he hardly needed to. He had caused mayhem among Hampshire's second XI opponents when he first played for the club in 1973 and the following year, when he took over 100 wickets for the first team, he had attracted further notoriety by felling Cowdrey at Basingstoke. While anxious fielders huddled round the stricken figure collapsed in the crease, Roberts had stood several yards away, waiting impatiently for the next batsman to be brought on. He was, in any case, a man of few words. Gordon Greenidge, a fellow West Indian who played with Roberts at Hampshire, said that Roberts was talked of as a Black Agitator and dressing-room rebel. Greenidge was not sure about the validity of the first comment because, although they shared a flat together, Roberts said so little Greenidge had never had the chance to find out.

Roberts certainly had some rather disturbing habits, such as his fascination with cartoon books. They were full of guns and death, and Roberts seemed only too willing to take his Zaps and Kapows out on to the field with him. And he had some formidable weapons in his own armoury. Apart from a devastating yorker, he possessed a quite lethal two-ball combination, bouncers of varying speeds with no discernible change of action. He would bowl a short ball just slow enough to encourage the batsman to think he had the measure of the Roberts bouncer, and then send down another, much faster, one. The batsman, sensing something familiar, would shape to hook, only to find the ball rushing down on him and just the time to think, 'Oh God, I've got this one wrong.' That was exactly what happened to Cowdrey and, as in his case, the results were often horrifying. Barry Stead, of Nottinghamshire, scarcely a bona fide batsman, had his jaw broken by the Roberts one-two but even if you were as good a batsman as Cowdrey it was a pretty mean trick.

It was not that Roberts was the only one to employ the tactic – any fast bowler worth his salt would attempt it – it's just that Roberts used it with more ruthless efficiency than anyone else. In this sense, he presaged the new age: chillingly calculating, frighteningly analytical of any weaknesses in a batsman's technical or psychological make-up. 'He was,' Lillee would say of Roberts, 'the most complete fast bowler I have seen.' Lillee versus Roberts in 1975–6 began to look like the world heavyweight championship of cricket.

Unfortunately, Roberts may have been up to the billing – he Zapped and Kapowed out 22 wickets during the six-Test series, including nine in the Test at Perth – but most of the rest of the West Indies team were not (although it was on this tour that Holding found out just how fast he could bowl). In fact, it turned out to be the greatest mismatch in years. West Indies were on the canvas in the first round, rallied briefly with some flashy blows in the second, but were comprehensively outpointed in all the remaining rounds. Their battering was so severe that, had they been able, they would gladly have left the ring long before that final bell.

England may have been in disarray by the second Test of their tour; for West Indies, it came a lot sooner than that. A young and inexperienced team – Michael Holding was making his first Test tour, Gordon Greenidge, Viv Richards and Andy Roberts their second – they were intimidated by the unexpected pace and bounce of Australian pitches, the sheer speed of Lillee and Thomson and the hostility of both the crowds and the opposition. (Richards said he found it difficult to concentrate when someone was snarling, 'Fuck off, you black bastard,' which is understandable enough.)

In the first Test at Brisbane, they scarcely knew what had hit them. West Indies were by nature uninhibited but undisciplined strokeplayers; against this torrent of violent, short-pitched bowling, they lost all self-control. In their panic, they tried to hit everything: blades flashed in the sun like a sabre display; you've never seen so many cuts, slashes, pulls and hooks –

especially hooks. These shots brought them runs – and much-needed psychological relief – but also cost them wickets, and at an exchange rate Australia were gladly prepared to pay. West Indies' first innings at Brisbane lasted only 299 balls; their first innings at Melbourne only 374; their second innings at Sydney 317; their first at Adelaide 338; and their first at Melbourne again just 243. Over the series as a whole, they lost a wicket every 49 deliveries. It was hardly surprising Australia put so much faith in fast bowling.

Losing was in fact the least of the West Indies players' worries. Lillee-and-Thomson was all that occupied their thoughts. Greenidge, who made a pair at Brisbane, admitted that he was in a state of near panic there, not just nervous but genuinely fearful of what might happen. Richards said he had never before seen a pitch as quick as the one at Brisbane and was so totally overcome by nerves that he ran himself out in the second innings. Who cares about losing when your life is at stake?

West Indies became known as the Happy Hookers. They were so hooked on the hook shot that it cost them sixteen wickets during the six Tests. They gave hooking a bad name. They were like drug addicts, simply unable to give it up. During the fourth Test at Sydney, Greg Chappell (who had succeeded his brother to the Australia captaincy) deliberately deprived West Indies of bouncers and then fed them to one batsman after another. Roy Fredericks, Richards and Alvin Kallicharran, all unable to resist, duly hooked themselves into oblivion.

The Happy Hookers had their day, though. For once, at Perth, everything they tried came off, especially for Fredericks, who hooked his second ball, from Lillee, off the edge for six and after that never looked back. On perhaps the fastest pitch in Australia, he hooked, drove and cut Lillee and Thomson like they were no more than medium-pace trundlers, and the harder he hit them the worse they bowled. Greg Chappell looked on in horror as they sent down bouncer, yorker, bouncer, yorker as though the needle had got stuck on a vaguely familiar and crackly old seventy-eight. The statistics relating to this incredible West Indies innings are perhaps as much an indictment of the batsmen as they are of the bowlers: Fredericks, whose fifty came off 33 balls and his century off 71, scored in all 169 off just 145 deliveries; Clive Lloyd, then still a batsman of uncontrolled aggression and taking advantage of ragged fielding, made 149 in three hours forty minutes; Lillee's analysis was 20 eight-ball overs, no maidens, 123 runs, two wickets; Thomson's 17 overs, no maidens, 128 runs, three wickets. Thus encouraged, West Indies continued to play in the same vein for the rest of the series, without achieving anything remotely like the same results.

Hooking was only one manifestation of West Indies' lemming-like behaviour. Kallicharran said that some players were so keen to get out of the firing line that they started to manufacture injuries. There was a suggestion, for instance, that Greenidge avoided playing in the last three Tests by claiming to have a bad back. Even those who did not fail completely found the tour a traumatic experience. Kallicharran and Lawrence Rowe both scored centuries in the second innings at Brisbane, yet both have only bad memories of the tour. Kallicharran said that it was a 'horrible, frightening tour . . . everyone was shot to pieces'; Rowe said, 'Not even God could have played that stuff.' Not that all the injuries were manufactured. Richards had his box broken by a ball from Thomson. In Sydney, Julien's right thumb was fractured, Clive Lloyd was hit on the jaw and Holding was hit in the face, all again by Thomson. In Perth, Kallicharran had his nose broken by Lillee.

The West Indies totally lost their grip. Many struggling touring teams start to imagine they are being hard done by with umpiring decisions, but after having an appeal for caught behind against Ian Chappell turned down, Holding sat down on the pitch in Sydney and actually cried in frustration (another myth shattered: fast bowlers are supposed to *eat* babies, not cry like them). The Chappell decision was obviously a distressing incident for the touring team, but one they allowed to get out of all proportion. Greenidge claimed it effectively decided the series, saying it 'broke us as a team and won the series for the Australians', and even Lloyd, the captain, admitted 'after that, our morale went to pieces'. (I've heard of some excuses for losing 5–1, but these are as good as any.)

Also, as the series went on, Richards's batting began to take on a surreal quality. Unable to come to terms with Lillee and Thomson's sheer pace, he came up with an extraordinary theory as to how to play them. *He tried to cut them off the front foot.* As if 0.44 of a second was not little enough time, he reduced it by going on to the front foot. Hardly surprisingly, it was a strategy that did not work, as Richards found himself being beaten by the ball's movement off the pitch. He then had another idea. He asked Clive Lloyd, his captain, if he could be promoted from number five to open the innings: he thought it would sharpen his concentration. You would have thought that facing bowling of 90 miles an hour would have kept you fairly focused at all times, but Richards was clearly in need of a heightened experience. As an opener, he found it. Playing, in the words of Kallicharran, 'like a man on drugs', he scored 30 and 101 at Adelaide and 50 and 98 at Melbourne. He even managed not to be fazed by Lillee's snarls and stares: he just stared back and did not flinch. Whether Richards knew much of what he was doing is questionable – he admitted that facing Thomson involved 'a silent prayer' – but he remembered enough not to want to open again. And he never forgot how to stare.

The man who lost his grip most completely, though, was Clive Lloyd. Against all the success he subsequently enjoyed as captain has to be set the fact that, when they were losing badly, as they were on this tour, he was unable to motivate his players. He finished the tour bemused and shattered. The Australians thought that he was washed up. Lillee said he looked to be 'at the beginning of the end'. Some of Lloyd's players felt he had badly let them down.

But these tours of Australia by England and West Indies were to have consequences not yet apparent. Thomson had delivered a slingshot that had been heard around the world.

3

Nice Guys Never Win

Clive Lloyd is supposedly the man behind the Great Idea of modern cricket: the idea that changed the way the game was played; the idea that once led someone to observe that – because few other countries have been as blessed as the Caribbean nations with such an abundance of fast bowling talent – there were now two types of Test cricket, one that involved West Indies and one that did not. The Great Idea was, of course, that the surest way to win at cricket was to load your side with fast bowlers. In short, the fastest way to scramble the minds of the opposition was to put all your eggs in one basket.

This is a remarkable theory, because one of the few things that most critics agree on about Lloyd's much-debated ten-year leadership of West Indies is that it was notable for its absence of on-field innovation. Stasis was more apparent than spark. In the early years, he was regarded as easy going to the point of weakness. Mike Brearley felt that when Lloyd captained the ordinary Lancashire attack (which he did for four seasons between 1981 and 1986) there was a 'lack of ideas', and even went so far as to say, 'I never felt he had a cricketing brain.' Richards and Greenidge criticized Lloyd for lack of leadership on their first tour of Australia. Michael Manley, prime minister of Jamaica, in his history of West Indian cricket, observed that Lloyd led 'without seeming to drive'.

Let's face it. Lloyd did not choose to rely on fast bowling, he was pushed into it. Is it not significant that the first two times Lloyd's fast bowlers were accused of intimidating the opposition – at Kingston, Jamaica, in April 1976 and at Old Trafford in July 1976 – were in matches in which West Indies had been up against it? This was not bowling to a master plan, this was desperation time. Far from devising life in the fast lane, Lloyd was slow to follow the example of Australia, who had demonstrated the potency of pace during the series with West Indies in 1975–6, regularly using three fast bowlers and once, at Perth, four (Lillee, Thomson, Gilmour and Walker). All Lloyd did was play to his strong suit and in doing this he was certainly not the first. Who was the first Test captain of modern times to stack his side with bowlers of the same type? The answer is not Lloyd, nor even Greg Chappell, but the Nawab of Pataudi junior, who went into the field at Edgbaston in 1967 with Bedi, Chandrasekhar, Venkataraghavan and Prasanna. They were all spinners.

What Lloyd did have when he took over the West Indies captaincy was a flint-hard competitiveness, a professionalism then alien to most West Indies cricketers. He had acquired it partly through the straitened financial circumstances of his upbringing – his father had died when he was twelve – and partly from his early years in Lancashire, where he had played either in the leagues or for the county in every season since 1967. He simply hated losing and was determined to alter the happy-go-lucky nature of West Indies cricketers, who were often uncontainable when things were going well but who folded when the going got tough. What had been so disheartening for Lloyd about the tour of Australia was that it had entirely confirmed these impressions. West Indies needed discipline and direction, and Lloyd was going to give it to them. If anyone was going to get ground into the dirt, it was no longer going to be them. What the Australia tour also confirmed for Lloyd was that nice guys never win. 'I developed the killer instinct . . . I was determined to be a winner,' he said. This was the Great Idea Clive Lloyd had.

Thus, when he returned home from Australia to lead West

Indies in a four-match home Test series with India and within weeks suffered a humiliating defeat in the third Test match, equal to any of those experienced at the hands of Lillee and Thomson, Lloyd resolved that things had to change. (For one thing, his own record as captain. He had led West Indies in 14 Tests, won five and lost eight. The vultures must have been circling.) In that third Test, Lloyd, having been in control for most of the match, had left his opponents ten hours to save the game or, alternatively, score 403 to win. The latter had seemed such a remote target that, for most of those ten hours, India themselves did not seriously consider as a possibility what would have been one of the most remarkable victories in Test history. But they won by six wickets with seven overs to spare. Just to rub salt into the wound, the match took place in Port of Spain, Trinidad, where the population is largely of Indian descent and many locals celebrated India's victory as their own. West Indies looked like everyone's fools and Lloyd's declaration looked like going down in history as the Stupidest Idea of modern times.

Because it had been known that the Port of Spain pitch would turn, Lloyd had gone into the match with three spinners but, with Lance Gibbs effectively in retirement, all three were inexperienced: Jumadeen had only four Test caps and Padmore and Imtiaz Ali were making their Test debuts. On a pitch which did indeed take turn during India's second innings, they let their captain down badly, although so too did Holding and Julien, who bowled so loosely with the second new ball that India were encouraged to think in terms of victory for the first time. It should also be remembered that Gavaskar and Viswanath, who scored centuries for India, were great players of spin. Lloyd nevertheless laid the blame squarely at the door of the spinners. In the dressing room afterwards, he called the three bowlers before him and asked: 'Gentlemen, I gave you four hundred runs to bowl at and you failed to bowl out the opposition. How many runs must I give you in future to make sure that you get the wickets?' In fact, there was not going to be much future for any of them. Lloyd never forgave them. Imtiaz never played Test cricket again, Padmore played once more and Jumadeen five more times.

Even then, Lloyd was not converted to the power of pace – he retained Jumadeen for the final Test at Kingston – but he did now embrace the killer instinct. He wanted victory at Kingston at any price, and he got it. And what a price. Never again would anyone call West Indies a soft touch. In the absence of Roberts, who had withdrawn from the series after the second Test because of exhaustion, the Zapping and Kapowing was left to the inexperienced new-ball pair of Holding, aged twenty-two, and Wayne Daniel, aged twenty and playing his first Test. As a combination they were scarcely less of a gamble than the spinners at Port of Spain but they were raw, hungry for success and menacing. Daniel was tall and broad and used to run in like a rickety express travelling down a South American gorge. The son of a Barbados farmer, he was already an imposing figure at the age of fourteen – it was said he lived off the milk of his father's cows – and he struck terror into the hearts of his school contemporaries. Even Malcolm Marshall admitted, 'There was one boy we all dreaded facing.' Holding was even taller than Daniel but was wispish and nowhere near as physically intimidating. The only thing about him that was menacing – apart from his bowling – was a pair of incisors of which Dracula himself would have been proud.

The killer instinct was on show from the start. On a pitch offering bounce but little real pace, Lloyd's fast bowlers, Holding, Daniel and Holder, persistently dug the ball in short. To make matters worse, the pitch had recently been relaid and there was a ridge at one end which made the bounce there vary alarmingly. Holding repeatedly bowled bouncers and even resorted to going round the wicket. Several times the batsmen were struck on the body and fingers. Nevertheless, India, having been put in by Lloyd and shown great courage, finished the first day on 178 for one.

Then a remarkable thing happened. During the night, a

noticeable layer of grass sprouted on the pitch. It is hardly an exaggeration to say that this unusual sprouting changed the course of cricket history. Here were the green shoots of recovery that Lloyd had been looking for. 'It was immediately obvious that [the pitch] was going to be faster and more dangerous,' said Tony Cozier. Batting was an even more daunting proposition than it had been the day before. Viswanath had a finger both fractured and dislocated as he was caught off the glove to a ball from Holding; Patel, who had never looked at ease against pace even when making runs, took his eyes off a ball from Holder and edged it into his mouth and Gaekwad, after having survived seven and a half hours, was struck above the left ear by a delivery whose bounce bore no relation to its length. There were several other terrifying deliveries, including one to Viswanath which, according to Sunil Gavaskar, 'almost took his head with it'. With six wickets down, Bishen Bedi, the India captain, did what no other captain has had the temerity to do (although many in their time must have longed to do so) by declaring the innings closed in order to protect himself – and Chandrasekhar – from the risk of being hurt. ('It's not that I'm afraid to die. I just don't want to be there when it happens . . .') When India batted again, five men were absent hurt; Gaekwad (who had spent nearly two days in hospital), Viswanath and Patel were all incapacitated with their first-innings injuries, while Bedi and Chandrasekhar had apparently damaged fingers attempting return catches.

Most of the Indians had had enough long before the end. The turning point was the blow to Gaekwad, which not only ended his long resistance but also knocked his spectacles to the ground, thereby transforming him from a picture of determination to a vision of vulnerability at the drop of a bat. Even Gavaskar, India's leading batsman and a fine player of fast bowling, was shaken. 'Fast bowling of that speed is barbaric,' he said. Bedi was so upset he called a press conference on the rest day of the match to make his complaints known, claiming that West Indies were conducting 'a war' (he didn't yet know that nice guys never win) and saying that he had declared his first innings 'in disgust'. There was later the suspicion that Bedi had also declared his second innings in protest at Lloyd's tactics, because the hand injuries to himself and Chandrasekhar that supposedly prevented them holding a bat had not stopped them bowling several hours earlier. Bedi also pointedly refused to take the field when West Indies went out to score the thirteen runs they needed to win. It is the nearest anyone has ever come to surrendering a Test match.

This match was not played in a good spirit: the stakes were too high for one side for that. In fact, things got badly out of hand. There were distinct racial undertones to what occurred and this time the crowd was strongly behind West Indies, especially Holding, who was a local boy. Gavaskar wrote: 'To call a crowd "a crowd" in Jamaica is a misnomer. It should be called a mob. The way they shrieked and howled every time Holding bowled was positively horrible. They encouraged him with shouts of "Kill him Maan!", "Hit him Maan!", "Knock his head off, Mike!". All this proved beyond a shadow of a doubt that these people still belong to the jungles and forests . . .' When Gaekwad was hit, the crowd was 'stamping their legs, clapping and jumping for joy'. Even Richards, who is not the squeamish sort, admitted there were some 'pretty unpleasant jibes'.

Afterwards, Lloyd never even blinked, let alone failed to keep a straight face. 'Some Indian batsmen felt that when Holding went round the wicket to them, he was aiming at their bodies. Quite simply, it was a ploy to change his direction against batsmen who were not getting into line and who would then snick the ball to the wicketkeeper or to the slip cordon . . . I can't say I was greatly upset. Because a wicket is quick, and batsmen get into difficulty, you can't bowl half-volleys, you still do your best to get them out. That's the game. If you can't play quick bowling you shouldn't be in the game at international level.' This could have come straight out of the Ian Chappell Book of Cricketing Etiquette. Lloyd had well and truly gone over to the other side. So had most of his players, many of whom (lest it be forgot) had lived through the tour of Australia: Holding made no bones about the fact that 'it was war' at Kingston; Richards stated calmly that the Indians 'over-dramatized the dangers'. The West Indians, reanimated by the sorcery of Lillee and Thomson, were chanting the mantra like some sort of walking dead. (Maybe that really was Dracula running in from the pavilion end.)

Even if Lloyd was not responsible for the Great Idea people thought he was, it was undoubtedly an achievement to get a team drawn from various islands and cultural backgrounds on to the field with the necessary commitment to pursue that idea; in the words of Imran Khan, to 'bring them all together and make them play'. Thus, after India had returned home like Napoleon's troops on the retreat from Moscow, battle-weary and enveloped in plasters and bandages, the West Indians left for England to fill the visitors' dressing rooms with subdued voices and steely eyes. 'Jokes,' Viv Richards remembered, 'were out.'

Don't you know? Nice guys never win!

In England there was much wailing and gnashing of teeth. They knew that the rules had changed, and that they were missing out. You couldn't get anywhere these days without a top-class fast bowler. Dammit, everyone seemed to have one except them. There was a party going on and they weren't invited.

As if Thomson and Lillee hadn't been enough, here were the West Indies, only in the country a few weeks and already they were picking off their chaps like they were coconuts in a shy. Holding had incapacitated Sainsbury, of Hampshire, and felled Amiss, effectively putting him out of the start of the Test series, psychologically if not physically. Daniel had broken Knott's finger and been warned for intimidation against Sussex. How were they going to keep up? All they had was the still lively but ageing Snow and the still coltish Willis. They were hardly going to have Richards and Lloyd hopping around the crease. It is their cannon against our peashooters. Something had to be done.

Over the next two years the country was gripped by angst. The *Sun* newspaper ran a campaign to find a fast bowler, so did the *Cricketer* magazine; so too did the self-appointed wiseman Ted Dexter. Alec Bedser, the chairman of selectors, simply bemoaned the fact that young English county players weren't exposed to top-flight fast bowling every day of the week (this was in the days before every county signed a West Indian quick as their overseas fast bowler). But no one really did anything very meaningful. The *Cricketer*'s search produced a shortlist of fifty young fast bowlers, but nothing much would come of any of them. Dexter came up with Tom Stancombe, who found the publicity hard to bear and soon returned to his native Devon. They used to say in the old days that all England had to do if they wanted a fast bowler was whistle down a mineshaft, but this was little more than whistling in the wind.

Despite the lack of firepower, Greig, being Greig, talked big. He had seen West Indies play in Australia and reckoned he could stifle their batsmen, but pursued the policy erratically during the Test series and largely without success. (When he first held the upper hand in pace-bowling strength, in India the next winter, Greig used his advantage superbly. Knowing the Indians were fine players of spin – tell Clive Lloyd about it! – Greig employed as his cutting edge Willis, Old and Lever to win him the first series by an England side in India for over forty years.) He had, at first, more luck with the batsmen he chose to hold Roberts, Holding and Daniel at bay. He had been responsible for finding David Steele the previous summer by canvassing opinions on the county circuit. Now he introduced Brearley, brought back the almost dementedly brave Brian Close at the age of forty-five, and before the summer was out had successfully rehabilitated Amiss.

Greig never talked so big or so badly, though, as the day in May 1976 that he gave a television interview on the balcony at Hove and stated, in his harsh, unsympathetic, South African accent, that he intended to make the West Indies 'grovel'. If he couldn't hold the upper hand in fast bowlers, he was determined to hold the upper hand in administering inferiority complexes. Unfortunately, he had misjudged the mood – and stuck his size thirteens into the dark, politically charged mood of Caribbean revivalism. The West Indians suspected Greig of having a racist dig – someone told them the word 'grovel' was often used to put down blacks in South Africa – and the next time they held a team meeting, they resolved to punish him. In effect, a whole collection of demonically charged fast bowlers joined Dennis Lillee in walking down the pitch to Greig and making the mark of a cross on their foreheads. Greig's assurances that he never intended his remarks to carry political undertones were too late. Before the summer was out he would be back on a balcony to give a television interview – this time after the fifth Test at the Oval – and add his voice to the growing clamour. *Find me a fast bowler!*

Clive Lloyd did have at least one other very important idea. It played a vital part in his ability to take control of matches, something he had not been very good at in his early career as West Indies captain. His experiences in the field against Australia and India taught him that if you cannot get a batsman out, then it is best to cut off his oxygen supply. In Australia, West Indies had bowled their overs more rapidly than their opponents; all that had done was contribute to their own downfall. When Lloyd set India 403 to win, West Indies had obliged them by bowling 147 overs in nine and a half hours; had fast bowlers operated all the time, India could not possibly have won. They wouldn't have received enough balls.

Lloyd was undoubtedly the first man to think of fast bowling as a means of defence as well as attack. In England in 1976, West Indies plumbed new depths for a Test series in England by bowling their overs at 13.91 per hour (Greig responded by having his bowlers deliver them at the rate of 14.44). This was as potentially damaging to the minds of opposing batsmen as the fear of injury. John Edrich declared himself 'bored' by the meagre diet of deliveries that West Indies gave him to hit; Graham Gooch, in a rare burst of imagination, would say that the West Indies 'dripped away at you like water on a stone'. Lloyd may have given the impression of letting things on the field run themselves, but at least they were running themselves at the tempo he wanted.

That summer, as in their series with India, West Indies only emerged with a clear advantage once they came across a dodgy pitch, which they did in the third Test at Old Trafford. The pitch there must have resembled the one on the second day at Kingston: undulating and grassy, lively and unpredictable in bounce. There was actually an inch-wide crack in the pitch which the groundstaff did their best to fill in. The following year, Greig was fined for criticizing the standard of the pitch for this match, but his remarks were quite justified. John Woodcock, cricket correspondent of *The Times* for over thirty-five years, later recalled that he had never thought it more likely that he would see a fatality at a match than at Old Trafford in 1976. One of the outcomes of this match was that England, who were dismissed for a mere 71 and 126, were persuaded over the next fifteen years to prepare bland pitches against opponents whose strong suit was fast bowling. What England forgot was the need to be aggressive themselves in the field, and that West Indies had struggled in their first innings, to 211 all out, and were vulnerable themselves in circumstances which assisted the bowlers. (The next time West Indies encountered a really helpful pitch in England, at Headingley in 1991, they lost, their first defeat in the country for twenty-two years.)

Old Trafford 1976 is the worst nightmare in the consciousness of modern English cricket. Though the West Indies bowling was consistently hostile in its speed – and one ball to Pocock, the nightwatchman, caressed the tip of his nose like a feather – there was really only one passage that caused concern. It was the eighty minutes Edrich and Close, the England openers, survived on the Saturday evening after their side had been set the absurdly high target of 552 to win in thirteen and a quarter hours (Lloyd, as you can see, was not taking any chances this time). The bowling they faced was so hostile that Holding was warned for intimidation by umpire Alley after delivering three successive bouncers to Close and the mood so ugly that Padmore had to be brought on to allow things to cool down (his three overs were the only overs of spin that the West Indies bowled in the match). Close, who was hit several times, more than once buckled at the knees and almost collapsed, and also had his box cracked by a ball from Roberts; Edrich was so angry and frightened he almost walked off. When they returned to the pavilion, 'the whole dressing room,' Pocock said, 'stood back and stared in genuine awe.' Edrich then burst out laughing. 'D'you know what your score is, Closey? One! All that for one! Closey, was it worth it?' Close immediately sent off Randall, the wide-eyed twelfth man, for a large Scotch and swallowed it at a gulp.

Several snapshots survive concerning this terrible evening. One is of Lloyd, after the match, coming as near to an apology as he dare: 'Our fellows got carried away. They knew they had only eighty minutes that night to make an impression and they went flat out, sacrificing accuracy for speed. They knew afterwards they had bowled badly.' Another is of the silence in the England dressing room during those eighty minutes, and of some of the players being unable to watch. Then there is Woolmer, standing on the balcony, 'as white as a sheet'. There is Pocock, catching sight of Close's torso covered in 'small clusters of livid bumps, as if somebody had forced handfuls of marbles beneath his skin'. There is Willis, who found it 'frightening to watch', saying that it was the 'most sustained barrage of intimidation' he ever saw. Then there is Close himself, describing how he had to have 'a long session with a pain-killing injection before I could lie down in bed, let alone sleep'. (Nevertheless, the day after the Test finished, Close was back in the fray, playing a belligerent innings of 69 for Somerset in the Gillette Cup despite being struck on the body by Willis.) What

Frank Hayes – who was rumoured to be of such a nervous disposition that he was sometimes sick before a major innings – thought of it all, goodness only knows.

Old Trafford took the greatest toll, however, not on Close, not on Edrich, but on Greig. Perhaps it was not so much this match itself as the accumulated effect of the series up to this point. Greig's 'grovel' remarks had inspired the West Indies fast bowlers to find an extra two yards of pace for him and by the end of this third Test his batting average was a mere 7.6. He was no longer able to leave his fear behind in the dressing room: it walked out with him when he went in to bat. 'When my turn came, it was the first time in my career I felt frightened,' he said. 'For tuppence I'd have given the game up there and then. I felt as though my world had collapsed. The quick men had got to me,' he said. He was so shattered that even the vote of confidence given him by the chairman of selectors was not enough; he had to be given a lecture by Knott before he could be persuaded to carry on ('Has anyone seen the fags, skip wants a fag'). Knott is quite clear about why Greig had to carry on: 'I don't believe in ever dropping yourself,' he said. 'Poor form is one ball. A whole game can change in one ball. A lot of people get down and think they should give someone else a go. It was the same for me at that stage in seventy-six. I was also not in the best of nick.'

Knott's talk worked. Briefly. In the next Test at Headingley, Greig, having sharpened up beforehand against bowling from eighteen yards, rediscovered his confidence and took on Holding and Roberts as he had taken on Lillee and Thomson (his innings of 116 and 76 not out were largely responsible for England losing by only 55 runs); but by the time of the Oval, he had also relocated his mouth, and had provoked Holding to bowl him as fast a ball as he had ever faced (it not only shattered his stumps, but provoked a pitch invasion by joyous West Indians celebrating the downfall of the Man They Loved To Hate). After that, Greig was again no longer keen to get out in the middle, and during the one-day international at Lord's even allowed several young and inexperienced batsmen to go in before him to confront a rampaging Roberts on a damp pitch.

It was hardly surprising that by the end of this Test series even Lloyd had begun to realize he could rely almost exclusively on his fast bowlers. He had started to experiment with an all-pace attack and even used one on a dry and dusty pitch at the Oval for the fifth Test match, a decision which aroused considerable debate (on subsequent, similar occasions, his argument would be that any pitch that might wear and help a spinner would also be unreliable enough in bounce to make the fast bowler even more dangerous). The Oval pitch was so slow that the ball rarely rose above waist height; Greig and Knott both described it as one of the slowest pitches they had ever played on. Yet on this surface, Holding took 14 wickets for 149 runs, claiming, on average, a wicket every 23 balls. After the strictures which had followed Old Trafford, and with most of the England batsmen encouraged into coming on to the front foot, he pitched the ball up and beat them with pace through the air, although, had he not been so inexperienced, he would probably not have sought to bowl so fast on so dead a track (his more worldly colleagues stuck to a good line and length). Twelve of Holding's wickets were bowled or leg-before and Greig and Knott both felt he was as fast through the air as anyone they ever encountered and that only Thomson, who had considerable assistance from the Australian pitches, was faster overall.

Though there was a similarity in speed, Holding and Thomson could not have had more different methods. With Thomson, there was an obvious climax of effort: the V-shaped back, the catapult action. With Holding, it was as though he was out on a gentle jog during which his main purpose was to remain as graceful as possible. Barely a blade of grass was disturbed as he loped in; barely a muscle rippled as his tall, slim-shouldered body slid through delivery. Umpires and players alike were astonished that such an ethereal being could generate such speed: so it was that Dracula became known as Whispering Death. Lloyd must have watched with interest as England's batsmen sought to avoid Holding by getting up to the other end to face Roberts. Caught between the devil and the deep blue sea.

The only man who was able to keep Holding at bay at the Oval was Amiss, who had returned to the England side for the first time since Lillee saw him off the previous year and who sensibly eschewed front-foot methods in favour of a technique, borrowed from Ian Chappell, of moving back and across his stumps to get in line. With few of the bouncers around that had got him into such trouble when he batted for MCC against West Indies earlier in the season, Amiss was able to demonstrate again his penchant for building large innings by making 203 in the first innings, but it was not enough to save England from defeat and – as subsequent events showed – it proved little about his ability to play the short ball.

During the series, 84 of the 91 England wickets that fell went to the fast bowlers, only three to spin, and Lloyd had glimpsed what the future would hold. 'Even when people kept on at me saying, "You must play a spinner here or a spinner there",' he would say, 'I remembered Australia and how effective that fast-bowling combination was.'

Hardly surprisingly, batsmen had started to demand protection. They wanted physical protection and the protection of the laws. They started to arm themselves. Before Thomson came along, they wore little that would lessen the impact of the ball. When England began their tour of Australia, there were no chest guards, arm guards, or inner-thigh pads, and certainly no helmets. When Cowdrey was called up, he had the foresight to get the physiotherapist to sew some rubber into one side of his vest, and it was not long before his team-mates took up his lead. Other, more sophisticated, types of body armour quickly followed, including gloves designed to reduce the growing number of hand and finger injuries. By the time Steele joined the England team in July 1975, he was taken aback to see Amiss kitting himself out before going in to bat. Steele's habit against the quicks was to stuff a towel down the side of his flannels; Amiss, he said, 'looked like a knight in armour'. The injury to Chatfield fuelled debate about the possibilities of headgear but the idea rarely got beyond the discussion stage. Early in 1976, Greig was photographed in a crash helmet, but aroused amusement rather than admiration. There were no takers, certainly not Greig himself.

There was much talk of the New Bodyline, much talk of imminent fatalities – Dr R.W. Cockshut, a vehement critic of short-pitched bowling, warned that in 1976 up to ten deaths and forty irreversible brain injuries should be expected from the impact of cricket ball on skull – and much talk of the need to curb the fast men. At its annual meeting in 1975, the then International Cricket Conference insisted that the law concerning intimidation was sufficient. It stated, 'The persistent bowling of fast short-pitched balls is unfair if in the opinion of the umpire at the bowler's end, it constitutes a systematic attempt at intimidation.' By the following year, when its meeting took place only a few days after the dark deeds at Old Trafford, it spoke out more strongly, condemning intimidatory fast bowling and bouncers aimed at non-recognized batsmen (although this term itself was open to interpretation), and calling on umpires to enforce the laws.

The main problem was that there were almost as many lily-livered umpires around as there were batsmen. Lillee and Thomson – and Greig for that matter – had been treated with leniency in Australia, as had Holding and Daniel in Jamaica (despite Gavaskar at one point walking down the pitch to ask umpire Gosein what, exactly, was his definition of intimidation). The fact was that despite all the bouncers, all the smashed fingers, broken ribs and cracked skulls, despite all the ashen-faced tailenders, despite, even, the horror-stricken looks of the slips (the men who could usually be counted on to urge on Fot, Two-Up, Whispering Death or ol' Mean Eyes), only one umpire – Alley at Old Trafford – had so far had the fibre to be seen to be warning a bowler for intimidation.

When Lloyd and the Chappells pleaded that it was not up to them but up to the umpires to interpret the laws – and this applied not only to intimidation but also to over-rates – they did so safe in the knowledge that there were not many officials around who had the guts to do so. When one umpire did apply the law – Dickie Bird warning Marshall for intimidation at Edgbaston in 1984 – Lloyd showed how much he cared for the laws by tossing the ball away in disgust. And once the matches were over, what could be done then? After the battle of Kingston, the India players, feeling that the spirit of the game had been violated, made a formal protest to their board about the West Indian tactics. It was the last they ever heard of it.

Captains who had pace bowling at their command had the only power that really mattered. When, in July 1978, the International Cricket Conference attempted to get to grips with the problem by introducing an experimental law – only an *experimental* law be it noted – that in Test matches bowlers should be limited to one bouncer per over, the first series to be played after the introduction saw one of the teams, Pakistan, take not the blindest bit of notice. When Imran Khan and Sarfraz Nawaz first bowled, they subjected Gavaskar to such a barrage of bumpers at Faisalabad that the Indian opener called Bedi, his captain, on to the pitch to protest at his treatment. Only then did Pakistan desist. The umpires did nothing. Two weeks later, Bedi did what he had almost done at Kingston and conceded a match in protest at his opponents' use of the short-pitched ball; with India needing 23 runs from 20 balls to win a one-day international at Sahiwal, he called his batsmen from the field after Sarfraz had bowled his fourth successive bouncer.

Bedi had made his point, but no one really wanted to listen. Those who had the power were not going to be curbed; most of those who did not have it were too busy falling over each other in the rush to get a piece of the action to worry much about curbs either.

Who cared any more about the health of the sport? The heart of cricket had been ripped out with a broad, bare hand and tossed on to the table around which sat the game's administrators, before another hand had driven a stump through its still-quivering centre.

Didn't I tell you? Nice guys never win!

'Oh God, I've got this one wrong . . .' Colin Cowdrey falls for Andy Roberts's faster bouncer at Basingstoke in 1974. Seventeen years later Cowdrey was instrumental in the introduction of the one bouncer per over rule in Test cricket.

Keith Fletcher is made to regret sledging Dennis Lillee as he is hit on the head by a ball from Jeff Thomson at Sydney in 1975. The ball bounced out into the covers and was almost caught by Ross Edwards.

The night of shame: Michael Holding bowls another bouncer to Brian Close during the final session of play on the Saturday of the Old Trafford Test in 1976. At the end of the day, Close's torso was so bruised it looked as if someone had 'forced handfuls of marbles under his skin'.

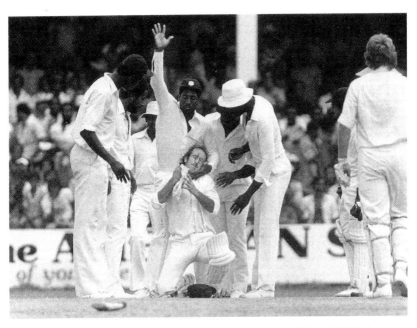

Peter Toohey pays the price for missing a bouncer from Andy Roberts in Trinidad in 1978. It was the first Test match Australia had played against West Indies since they had beaten them 5–1 two years earlier.

Bob Willis, bowling from around the wicket, makes nightwatchman Iqbal Qasim regret hanging around so long at Edgbaston in 1978. This incident led to an ill-fated attempt to introduce an immunity for 'non-recognized batsmen'.

Allan Lamb is discomfited by Imran Khan at Lord's in 1982. Lamb reckoned Imran was as dangerous as any of the West Indies bowlers he faced.

Botham misses an attempted hook against Imran at Edgbaston in 1987. 'I don't think he actually relishes the real bouncer as much as he thinks he does,' Lawson said.

Nobody pursued bouncer wars with more relish than Ian Botham. Here, at Headingley in 1985, he makes Geoff Lawson wish he had not bowled him a couple of beamers at the same ground four years earlier.

Fast-track bully meets flat-track bully: Curtly Ambrose introduces Graeme Hick to some of the niceties of Test cricket at Trent Bridge in 1991.

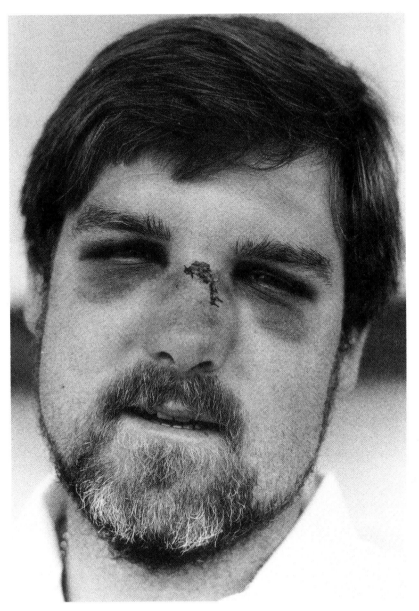

What happens if you miss . . . Mike Gatting after meeting Malcolm Marshall in Jamaica in 1986.

The guys you've got to feel sorry for are the tailenders: Michael Holding makes Derek Underwood jump for his life at Old Trafford in 1976.

Craig McDermott can remember only one ball being pitched up to him during the Tests in the Caribbean in 1991. This was it: a yorker from Patrick Patterson in Jamaica.

4

Gangsters

Thus began cricket's era of gang warfare. The authorities had surrendered control, lawlessness was rife. Fast bowling was not simply intimidatory, it was violent and bloody, and teams roamed the cricket grounds of the world committing violent and bloody deeds. Ian Chappell's language of the underworld became common parlance. Everyone had one fast bowler, many two, some three; the West Indies were on their way to settling for no fewer than four. It made for a lively and interesting time, as long as you weren't in the middle taking the flak. Gunsmoke constantly filled the air. No one spent much time talking of peace: everybody was too busy fighting fire with fire. It was absurd. It was as though the characters in Andy Roberts's cartoon-books had come to life and were Zapping and Kapowing each other all over the place.

All the new fast bowlers – and there were plenty of them – were desperate to be thought of as terrifyingly fast but, whatever they may have imagined, most couldn't hold a candle to Thomson or Holding for speed. In fact, many of them weren't of the highest pace at all and tried to disguise the fact by showing off their bouncer, displaying it as they might a gun holster from beneath a pinstripe.

The rivalries were most intense among the fast bowlers themselves. It was not just that they all wanted to bowl fast, faster, fastest. Everyone had seen the effect Lillee, Thomson, Holding and Roberts had had on batsmen. Theirs was the power to *scare*. Now everyone wanted to be not only fast, faster, fastest; but to scare, be scarier, be the *scariest*. Bowling fast had become a powerful masculine statement. 'Fast bowlers are basically bullies,' Viv Richards said. It was no longer just about machs, it was about machismo.

This manifested itself most clearly in the bowlers' on-field encounters, when they had to bat against each other. These were the plays-within-the-play. The days of the Fast Bowlers' Union were well and truly at an end. Now, they were always trying to knock hell out of each other; seemed to go round the world for no other purpose. At Northampton, Sarfraz Nawaz took on Thomson; in Melbourne, Hogg put the frighteners on Botham; at the Oval, Willis crossed swords with Lillee; in Kingston, Imran sparred with Roberts; in Christchurch, Botham pursued Hadlee; in Lahore, Sarfraz terrorized Willis; in Kingston, Hadlee chased Garner. And so it went on, this constant settling of scores, no one rightly remembering – or caring – who had first done what to whom. It was all part of the challenge, the challenge to see who was the worthiest, who nearest to being the biggest shot in town: the World's Fastest Bowler.

Or at any rate, if not the fastest, the scariest.

One newcomer *had* to be taken seriously. Virtually overnight in 1977, Kerry Packer, an Australian media magnate, created the biggest and most dangerous gang of them all when he signed many of the game's leading players to appear in his own matches. To draw the crowds, Packer highlighted the game's confrontational aspects and hostile fast bowling was an integral part of the process. Most of the bowlers he signed were quick men – this in itself created demand for fast bowlers because during the two-year life of Packer cricket most Test countries refused to select his players – and the more dangerous they were, the more he liked them.

Packer was the godfather of fast bowlers. He not only gave them work and paid them well, he glamorized them and re-packaged them, securing them a place at the centre of the game.

Packer was anti-establishment in many ways, one of which was to actively encourage his fast bowlers to be dangerous. He made their very anarchy a virtue. Come to the match and see what *might* happen.

Packer, of course, did this for a purpose beyond simply being nice to a group of sportsmen. They were essential to his financial success. He had to draw the public away from established cricket (i.e. Test cricket) and to his own matches (which comprised Supertests and, his speciality, a bevy of one-day games), and sought to do so by the most aggressive marketing the game has ever seen (Packer, whose original dispute with the cricket authorities was over television contracts, owned Channel 9 in Sydney). This involved concentrating on the dangerous aspects of the game: the bouncers, the helmets, the violent injuries, the slog. With the assistance of sophisticated advertising and television coverage, Packer succeeded beyond even his wildest dreams. The atmosphere at many of his one-day matches, particularly those staged at night under floodlights, was absolutely electric (and led to his most memorable slogan: 'Big Boys Play At Night'). He would have got nowhere without his fast men.

Things were not so mouthwatering for the batsmen. Almost every ball they faced was from one of the world's fastest bowlers; almost every ball, it seemed, was a bouncer; almost every bouncer, for sure, raised a cheer from the crowd. If you once got out of form it was almost impossible to recover, for there was little medium-pace or spin bowling against which to get your eye back in, and what there was of course was of the highest class. Injuries were frequent (according to Amiss, twenty-three batsmen were hit on the head during Packer's first season); sympathy hard to find. Anyone who tried to stick it out often fell prey to frustration. In one match, Greg Chappell, having been repeatedly hit on the shins by Garner, could take no more and threatened to hit him with his bat if he did it again; Garner just smiled and, shortly after, had him caught. In another, Lawrence Rowe had a narrow escape when he failed to pick up a bouncer from Lillee and was hit on the temple guard, a piece of protective equipment he himself had pioneered. Despite the guard taking much of the impact, he suffered a depressed fracture. Greg Chappell, who was fielding at the time, said the guard saved Rowe's life: 'It sounded terrible – I thought he was dead.'

Under such intense pressure, many batsmen found their technique splintering like firewood. And once they had lost faith in their technique, they lost faith in their ability to defend themselves, and then they became exposed to fear itself. They started to develop the heady humour of war, the kind of humour that hides fear. Barry Richards, the gifted South African who had been deprived of cricket at the highest level since 1970 because of sanctions against apartheid, could not believe what he found when he joined Packer, and predicted that it would not be long before Packer's matches were played by batsmen wearing armour against bowlers who only bowled fast. There would, he said, be no fielders because the batsmen would be unable to run and runs would be awarded according to how far the batsmen hit the ball, their shots measured by concentric circles around the outfield. And make no mistake, it *was* cricket of the highest level. Viv Richards, who has the perspective of a long Test career, remembers Packer cricket as 'some of the hardest, meanest cricket that I have ever played in. With all those great players on the park it was impossible to relax for a second. The competition was as fierce as any Test match, fiercer if the truth be told ... Every bowler wanted to intimidate you. It was gladiatorial cricket at its finest.' So there you are, Barry. Worth the wait, was it?

Nor could there be any running away. All Packer's players were obliged to live up to the superstar status he had created for them. David Hookes was a classic example. When he first played for Packer he was twenty-two and had six Test match appearances behind him. He started to believe all the hype about being a Supertest superstar. After a few weeks, in December 1977, he came up against the West Indies XI on a bouncy pitch at the Showground, Sydney (there were three teams in Packer:

an Australian side, a West Indian side and a World XI). Hookes felt he had to take them on. He was a boy on a man's errand. He took 17 runs off an over from Garner, 22 off another from Holding, then had his jaw smashed by a ball from Roberts. There was no ambulance on the ground and he had to be taken to hospital in Packer's own Jaguar. People who had doubted the seriousness of Packer's matches realized then that it was for real.

Hookes made a full recovery but some batsmen were permanently scarred. Majid Khan never fully adjusted to the preponderance of pace; Mushtaq Mohammad, according to Imran, 'vanished into oblivion'; while Greig, who ironically was instrumental in bringing the whole thing into being (the idea of the big stage was too tempting for the Great Showman), found his technique cruelly exposed by the barrage of short-pitched bowling.

Packer did still more for his fast bowlers. He raised their standards in several ways. By signing up so many of them, he created competition among them for places in his teams; he also obliged many of them, particularly those in the World XI, to work together, sharing their skills in a way they might not otherwise have done. Garth le Roux, another South African with no opportunity to play Test cricket, was a classic case. Given the chance to take part in a highly competitive atmosphere, he bowled superbly and was reckoned by some to be the best fast bowler in the world by 1979. His spell with Packer launched him on a county career with Sussex and, although he rarely bowled as well in England as he had in Australia, he and Imran almost took the county to its first-ever championship title in 1981. Packer also raised the fitness of all his players to new levels, introducing the practice of each team having its own physiotherapist and inspiring the West Indians, in particular, to be not simply fit but, in Lloyd's phrase, 'fit to compete'.

Perhaps most importantly, Packer's brand of cricket made the wearing of helmets commonplace. Laughter greeted the skullcap that Brearley sported in the Test series against Australia in 1977, and the crash helmets which Yallop introduced to Test cricket and Amiss to English county cricket in 1978. The laughter went when Amiss, wearing his crash helmet, was the only batsman that season to score 2,000 runs, and when rapid improvements were made to the early cumbersome designs. By the time of the first Ashes Test at Brisbane in December 1978, players were buying up helmets like hotcakes.

With the introduction of the helmet, the psychology of cricket changed. A slice of tension was removed. Batsmen felt safer – although not completely safe because even with a helmet on some of them sustained nasty head and face injuries – and braver, although there was a certain loss of pride involved in even donning a piece of protective headgear. 'Better yellow than dead,' they were obliged to mutter. But the helmet helped the fast bowler, too. It gave him licence to bowl even more bouncers and, while batsmen may have been physically less vulnerable, many of them were technically even more exposed.

And that situation still exists today.

The first man to issue a challenge to the established powerhouses of pace was Imran Khan. And he could have found no better, no more provocative place to do so than in Sydney, Thomson's own backyard. Talk about working your rival's pitch!

It was January 1977: the final Test of a three-match series between Australia and Pakistan. Imran was twenty-four at the time, the same age as Thomson when he first won a Test match. Not that Thomson was playing now: on the first morning of the series he had dislocated his collarbone in a collision with Alan Turner and put himself out of action for four months. (Batsmen around the world wept openly.) But for Thomson's injury, Pakistan would probably have fared as badly in Australia as England and West Indies had before them. Even as it was, Lillee and the hostility of the crowds got to Mushtaq Mohammad and his men and they went to Sydney one down in the series and with a side stacked with batting, their only ambition to escape with a draw.

The conditions there were ready-made for Lillee: a heavy, humid atmosphere; a pitch hard and mottled green. There were widespread predictions of an Australian win inside three days and Greg Chappell showed his contempt for Pakistan's bowling by choosing to bat first. It was an act of hubris for which he paid dearly. Australia were dismissed for 211 and 180 and Imran, finding a rhythm that had previously eluded him, got through 45.7 eight-ball overs and took twelve wickets for 163 runs. In the stifling conditions his shirt became so soaked in sweat that one of the sleeves eventually gave up the ghost and fell off. So, too, did the Australian batsmen. Pakistan, having lost the previous Test by 348 runs, won this one by eight wickets. 'To avenge any type of affront,' Imran would one day write, 'is very much part of the Pathan character.'

Imran's reputation was made overnight. He had shown that Australia were not invincible and there was even talk that he was bowling as fast as Lillee. His arrival in the West Indies a few weeks later, for a five-match Test series, aroused considerable interest. Sir Garry Sobers took an early look at him in the nets and dismissed the suggestion that he was Lillee's equal for pace but Imran bowled with enough venom in the Tests to show that Sydney had been no fluke. He took 25 wickets and by the end of the series was exchanging bouncers with Roberts, a sure sign that he had been accepted into the brotherhood.

Exchanging bouncers with the world's best had been a cherished ambition of Imran's. He had taken up bowling at the age of fifteen not so much because he was interested in taking wickets as because he liked to see batsmen hopping around the crease. His early methods were not very sophisticated. He had, in his own words, 'a slinging action, somewhat similar to that of Thomson, only wilder'. He bowled a diet of inswingers and bouncers from wide of the crease and whenever he tried to bowl fast or intimidate batsmen he lost control. Worcestershire, whom he joined in 1974, encouraged him to become a stock bowler but he was intelligent enough to ignore their instructions and develop his fast bowling skills. By 1976, he had realized that he would never get anywhere as a Test match bowler unless he increased his pace. He worked further on his action and enhanced his training. The month before the Australia tour, he was ordered out of the Pakistan attack in a Test at Karachi for bowling three successive bouncers at Richard Hadlee.

Imran developed into one of the finest and most complete fast bowlers there has been. By 1982–3, he had put a jump into his run-up, was generating considerably more pace and had added the outswinger to his repertoire. He was at his peak during the home series against India that winter. Despite being confronted by a powerful batting line-up and easy-paced pitches, he took 40 wickets in six Tests at 13.95 each, including spells of five wickets for seven runs at Karachi and five for three at Hyderabad, the latter the fastest spell Imran reckoned he ever bowled.

The bouncer, though, remained an integral part of his attack: he used it to anyone coming forward and, if they retired on to the back foot, would attempt to beat them with swing. His was a dangerous bouncer too, bowled from wide of the crease and boring into the batsman's body. There was little chance of escape. Allan Lamb, something of a specialist when it came to facing fast bowlers, reckoned that by 1984 Imran was the most dangerous he had faced: 'He can be as fast as Malcolm Marshall – and as nasty – when he is in the mood.' Imran's aggression often got the better of him, as it did at Edgbaston in 1982, when he became so obsessed with trying to hit England's tenth-wicket pair, Bob Taylor and Bob Willis, that they were allowed to add 79, a partnership that contributed to Pakistan's defeat. Even when he took part in a fast-bowling competition in Australia in 1979, Imran couldn't resist dropping the ball short. Had he bowled at the stumps instead, he might have gained that extra one mile per hour that would have moved him into second place ahead of Holding.

For some reason, Imran's bowling in Test cricket rarely resulted in batsmen being badly injured. He forced only one batsman to retire hurt, Mohinder Amarnath ducking into a short ball at Lahore in November 1978 (it tells you something about the bowler that a photograph of this incident appeared in his autobiography). Perhaps when it came to the crunch, he didn't really want to hurt people, just rough them up a bit. It's not your bones they want to break, but your nerve.

Imran put down his liking for the short ball partly to the pitches in Pakistan, which gave fast bowlers so little help that once the shine had gone from the ball the bouncer was one of your few remaining weapons. Even medium-pacers would often deliver two or three bouncers an over. Certainly Sarfraz Nawaz, who fell short of being among the fastest of fast men and was Imran's regular new-ball partner for several years, used the bouncer frequently and indiscriminately. He was an unorthodox and unpredictable character and was mistrusted by most of his early Pakistan captains. Later, he found himself overshadowed by the glamour of Imran's personality and achievements, and remained an underrated player, a process that history will be slow to repair after the publication in 1992 of allegations by the England batsman, Allan Lamb, that Sarfraz taught younger Pakistan players how to interfere illegally with the ball.

Together Imran and Sarfraz formed a potent strike force. In the Caribbean in 1977 they demonstrated that there was still a brittleness about the West Indies batsmen who had scored so many runs in England the previous year by taking 41 wickets between them at an average of 33.39. At home to India two years later, their reliance on the short ball led to Gavaskar's protest at Faisalabad and Bedi's dramatic concession at Sahiwal. Sarfraz did, though, have a few moments of unshared glory in his career and he produced one of the greatest spells of fast bowling in Test history when he took seven Australian wickets for one run in 33 balls at Melbourne in March 1979.

Even by the standards of cricket's new underworld, Sarfraz was a tempestuous character. He had a lot of aggro in him for someone who wasn't that quick. Once, while playing for Northamptonshire against the Australians in 1975, he went completely off the rails. Incensed at a bouncer from Thomson, his response was direct and laced with real thuggery. When Thomson batted, he ran up to bowl, overstepped the delivery crease by two paces and unleashed a beamer from some eighteen yards. Fortunately the ball missed its target, although Sarfraz's words did not: 'Thomson,' he spat, 'there's a spare plot in the cemetery. It's got your name on it.'

Sarfraz was accused of dabbling in the intimidation business even after his playing days were over. In September 1992, he was charged with imprisoning, assaulting, and stealing the clothes of a woman he had met at a party in Middlesex. Azra Rauf, a dancer, said Sarfraz had given her a lift home after she had performed for guests at the party and then held her captive at a flat in Chelsea. But, as with the intimidation he was sometimes accused of practising on the cricket field, charges were not pressed. Sarfraz walked free from the Old Bailey a year later when Azra Rauf declined to give evidence.

If Imran was keen to avenge an affront, so too was Bob Willis. He has not, even now, forgotten the terrors that England experienced on their tour of Australia in 1974–5, never forgotten how Lillee and Thomson treated them. Throughout the remainder of his career, they were to remain his *bête noire*. Brearley reckoned that, even by the time he had become England captain, Willis was still so fazed by Lillee that his effectiveness was reduced when he bowled to him and, certainly, one of Willis's worst lapses was when he was being carted around the Oval by Lillee in 1981 and in frustration deliberately overstepped the mark – in fact, did a Sarfraz – and delivered a ball to him from nineteen yards. Willis seemed to feel, though, that the intimidatory tactics adopted by Lillee and Thomson justified him in bowling as aggressively as he liked on the basis that nothing could ever be as bad as what they had done. For instance, when Willis went round the wicket and hit Iqbal Qasim, the Pakistan nightwatchman, in the mouth with a bouncer at Edgbaston in 1978 – an incident which caused a storm of controversy – he tempered his regrets with the remark that it was 'not as callous as Lillee and Thomson'.

Willis, who first began to realize his own considerable bowling potential during Mike Denness's ill-fated 1974–5 tour of Australia, subsequently gained a reputation as an unsympathetic hit man which was at times not altogether undeserved. Although he claims to have held no grudges against batsmen ('Perhaps I would have been a better bowler if I had hated them more'), there was undoubtedly a spiky hostility about much that he did. He bowled from an awkward angle, speared the ball into the batsman's body nastily, produced awkward bounce (he was 6 foot 6 inches) and was genuinely quick. He could seem psyched-up and remote from his team-mates when he was bowling ('I didn't want any distractions ... I didn't want people talking to me or asking me if I wanted the field changed ... I wanted to concentrate on what I was doing') and remote from his opponents at almost any time. There was even a certain spikiness about the length of his career – he has still played more Test matches (ninety) than any other specialist fast bowler – for it can have been determination alone that brought him back from so much surgery on his knees.

Willis himself accounted for his detached manner by saying that it all went back to the Centenary Test at Melbourne in 1977 when he had rushed to the aid of Rick McCosker, who had gloved a ball from him into his jaw. 'The sight of the injury, and its clear extent [the jaw was broken], lessened my effectiveness as a bowler for the remainder of that game,' Willis said. He resolved never to make the same mistake again, and he never really did, although he gave himself some fairly stern tests one way and another. Iqbal Qasim's mouth, Max Walters's nose, Rick Darling stretchered off unconscious after being hit under the heart: none of these can have been easy to walk away from.

Willis's coshing of Iqbal Qasim in June 1978 led to one of the few attempts to negotiate an end to the warfare. A bouncer immunity for non-recognized batsmen was created. The plan was fanciful in the extreme and did not survive beyond a year, demonstrating how hard it is to legislate over something as open to interpretation as intimidation. The breakdown occurred during the series between Australia and England the following winter. Graham Yallop and Mike Brearley, the two captains, identified which of their players they felt were entitled to immunity, but the list was negotiable and a tailender could lose his immunity if he stuck around at the crease long enough. When England decided during the second Test that they wanted to bowl bouncers at Rodney Hogg, Australia's number nine, they had to surrender immunity for their own number nine, John Lever, in order to do so. The difficulties were that the scheme depended too much on trust (Hogg bowled a bouncer at Willis, who was supposedly immune, during the final stages of the Melbourne Test) and was too open to interpretation (Brearley had several disputes with umpires about how long a tailender had to be in before he could receive a bouncer). In any case, Brearley had a stronger fast bowling attack than Australia and little sympathy for the plan, which he felt displayed 'undue namby-pambiness'. More lastingly, the Iqbal Qasim incident led to the understanding that a nightwatchman was a recognized batsman and entitled to no special protection.

Willis's most regular new-ball partner for England was Ian Botham. Botham had not been on the tour of Australia in 1974–5 – he was too young – but he desperately wanted to join in the fight and mixed it with the old enemy at the earliest opportunities. In 1975, aged nineteen, he declared himself unhappy at the bouncers they bowled him when he first played against them at Taunton. In 1976–7, aged twenty-one, he encountered Ian Chappell in a Sydney bar, got into a frank exchange of views and removed the former Australia captain from his stool. In 1977, still aged twenty-one, he was withdrawn from the MCC attack in a match at Lord's for bowling too many short balls at Rod Marsh. Two months later he took five wickets on his first day of Test cricket against Australia: they included Greg Chappell bowled by a long hop and Marsh, softened up with a bouncer, leg-before. In 1980, on first encountering Ian Chappell on a Test match field, Botham made sure he gave him a first-ball bouncer.

If there wasn't an Australian around for Botham to have an argument with, another fast bowler would more than suffice. He got stuck into Richard Hadlee on the tour of New Zealand in 1977–8. When Hadlee was bowling to him, he would encourage him with abandon to bowl bouncer after bouncer: 'That's that,' he would shout after hooking a ball to the boundary, 'now give me another'. When Hadlee was batting, Botham couldn't resist the temptation to drop it short, although he paid a heavy price for doing so in the second Test match at Christchurch when Hadlee began flat-batting him over the slips for four and Botham then lost his cool completely ('He smashed me all over the ground'). It was during this Christchurch Test that Botham also crossed swords with Ewen Chatfield, who was playing his first Test against England since his near-fatal accident, and who aroused their ire during the second innings by running out Randall at the non-striker's end for backing up too far. Chatfield then threatened to do the same thing to Botham if he left his crease. 'Just remember one thing, son,' Botham said to a man five years his senior. 'You've already been killed once on a cricket field.' Welcome back, Ewen.

Like Kapil Dev, who emerged during this period as India's first genuine fast bowler for a generation, Botham for several years possessed a potent combination of pace and movement. Botham produced some devastating performances, perhaps most notably his completion of figures of eight for 34 against Pakistan at Lord's on a cloudless morning in June 1978, while Kapil Dev must be one of the few men who, at Madras in January 1979, has fought and won a bouncer war with West Indies. By the time they had reached their mid-twenties, though, both had been reduced by immense workloads to relying more on swing than speed. Kapil Dev took to this more easily than Botham, who persisted in bowling bouncers, too many of which landed in his half of the pitch and begged to be hit. But once Botham had got it into his head that he could bounce someone out, he was not easily dissuaded from his plan, however expensive it was proving: witness what happened with Des Haynes and Gordon Greenidge at Port of Spain in 1986. Five overs for 39 runs. Talk about surrendering the initiative!

Of all Australia's opponents, though, the ones with thoughts of revenge on their minds were West Indies. They had been gathering their strength ever since their roasting in Australia in 1975–6 and by the time the countries next met they had henchmen galore. It must have been an immense disappointment to them that when the series in the Caribbean in 1978 arrived, many of the leading Australians were away with Packer (the only survivors from the previous series were Cosier, Yallop and Thomson). Everyone on both sides was aware that no holds would be barred; you could tell that because the administrators were at pains to draw up a clause in the tour regulations limiting bouncers to no more than three every two overs. They might as well have gone down to the beach and commanded the waves to stop breaking on the shore; after what had happened in Australia, there was no way West Indies, now that they held the upper hand in pace, were going to be curbed. They pitched short relentlessly and there were times during the Bridgetown Test in particular when they bowled up to four bouncers an over, yet they were rarely warned.

It cannot have been long before the Australians were regretting the excesses of their predecessors. On the first day of the series, on a Port of Spain pitch of poor quality, Andy Roberts, Colin Croft and Joel Garner dismissed them for just 90, the innings lasting only 35.1 overs. One of the few batsmen to appear at ease, Peter Toohey, was hit over the right eye hooking at Roberts and had to be taken from the field to have stitches inserted in the wound; when he returned, he had his thumb fractured by the same bowler, an injury that kept him out of the remainder of the match and the second and third Tests. West Indies won the first two Tests in three days each and had not a dispute then led to the absence of their Packer players it is possible that they would have completed a clean sweep in the

five matches. As it was, they won the series 3–1. Just how
strong the West Indies now were in fast bowling can be judged
from the fact that they could win so comprehensively without
making undue demands on the likes of Holding (who was hampered by injury), Daniel (who was overlooked entirely) and
Sylvester Clarke, who performed ably in the Test at Georgetown
before losing his place through injury.

Croft and Garner had both emerged during Pakistan's tour
of the Caribbean in 1977, the one on which Imran had done
so well. With Holding and Daniel out through injury, places
were up for grabs and Croft and Garner grabbed them at the
first opportunity. Playing for the West Indies Board President's
XI in the touring team's second match of their tour, they
exploited a fast and bouncy pitch at St Lucia to devastating
effect, returning a combined match analysis of 17 for 195 from
63.2 overs and establishing a psychological ascendancy over
Pakistan which was not broken. With Roberts displaying signs
of tiredness, they dominated the Test series, Croft taking 33
wickets and Garner 25.

By the fifth Test match at Kingston, Pakistan were both physically and metaphorically on the back foot, even though the
series was level. They were only too aware that it was on this
ground a year earlier that India had been destroyed with so
many casualties. Before the game, Mushtaq Mohammad, the
captain, questioned the actions of Roberts and Garner (an
absurd idea) and on the first evening a hostile spell by Roberts
on the fast, uneven surface sent shock waves through the dressing room that no one was able to still. The next morning, Imran
said, 'We felt as though we were going to a funeral . . . Our
batsmen were living in fear, and got themselves out to wild
shots.' It was, he added, a 'fiasco'. The West Indies crowds,
too, were learning. Just as the Australian crowds had spurred
on Lillee and Thomson, they now encouraged Roberts with
chants of 'blood, blood'.

Croft didn't enjoy playing cricket and it showed. He was
moody and uncommunicative. He was also 'genuinely nasty'

(Imran); showed 'snarling aggression' (Marshall); was 'full of hatred' (Roebuck); and 'didn't appear to care whether he hit you or not' (Gatting). Because he bowled from wide of the crease, slanting the ball into the batsman's body, and because he was so fond of the short ball, Croft hit you quite often, and quite often on the head. One of the most distressing injuries he caused was to Ian Gould, of Middlesex, who was struck by a Croft bouncer during a county match with Lancashire at Lord's in 1978. 'It took nearly five minutes to get a doctor on the pitch,' Gatting recalled. 'Ian was shaking and we weren't sure if he was concussed, unconscious or what.' If Croft did hit you, he would stand over you like the Angel of Death and stare, as though he was just checking to make sure you *weren't* all right.

For some, Croft represented the unacceptable face of West Indies cricket, although most of his team-mates were probably as embarrassed as everybody else by some of his behaviour. It was typical that when the West Indies became totally disenchanted with the umpiring in New Zealand in 1979–80 (even the New Zealanders admitted it was unacceptable), it was Croft who was the most demonstrative, flicking off the bails and barging into umpire Goodall as he ran in to bowl. The New Zealand board wanted Croft left out of the next Test as punishment but Lloyd failed to take any disciplinary action, as he did against any of his players during an unruly tour. But it was during Australia's visit to the Caribbean in 1978 that Croft produced one of his most destructive performances. Playing for Guyana against the touring team three weeks after Roberts had fixed Toohey, Croft fractured Yallop's jaw and hit Yardley on the head, and prompted a heated response from Fred Bennett, the Australia tour manager, who issued a statement objecting to Croft's overuse of the bouncer which, he claimed, was a 'direct contravention of both the law and tour conditions'. How quickly the tables are turned!

Croft and Garner made a strange pair: Croft seemed to want to hit people and Garner didn't. If they had been assassins,

Croft would have blown you away with a shotgun, while Garner would have finished you with a single shot – although he'd rather not have killed you at all. Garner was perfectly made for fast bowling – he was immensely tall (6 foot 8 inches) and solidly built (he weighed seventeen stones) – but he rarely sought to bowl at his highest pace. He was temperamentally more akin to the medium-pacer who concentrated on long spells of line and length to frustrate batsmen into making errors, and this often suited Lloyd's purpose, for he liked to use Garner to block up one end while the rest blasted away at the other. Garner would fire the ball in from wide of the crease (and often from above the height of the sightscreen), force the batsman on to the back foot, get him thinking about his ribs, and then throw in the yorker (and Viv Richards reckoned Garner's fast yorker was the best he'd seen). There was little need for him to resort to bouncers. Greg Chappell's description of Garner's bowling was simple: 'Everything looked like it was going to be short yet he kept hitting me on the foot.' Garner so rarely bowled a bad ball that Gower said you felt you would never score a century against him. But don't be fooled: Garner could be decidedly quick. The farthest Knott ever stood back for anyone was for Garner in a Packer match at the Sydney Showground – and that was only partly because of Garner's ability to make the ball carry. And remember Coney. If you can break a man's arm when it is protected by a cast, you're quick.

Garner had a great ability to remain cool but woe betide anyone who found him in an aggressive mood. Then, he would start rolling his fingers over to cut the ball, start hurling down bouncers and generally behaving like . . . well, like Colin Croft. Often, he needed to be provoked to get into this state and sometimes team-mates sought to wind him up deliberately. Viv Richards managed it once to great effect when they were playing together for Somerset before a Gillette Cup quarter-final tie against Kent in 1979. Richards told Garner that he had heard that the Kent captain, Alan Ealham, did not rate him for speed. The result was explosive. On a fresh pitch, Garner whipped up a fierce pace, took five wickets for 11 runs in 9.4 overs as Kent were dismissed for just 60. The hapless Ealham, no doubt unaware of what he was supposed to have said, was out, bowled Garner, for a duck.

Sylvester Clarke and Malcolm Marshall would not have got their chance in the West Indies team as early as they did had not Roberts, Holding, Croft, Garner and Daniel been signed up by Packer, and for two or three years you could tell they were sixth and seventh choices. In their anxiety to prove themselves they were overly hostile, desperate to show that they, too, could put the wind up people. (Neither, in fact, ever lost this sense of hostility.) The difference between them was that when the Packer players returned, Clarke went back to being a sixth- and seventh-choice bowler, while Marshall moved ahead of Daniel in the pecking order, first reserve if any of the Big Four was injured. When Croft was banned for joining a rebel tour of South Africa in 1982, Marshall was ushered into the inner circle and within a couple of years had become grand master to them all. Whatever Lamb might have said about Imran, Marshall was the most frightening bowler of all.

It should have been the other way round. Physically, Clarke looked the more likely of the two to survive. He was not yet as broad-shouldered as he later became but he had powerful legs and, in Marshall's words, possessed 'pace, bounce and strength'. But although he did a nice line in aggression – he angled the ball into the right-hander and was only too willing to go round the wicket to anyone who blocked him – there was a question mark over his commitment. Lamb said that Clarke could be among the most fearsome bowlers in the world 'when he put his back into it'; Imran said, 'I never felt he was particularly interested in the game.' Certainly, when the Packer players returned, Clarke seemed content to go back to filling the small fry of the county circuit with lead. He particularly enjoyed terrorizing tailenders. Jonathan Agnew, one such tailender, said: 'You can keep your Marshalls, Pattersons, and Daniels. This man is the most feared in county cricket.'

Marshall, meanwhile, found his physical limitations a handicap in his early years. Instead of bowling in a way that was comfortable, he attempted to match the bowlers he was trying to replace in the West Indies team, all of whom were taller, stronger and more experienced than himself. He strove so hard to rival the pace of Holding in the Kingston Test against England in 1981 that he strained stomach muscles and had to leave the field; eight months later he put himself out of a tour of Australia trying to bowl through a back injury. But Marshall was extremely predatory by nature, coveting not only wickets but also Holding's position as the premier West Indian fast bowler. He put aside the petulance with which he had greeted early setbacks in favour of acquiring the variety which could help him claim Holding's mantle. And in the end he got what he wanted. Marshall regards as one of the highlights of his career the day at Kanpur in October 1983 when he was first given the new ball in a Test match. He did not waste it: his opening eight-over spell claimed four Indian wickets for nine runs. Gavaskar thought his speed 'amazing'; Richards described it as 'ferocious . . . the best I have ever seen from him; his pace and accuracy were just mesmerizing'.

The funny thing about Marshall was that he was so unintimidating in stature, so cherubic-cheeked, so boyish in his run-up to the wicket, that he couldn't be the most feared hit man in the game, could he? And yet, no bowler ever made a more searching examination of a batsman's weakness to the ball flying around his face; no bowler did more to give credence to the idea that West Indies were infringing the spirit of the game's laws. But blame him? How can you blame a fast bowler who stands only 5 foot 11 inches tall and whose deliveries naturally go through to the batsman at around head height? How can you blame a bowler whose arm action is naturally so fast that it gives the batsman little time to pick up the flight of the ball? Nasty injuries are bound to follow, aren't they? Andy Lloyd takes his eyes off the ball, gets hit on the head, is carried off to hospital; Marshall says, 'Lloyd's injury was not my fault

and he acknowledged as much when I saw him later.' Mike
Gatting misjudges a hook, gets his nose broken, is carried off
to hospital; Marshall says, 'I went to see Gatting, who had
played his hook shot too late, and when he told me it had been
his fault, not mine, I was greatly relieved.' And so on, through
countless other smashed noses, broken teeth and cracked heads.
Never his fault. In which case, why did he need to say, as David
Boon alleged in his autobiography, 'Are you going to get out,
or do I have to come around the wicket and kill you?'

Not that Marshall need have worried. He was far from the
only chilling customer in the game. The Australians had some
of the worst, perhaps because they, above all others, were trying
to emulate Lillee and Thomson; become, in fact, the next Lillee
and Thomson. Len Pascoe and Rodney Hogg were two who
were regarded by the Australian public – indeed, regarded themselves – as their successors. Pascoe, who was of Yugoslav stock
and had changed his name from Durtanovich, had the ability
to bowl with real pace (in the competition organized by Packer
in 1979 he finished ninth, not far behind Lillee) but lacked the
control to make the most of it; Hogg relied more on accuracy
and the ability to move the ball either way, bowling fast only
occasionally, although Randall said that at times he was as fast
as Lillee had been in the Centenary Test of 1977. Hogg was
hampered both by asthma, which restricted him to bowling in
short spells, and the fact that, when he first played for Australia,
he had to carry the attack virtually single-handed, Lillee,
Thomson and Pascoe having all joined Packer. Despite this, he
took 41 England wickets in his first Test series.

They, too, had nice lines in aggression. Hogg, charged with
the task of answering English hostility during the 1978–9 series,
displayed all the necessary attributes: he was highly verbal;
spattered more than his fair share of skull-crushers; went round
the wicket to attack Boycott; got into a feud with Botham; and,
before the Tests had even started, had put blood on the pitch
and eight stitches in Clive Radley's forehead. He had to have
things going his way though: during Australia's tour of India

in 1979–80, for instance, he became so badly demoralized at losing his rhythm that he kicked over the stumps in frustration during the second Test at Bangalore and finished the series with only 11 wickets in the six Tests.

Pascoe was even more volatile; was, in fact, quite unable to handle the role of macho fast bowler. The legacy of Lillee and Thomson was just too much. He was, in fact, a friend of Thomson and had played Sydney grade cricket with him. He was warned for bowling too many bouncers the first time he confronted Boycott in a Test match and in one of his first meetings with Viv Richards; he was also warned during the Centenary Test in England in 1980. Batsmen tell of all sorts of threats from Pascoe: he was going to kill them, maim them, would warn them they were going to end up in hospital; and then he would lose control trying to carry out his threats. Border wrote in his autobiography in 1986 that he reckoned Pascoe was the worst player for sledging he had ever come across (although that was 1986, before Border's captaincy entered its mean period); and Gower said Pascoe was 'genuinely off his rocker . . . he really did flip at times'. Not for nothing was he nicknamed 'Loosehead'. Pascoe was about as subtle as an oversized man with oversized hands walking down the street with a violin case under his arm.

Perhaps the most sophisticated fast bowler of them all, though, was not a West Indian, an Australian, a Pakistani or an Englishman, but a New Zealander. In his youth, Richard Hadlee was as wild as any other would-be quick, hurling down the ball as fast as he could and grossly overdoing the bouncer. He was stereotypical of his breed: obsessed by his own skill, that of being able to propel a cricket ball quickly, he forsook all others. He was aggressive, bullying, selfish, uncontrolled and uncontrollable. He was fiercely envious of his elder brother Dayle, who preceded him into the Canterbury and New Zealand teams, so much so that he once announced to the rest of the family that he intended to 'bring [Dayle's] head home on a silver platter'.

But then one day, around 1980, Hadlee suddenly – and inex-
plicably to most people's eyes – changed. He decided he was
wasting his time trying to blast out opponents. He was lean
and unmuscled, gained most of his speed from a side-on delivery
and a long, whippy bowling arm, and had the strength to bowl
at high speed only in short bursts. He decided that, in that case,
he needed to pick off his victims rather than blow them away.
So he revised his methods. He cut down his run-up, employed
the bouncer only as a weapon of surprise, and replaced the
verbals with the stare. He bowled wicket-to-wicket, developed
the ability to move the ball either way and concentrated on
rhythm and swing. He spent hours studying videos of the
world's best batsmen, searching for chinks in their armour, and
analysing the methods of Lillee, the bowler he most admired.
And it worked. If the ball could swing, he would make it; if
there was anything in the pitch, he would find it; a combination
of the two, and he would be absolutely deadly.

At this time, when the whole cricketing world was obsessed
with knocking each other's heads off, this was a remarkable
thing for anyone to do. Many New Zealanders were appalled
at Hadlee's volte-face. They had come to rely on him running
in off twenty-yards to kick ass on behalf of a Test team that
spent a lot of time having its own ass kicked. Don Cameron,
one of their leading cricket reporters, bemoaned 'New Zealand's
heaviest artillery operating off a pop-gun run-up', a jibe that
stung even Hadlee. Hadlee has often been described as a solitary
man – as New Zealand's one bowler of match-winning potential
he inevitably had to be – but in this respect Hadlee chose the
solitary course. He was the tearaway fast bowler who turned
his back on the greatest bun fight in cricket history to ply his
trade as seam-up-and-swing-it merchant. Hadlee could not have
surprised people more if he had announced he was going off to
join the local ballet company.

For the last ten years of his career, Hadlee ploughed his lonely
furrow. He was known as a ruthless operator. Derek Randall
said he could be 'one of the nastiest pieces of work I have

come across'; Greg Matthews described him as 'one of the most aggressive bowlers I've ever faced. He uses eye contact – he has a presence'. Although he did once give Peter Roebuck a working over after Roebuck had described him in a newspaper article as 'austere and morose', and he had his inevitable run-ins with Botham, he largely eschewed the rough stuff in favour of more constructive behaviour. He occasionally played difficult, sometimes with his own team-mates, perhaps because, as David Gower once observed, 'he tired of being considered a quiet man'.

But at the end of it all, Hadlee got what he wanted. He did not want to hit a batsman between the eyes as he stretched defensively forward; he did not want to hit him in the teeth after deceiving him with a quick bouncer; he had no desire to break fingers, thumbs or ribs. He simply wanted to be top of the pile. Not the fastest, not the scariest, just the best.

And in the end, he was.

5

Riding the Roller Coaster

The most devastating thing you can do to a fast bowler is to hook his bouncer to the boundary. He hates it. It holds him up to ridicule. He has tried to unnerve you and you have turned the tables with the easiest-looking four runs you can make. The hook shot tells everyone that you've got his measure. And if you want to make him feel even worse, hook him to the square leg boundary rather than to fine leg: it shows that you've had oodles of time to dispatch his worthless trundlers. Hook him fine and it shows you were only just in control of the shot (if, indeed, you were at all); hook him square and it shows you had time to pick your spot; hook him *in front of square* and you've seriously impugned his status as a strike bowler and as a man. Not even the straight six can do that. There's only one thing worse than telling a fast bowler he's not quick and that's to prove it. Marshall? Fast? No way . . . watch this!

The hook is the stroke that every batsman would like to play. Everyone knows that trying to wear down a fast bowler by leaving alone every ball you don't have to play may be one way to win the duel, but it is hardly the most attractive (people talk about a battery of fast bowlers being dull to watch but it is the attritional batting that so often meets it that is really dull). For a start, it is an admission that you are the weaker force. But to hook is to execute a direct and deadly hit. It is not only like a blow to the solar plexus for the bowler, it also lifts the batsman. It is the sort of shot that makes you want to jog up the pitch (even though you know the ball is crossing the boundary), just so that you can turn and catch the eye of the hapless heavy and let him see how pleased you are. Make him realize that he is more of a leviathan than a Lillee.

The snag is that in order to play the hook shot you have to put your life on the line. To see the ball properly on to the bat you have to go back and across, get your body – get your *head* – behind the ball. You must make yourself stand there and watch the ball heading for your face; you must hit the ball in front of your face and never take your eye off it. It is hardly surprising that Len Hutton, when asked if he hooked Lindwall and Miller, replied: 'I once got to the halfway stage, but out of the corner of my eye I could see the local hospital. So I cut it out.' Even now, a helmet is of only limited help; even if it saves you from serious injury – and it may not even do that because not every batsman who wears a helmet wears a visor or grille – it cannot protect your morale from the shattering blow of having your skull rattled inside a tin can. Zaheer Abbas was once hit on the head in a Test match by a ball from Sylvester Clarke and had to retire, not because he had been physically hurt but because Clarke had put a two-inch dent in his helmet and an even bigger dent in his confidence. (You occasionally hear of a batsman 'duck-hooking', which, if accomplished successfully, is also known as having your cake and eating it, but it is not recommended as a long-term strategy for playing the short-pitched ball.)

Because it is the stroke that everyone would like to play, there is tremendous pressure on batsmen to hook. That's what did for David Hookes. He thought everyone wanted to see him hook Garner, Holding and Roberts. And he was right. Anything else would have left questions about him unanswered. Just as real fast bowlers must bowl bouncers, so real batsmen must hook.

Hooking is all a question of courage. You mustn't think about the possible consequences, or you'd never do it. When you hook, you mustn't be thinking, 'I don't want to end up like Gatting, Roland Butcher or Hookes.' You mustn't recall Viv Richards's words that if you play enough you are bound to get hit and the only question is how you will come back from it. You must be thinking that it is the most natural shot in the world, and play it confidently and decisively. There can be no half measures. You mustn't hesitate or flinch, or you are finished. The risks are great, but they are much greater if you start to think about them.

The courage of some players in the pre-helmet era was astonishing. Remember Colin Cowdrey, at the age of forty-one, hooking Thomson in 1974–5; Majid Khan insouciantly dispatching Lillee from beneath his bush hat two years later (he made Lillee a gift of that hat: a nice touch); Asif Iqbal and Wasim Raja taking it in turns to tackle Roberts, Croft and Garner head on in the Caribbean a few months later (Wasim Raja hit fourteen sixes during that series). And then, of course, there was Derek Randall, repeatedly hooking and pulling Lillee during his great hundred in the Centenary Test at Melbourne in March 1977, delighting England supporters frustrated by their recent dearth of strokemakers and impressing Australia who had rarely seen their fast bowler treated in such a way.

Randall annoyed Lillee not only with his hooking but also with his antics: when Lillee bowled a good ball, he would doff his cap in tribute or shout an acknowledgement ('That was a good one, Mr Lillee!'); when Lillee floored him with a bouncer, he would pick himself up, dust himself down and grin as though it were all a village match. Lillee didn't know what to make of all this (indeed, none of the Australians did; it was Randall's first Test match against them), except that he knew he did not like it. Was Randall mad? This was worse than Greig going down on one knee to signal his own boundaries: at least you knew where you were with him, at least he sledged you once in a while. But this guy?

Was Randall mad? He certainly liked to give the impression he was a bit daft – after receiving the man of the match award for the Centenary Test, he thanked Lillee for the bump on the head and said, 'If it had hit me anywhere else, it might have hurt' – but he was not so much mad as insanely courageous, as he had already shown in striking a swashbuckling 88 in a one-day international against the 1976 West Indies. It was courage alone making up for the nervousness and technical shortcomings that led to his shuffles around the crease as he prepared to face the next ball. (Lillee had once snarled at him: 'I hate bowling at you. It's so much harder hitting a moving target.') But if you are insanely courageous, what better way to spend your time than hooking fast bowlers?

Certainly Ian Botham, who bowled in the nets to Randall during the Centenary Test, wanted to join in the heroics. 'That's that . . . now give me another!' was what he shouted down the pitch not only to Hadlee but also, metaphorically, to Rodney Hogg, Kapil Dev, Dennis Lillee, Joel Garner and any other fast bowler willing to test his nerve against the bouncer. Botham's greatest hour was probably his duel with Lillee during the Old Trafford Test of 1981, when he took on the Australian armed with the new ball. Viv Richards has described hooking Lillee as one of the most dangerous shots in history. Three times in two overs, Botham hooked Lillee for six. Two of these deliveries were, in Brearley's words, 'exactly where Lillee intended, head high and dead straight'. Each time, Botham ducked his head but went through with the stroke, saying later that if he had missed the ball it would have 'caught me right in the middle of the forehead each time. Perhaps that was the reason I connected so well – out of sheer self-preservation.' Lillee was stunned: 'He kept hooking me, taking his eye off the ball. I was sure I would get him with the bouncer, but the more I fed him with it, the further the ball disappeared.' In all, Botham scored 45 of his 118 runs off the 24 balls he received from Lillee.

Perhaps even more extraordinary than that was the way Desmond Haynes took on Thomson in the Caribbean in 1978. He was playing international cricket for the first time and had never before faced Thomson. In the first one-day international at

Antigua, Thomson greeted the newcomer with a bouncer that flicked the peak of his cap. Instead of being overawed, Haynes responded with naked aggression. 'I decided to take up the challenge,' he said. 'This guy Thomson simply had to go.' He hooked him several times and during the course of 136 balls produced virtually every shot in the book in scoring 148. Although Thomson eventually bowled him, his ten overs cost 67 runs. Nine days later in Trinidad, Haynes did it again. It was his first day of Test cricket and he had gone in just over an hour before stumps; Lloyd had advised him to take it easy and concentrate on survival. When Haynes returned to the pavilion at the close the total was 79 for no wicket, of which his share was 53. His most sensational strokeplay came in one over from Thomson which cost, incredibly, twenty runs and included a hook for six.

If you think Randall, Botham and Haynes were crazy, you should have seen Rick Darling. He was a compulsive hooker and wouldn't have known which bouncer to not hook if it had come up and hit him between the eyes. The England team touring Australia in 1978–9 could not believe their eyes. They knew Darling liked to hook, so they put two men out in the deep for the shot, served up bouncers, and still he went for it – and got out to it – almost every time. Even nearly being killed in the Adelaide Test didn't deter him: he was struck under the heart by a ball from Willis that nipped back; his heart stopped, he swallowed his tongue, and only the prompt actions of John Emburey and South Australia's physiotherapist saved his life. In the second innings of the same match, chest padded, he was caught on the long leg boundary. And eleven months after Adelaide, Darling was hit near the right temple attempting a flamboyant hook at Kapil Dev in Bombay. After that, the only person ever to be twice carried from the field in Test cricket never played for Australia again.

And then there was Mohinder Amarnath. He too didn't seem to know what fear was. He had been taught by his father Lala, himself a Test cricketer, that the short ball was there to be hooked, and it was a principle he stayed true to throughout his career. The more often he was hit, the more determined he was to come back. Hit in the face by a short ball from Imran at Lahore in October 1978, he returned later and promptly got out hooking; unfazed, in his next Test he played, according to Imran, 'some incredible shots'. Touring England the following summer, he was hit on the head half a dozen times before failing to pick up a ball from Hadlee in poor light at Trent Bridge and sustaining a hairline fracture of the skull. Several months after that he re-emerged against Australia in Bombay wearing spectacles (the injury had affected his eyesight), an ancient topee belonging to his father and adopting an open-chested, crouched stance. Hogg immediately tested him with the short stuff: second ball, Amarnath tried to hook, failed to connect and overbalanced into his stumps. In Bridgetown in April 1983, he missed a hook against Marshall and retired with a cut lip, only to return and play shots which Marshall 'couldn't believe'.

If you really want to see the blood drain from the face of a fast bowler, forget about telling him he's not quick, forget about hooking him in front of square. Just do what Amarnath did: let him fell you once, then return to the crease, scars showing, and bat as if nothing had happened. It's not easy to do, but it'll really freak him out. It overturns everything he believes in. If he loses the power to scare, he has nothing left.

Amarnath did not always find favour with the Indian selectors – he was overlooked for three years after the Hogg incident – but his career was proof of the validity of the hook shot as a means of counterattack. During the Battle of Kingston, he was the only Indian to offer any resistance in their truncated second innings, scoring 60 out of the total of 97 with three sixes and seven fours. Two years later, he took 445 Test runs off an Australian attack missing its Packer players but led by Thomson. And by 1983, after he had scored 584 runs in six Tests in Pakistan (whose attack was led by Imran, then at his height, and Sarfraz) and 598 runs in five Tests in the West Indies (with an attack of Holding, Roberts, Marshall and Garner), he was generally acknowledged as the finest player of fast bowling in the world. Imran wrote in 1988: 'I have rarely seen such a classy batsman . . . had I been his captain I would never have dispensed with him – he's a player on whom you can depend when the going gets tough.'

Probably the only hooker in the modern game better than Amarnath was Viv Richards, who took the duel one stage further. Amarnath resisted all attempts by the bowler to break him; Richards tried to break the bowler. The hook provided the perfect opportunity. 'The fast bowler,' he said, 'is testing out your courage and your speed of reaction and you are trying to hit him either to, or over, the boundary. It is one of the game's great sights as the batsman rides the roller coaster of risk. You are telling the bully with the ball that you are not scared of anything he can send down at you.' Boycott said of Richards: 'Hooking is his passion – and the more violent the stroke the better he likes it. Not a shot to help the ball on its way but a totally aggressive, explosive attack, a challenge he can rarely resist.'

In fact, the challenge was so irresistible to Richards that some people in the game reckoned the best chance you had of getting him out was to give him a few bouncers early on and see if he would misjudge a hook before he got his eye in. The sooner you got him on that roller coaster, the better.

I said hooking was all a question of courage. That was not strictly true. It *used* to be all a question of courage. Things started to get more complicated as the sheer volume of high-quality fast bowling in Test cricket increased. Faced with attacks that could be sending down anything up to 250 bouncers a day, batsmen were forced to tighten up their techniques: they couldn't attempt to hook every bouncer they received, there were simply too many, so they had to decide which ones to hook and which ones to leave alone. Was the pitch too fast? Was the bounce too unreliable? The bowler too hostile? The ground too large? Did you have your eye in? You didn't want to get out hooking and be accused of irresponsibility, now did you?

The problem was more acute for some players than others. For those brought up in the West Indies, Australia and South Africa, where the ball bounced and came on to the bat, the hook stroke was one of the commonest and most natural shots in the world; it was an instinctive thing and the decision about which balls to hook and which ones to leave alone was easier to make. For those who learnt the game in England, where the pitches were slower, it was a stroke only rarely played, alien and unnatural, a stroke filled with mystery and danger. Just the sort of stroke to cut out if you wanted to give yourself a chance of surviving at the highest level. The real problem, though, was that if you did cut out the hook shot you seriously reduced your opportunities for scoring: 250 balls a day was an awful lot to let go by, particularly when many of the other deliveries you faced – such as those that were wide of the off-stump – could not be scored off either.

It was hardly surprising, therefore, that a lively old debate about the merits of hooking ensued in England. Randall was one of the characters at the centre of it. He had the courage to hook but he had this problem with judgement. He couldn't leave the bouncer alone. (Compared to Randall, Richards had no problem about hooking early in his innings.) On England's next visit to Australia after the Centenary Test, in 1978–9, Randall got into all sorts of difficulties, was hit on the head by Lawson attempting to hook against New South Wales and was caught hooking in the second Test at Perth and the fourth Test at Sydney. By the time of his first-innings dismissal at Sydney, second ball, the tour management was fit to gag. No one wanted to listen to Randall's pleas that the hook brought him lots of runs. Ken Barrington, the assistant manager, cornered him in the dressing room: 'It doesn't matter how many fucking runs you've picked up. You've got to look at the fucking wicket a few overs before you try a hook.' Doug Insole, the manager, got him in the car on the way back to the hotel: 'It's your responsibility to have a look at the bowlers, to get the pace of the wicket before you start hooking.' In the second innings, Randall made a concerted and successful effort to cut out the shot (exhorting himself with the rebuke, 'Twasack, don't hook!') as he battled almost ten hours for a match-winning innings of 150. But he failed to convince the people that mattered of any new-found discipline, especially when Brearley twice suckered him with the early bouncer in a county match at Trent Bridge in 1981. Then, in December of the following year, his luck ran out. He was hit badly in the face after attempting a hook at Holding on a dodgy pitch in Tasmania and was never the same against West Indies. Previously, he had always got into line against them ('All you could see when you bowled to him,' Holding recalled, 'was his feet') but this was not the case when next they met at Edgbaston in 1984. 'It ended my Test career,' Randall said. 'I made nought and one and didn't stay in line with the ball.'

The irony was that by the early eighties England had a side full of strokemakers who were increasingly reluctant to take the attack to the opposition. Gooch took on the West Indies fast bowlers in the Caribbean in 1981 but few of his team-mates felt confident of being able to do the same and the hook shot was rarely seen outside the nets. Boycott, for his part, was happy to leave the shot out of his repertoire altogether. He had regarded it as the riskiest of strokes ever since he ended up in hospital after first attempting to execute it at the age of eleven and his crisis of confidence in the mid-seventies was brought on by problems handling new-ball bouncers in the Caribbean in 1974. He had become uncertain whether to go through with the shot and sometimes hesitated alarmingly as he resisted the impulse to hook. Not that scoring runs was ever Boycott's priority. In nine Tests against West Indies in 1980 and 1981 he batted a total of forty-three hours and it was said that during that time he hooked Holding only once.

Gower, too, had opted for discretion. In his early days he was a natural hooker. He thought nothing of it (at that age, they never do). He would simply stand up and hook or cut the short ball; the thought of being hurt barely occurred to him. His first Test match against West Indies, at Trent Bridge in 1980, changed all that. It was his first ride on the roller coaster of risk. Roberts was faster in that match than anything Gower had previously faced and it brought home to him the dangers. 'Suddenly the physical risk became more apparent,' he said. He felt that the margin for error with the hook shot was so fine that it was best played 'when the opposing bowler is not really fast, but thinks he is, and when he is bowling on a slow pitch'.

Like many other batsmen at this time, Gower began to take the attitude that, tempting though it may be to hook, you could also discourage a fast bowler by swaying out of the way of his bouncers. This, he wrote in *A Right Ambition*, 'can be more disconcerting to the bowler than actually attacking him . . . you commit the bowler to a growing feeling of frustration, a loss of temper and control, or a change of tactics, which must work to your advantage . . . If he knows that you are prepared to hook him, then he does have the option of putting two men back and bowling in the hope that you might make an error and put up a catch.' Although Gower went cold on the hook shot, he developed a penchant for something similar, the pull to long leg. He was about as good at it as Darling was at the hook and his dismissal in the Adelaide Test of 1991, caught by one of three fielders positioned for the shot, was the beginning of the end of his working relationship with Gooch, the then England captain.

It got to the point that by the tour of Australia in 1982–3 virtually none of the England players was willing to meet the fast bowlers head on. The only one who might have done, Botham, who had hooked Lillee and Lawson with such success during the previous series between the countries in 1981, was deliberately starved of the short ball by the Australians. The result was that they gave a submissive performance during their defeat at Brisbane, a fact that Lamb partly attributed to the rule in county cricket limiting bouncers to one per over: English batsmen, he felt, had simply forgotten how to deal with the bouncer. This was backed up by Clive Lloyd, who said in 1984 that he felt one of the main faults of English cricket was that batsmen weren't encouraged to be aggressive enough.

Not that England were alone. India and Pakistan – who, on their low, slow pitches, were just as unfamiliar with the hook shot and the bouncer as England were – also began to favour passive resistance. When England toured the subcontinent in 1981–2, Fletcher, their captain, thought he'd had a Good Idea. He planned to repeat Greig's tactic of using pace to unsettle India's batsmen and even had his bowlers go round the wicket to bowl into the ribs (and at the heart) of Gavaskar, their leading player. But the Good Idea failed. India eschewed all risks. They left out the white-knuckle merchant, Amarnath, and refused to hook, and England came away frustrated and beaten. (This did not stop Fletcher giving the Good Idea another run when he returned to India as manager eleven years later, but India's strategy, and the outcome, was the same.) Imran Khan also learnt the value of restraint when Pakistan toured England in 1982 and he got out attempting a hook against Willis at an important stage of the first Test at Edgbaston. The match, Imran's first as Pakistan captain, was lost and he resolved to set his players a better example in future by eliminating the stroke altogether.

The funny thing was that even Australia started to change their approach. When West Indies toured in 1979–80 and started to grill Australia as fiercely as they had done in the Caribbean two years earlier (despite the fact that all the Packer players were available again), Australia decided that something had to be done. The principal target of criticism was their most brilliant and aggressive strokemaker, Kim Hughes, who was roundly condemned for taking risks against the fast bowlers by several former Test players. This seemed rather unfair, as he had been instrumental in saving the Test at Brisbane, where he had hit an unbeaten 130, and had made top score for his side at Melbourne with 70. His methods worked, and yet he was rebuked.

It was not long before the hook shot was back. In December 1982, Amarnath regained his place in the India team – he slipped back in partly because of his value as a seamer, although an astute selectorial ear might have caught the sounds of the *Ride of the Valkyrie* – and before anyone knew it he was hooking his way to one of the most prolific batting spells in Test history. Word got around. Batsmen realized they had surrendered the initiative and thought it was time to get it back. The bullies could not be allowed to have things all their own way.

By the 1983 English season you had county batsmen such as Peter Roebuck deciding they would hook again for the first time in years. Mind you, it did Roebuck little good. He found that hooking the ball for four only encouraged the bowlers to bang down the ball, their pride wounded, and by the second week of May he had been hit on the head four times, twice by Roberts. That was the trouble. It was always a roller-coaster ride.

Gavaskar was more successful. He reintroduced the hook against the West Indies in 1983–4, shortly after he had begun to wear a small skullcap (which protected his temples but little else), for the first time for India. He had been having a troubled time, scoring only modestly in the Caribbean several months earlier and making only nought and seven in the first Test at Kanpur, and he told Vasu Pranjpe, a confidant, that he saw no point in carrying on in the same vein. Pranjpe told him: 'Fast bowling like this cannot be contained, it has to be counter-attacked.' And so, in the next Test at Delhi, Gavaskar attacked. He decided to hook Marshall, the man who had dismissed him twice in the first Test, and it worked. In the first over at Delhi, Gavaskar hooked Marshall for four and six; he raced to his fifty off only 37 balls; reached his hundred off just 94 balls. In all, he struck 121 off 128 balls, with two sixes and fifteen fours, and even continued to hook when Marshall went round the wicket to bounce him. In the next Test at Ahmedabad, Gavaskar hit 90 off 120 balls and although he failed in his next five innings and considered standing down, he then scored an unbeaten 236 in the final Test at Madras. His double-century was a more subdued innings than the others, but he looked to attack Marshall at all times and began by taking fours off his first three balls.

Word got around about this too. Botham got to hear of it. He loved the roller-coaster ride and had never been struck on the idea of restraint. That summer, Botham came up against the West Indies and, with Gavaskar's example fresh in his mind, resolved to see Lloyd 'scratching his head'. He almost did. Most of the Tests were played on pitches of uneven bounce yet Botham stood still and hit hard. He took on Marshall, hooking him off his eyebrows as he had Lillee and even intervening on the fast bowler's behalf when Bird warned him for intimidation at Edgbaston. He made six scores between 30 and 81 in the five Tests and finished as England's second-highest run-scorer.

But when England toured the Caribbean eighteen months later the roller coaster had somehow become faster, steeper and more violent. The West Indies fed Botham off-stump bouncers, knowing he could not resist the challenge. He found himself getting out more and more often caught hooking or in the slips; found the runs beginning to fall away; found his strategy – despite winning a spectacular duel with Marshall in a county match at Taunton in 1985 and despite his own protestations – beginning to lose credibility. By the time England next toured the Caribbean, in 1989–90, they felt able to leave Botham behind and, although he altered his approach when he was recalled against West Indies at the Oval in 1991, it was too little too late.

Botham's fortunes against West Indies illustrate better than anything else the technical problems he had with the hook shot. He did not always get behind the line of the ball, did not always get back and across. Keith Andrew, the coach, felt that Botham hooked in the air because he loved to hit sixes and that he could have cut out the shot if he had wanted to. 'That's the only shot he plays that doesn't seem to be controlled,' he said. Keith Fletcher shared this view. 'He thinks he's a good hooker but he's not. He puts it in the air, he's a compulsive hooker. He should learn to duck under them, because he has so many other shots he doesn't need to hook.'

These days, the hook shot remains just one of the myriad options available to a Test batsman as he decides how to spend the next 0.44 seconds of his life, but he is less likely to choose it now than he would have been twenty years ago. Because of the predominance of pace, it has become a contentious shot, worthwhile if it comes off but if it results in the batsman's downfall woe betide him. Even Kris Srikkanth, who has played some of the most brilliant attacking innings of modern times (including a century off Australia in 97 balls, one off Pakistan in 118, and arguably the most destructive attack inflicted on the West Indies when he scored 136 runs off 141 balls in two innings at Bombay in December 1987), has been criticized for taking risks. 'He does not learn from his mistakes,' Gavaskar has said. 'He wastes his God-given talents.'

The days of the compulsive hooker, the days of Doug Walters, Rick Darling, Derek Randall and Andrew Hilditch (remember him?), are gone for ever. Even Haynes has changed his ways, and hooks only rarely. Perhaps the most enthusiastic and successful hookers in the game today are Aravindra de Silva and Richie Richardson, who employ the shot with a lack of repentance not seen since Amarnath. They have made their pacts with the Devil.

Perhaps there should be more like him. Perhaps Graeme Hick is someone who could benefit from his approach. Hick plays the hook shot devastatingly well at county level but still mistrusts it, fearful of the ball being in the air for so long, and has largely ruled it out at international level. Perhaps if he employed it he wouldn't look so suffocated against the fast bowlers in Test cricket.

Shall I go for it? Give the guy a taste of his own medicine? Ride that roller coaster one more time?

*   *   *

In case you're thinking I'm exaggerating the dangers, here's something that happened while I was writing this chapter.

It occurred in a North Lancashire League match between Whitehaven and Workington in Cumbria on 30 August 1993. Ian Folley, the Whitehaven captain, was batting against Graeme Cross. Folley was a former county professional, nine seasons with Lancashire and one with Derbyshire, a slow left-armer and useful tailend batsman. Cross was a fast bowler, although on this occasion he bowled at nothing like his top speed; in any case, Folley was averse to wearing a helmet. Cross dropped one short, Folley went back and across, but succeeded only in edging the ball up into his face. He was hit high on the cheekbone, underneath the right eye. He fell to the ground but left the field unaided and although he went off to hospital for treatment nobody thought anything of it. 'We all thought it was a routine four-stitches job,' Cross said.

That night, while under the anaesthetic for an operation to stop the bleeding, Folley died.

He had ridden the roller coaster one time too many.

— 6 —

Tour of Duty

If you now think the idea of playing in a Test match against West Indies is not such a good idea, just imagine what it is like to go on tour there. Or to Australia. Spending fourteen weeks in those places may sound like fun if you're a tourist, but for an international cricketer this can be the stuff of nightmares. Five Test matches and five one-day internationals (or whatever) provide an awful lot of opportunities for Curtly Ambrose and Courtney Walsh or Merv Hughes and Craig McDermott (or whoever) to explore the darker recesses of your psyche.

Touring is very different from playing at home. At home, you gather with the rest of the team before an international and disperse to your various county or state sides once it is over; afterwards, you might even get to go home and spend some time with the family. At home, you have a chance to refresh yourself before the next international encounter; if necessary, to forget a failure. On tour, there are no such opportunities. You are one of a group of sixteen or seventeen men, all there with one express purpose: to win cricket matches. For fourteen weeks, you share the same flights, share the same hotels (in some cases the same rooms), share the same dining rooms, the same buses to the ground, the same nets, the same dressing rooms, the same fortunes. Above all, the same fortunes. OK, so you may get an extended run in the side in the way you might not at home, but if you start losing, things can get very heavy. And when you're touring the West Indies or Australia –

the modern powerhouses of fast bowling – losing is something that touring teams do a lot of.

In the years directly after the Packer players returned to the establishment fold in May 1979, few visiting sides came away from either of these countries with much. In seven years, West Indies hosted five Test series and won them all; in six years, Australia hosted six Test series against countries other than West Indies and won five and drew one. Their combined record in these matches was played 45, won 28, lost 3, drawn 14. The three defeats were all Australia's and were all at Melbourne: one was by just three runs to England; another caused by a freak collapse chasing a target of only 143 to beat India; and the third was by an innings to Pakistan after the series had been won and Australia had persisted with a pace attack on a painfully slow pitch (Lillee, Thomson and Alderman bowled 89.3 overs without taking a wicket). The only break in the pattern was when West Indies themselves toured Australia: of these 11 Tests, the visitors won six and lost only two. Otherwise it was a long-running tale of failure against these two countries – right down to England's catastrophic tour of the Caribbean under David Gower in 1986.

During this period, fourteen weeks (or whatever it was) must have seemed an awfully long time. There can have been no escape. The more you played, the more you were beaten, the greater the psychological hold your hosts established. A siege mentality takes hold. You go back to your hotels each night and talk about your failures, the poor umpiring (away from home, there's always poor umpiring), show each other the bruises, talk of your absent families. Even if you yourself are not out of touch with the bat, hearing of the struggles of your team-mates can often undermine your confidence. And even if you avoid such ghoulish conversation, there's no avoiding the team meetings at which you discuss your tactics and prospects (what prospects?) for the following day. Talk of the punishment you are taking at the hands of the fast bowlers only heightens their menace and before you know it you are starting to expect the worst, to expect the lethal delivery every ball. And if these bowlers do not destroy you immediately, they will probably force you into some injudicious stroke by their unflagging accuracy and aggression. After several weeks of this, it is not always fear that makes you want to give up so much as all those sore fingers and sore ribs. You just become very *tired* of it all. How soon is it acceptable to start counting the days until you can go home?

Some of you, of course, do not have to wait until the end of the tour to go home. Injuries are frequent – especially among those in the front line, the batsmen – and some are serious enough to necessitate an early return flight. Reinforcements might be sent out. The comparison with fighting a war on a foreign field is too obvious to miss. One modern cricketer has indeed likened a tour of the Caribbean to the tour of duty American servicemen endured in Vietnam. 'It's hell on earth if you're there to play cricket,' he said. 'The unrelenting barrage wears down your emotional and physical resistance until you can stand it no more. When you see your team-mates being maimed by fast bowlers intent on causing injury, you'd need to be a masochist to derive any sort of pleasure from the experience.' In his diary he wrote of one day's play: 'It's so frightening – and painful – what we've been facing . . . Life in the middle is hell. There is no enjoyment out there. The last hour's play wasn't cricket – it was carnage . . . Up to three bouncers an over and two or three other deliveries into the ribs. They bowled to hit, and it was overdone.' These are the words of Richard Hadlee, describing New Zealand's tour in 1985, but they could belong to almost any other visiting cricketer of the period.

Nor was the atmosphere in these supposedly paradisean places pleasant. Post-Packer, beaches were the last thing you saw (unless you were on Gower's tour). In the Caribbean, you had more chance of experiencing a police escort, a crowd riot, a vandalized pitch, an anti-apartheid demonstration, or an umpire refusing to stand; in Australia, of being the object of physical or verbal abuse from spectators, of players throwing tantrums, scuffling or threatening to forfeit the match rather than accept an umpire's decision; in both, you could witness dissent, gamesmanship, sledging, and, of course, short-pitched bowling like you've never seen before.

Mentally and physically you were beaten, bloodied and bowed. Often you had given up before you got there. This was especially true when you reached a ground which was known to assist pace. During the late seventies and early eighties, the pitch at Perth was perhaps the fastest and hardest in the world. It was the home of Dennis Lillee, and Western Australia and Australia were regarded as virtually unbeatable on it. The surface was so hard and so shorn of grass that it glistened like glass, which was hardly an encouraging sight as you tapped your bat at the crease before looking up to see Lillee steaming in with the breeze behind him. When Pakistan played there in November 1981, admittedly on a pitch containing more than its usual moisture, they were dismissed in just 128 balls for 62, the lowest total in their Test history. Had it not been for a few lusty blows from Sarfraz towards the end, it would have been a lot worse. Lillee took five wickets, Alderman four and Thomson, who only got on for two overs, one. Zaheer missed the match with a rib injury which was widely rumoured to be a lot less severe than it was made to appear. Two years earlier, Mike Brearley's England side, which played the first Test of their tour at Perth, had problems with the thought not only of the pitch but also of the tales they had heard of Lillee's tongue. 'I think some of our batsmen,' Brearley wrote, 'were secretly unnerved by an image of Australian aggression. We lost touch with our own combative powers and surrendered to the legend of Lillee and the Perth pitch. Botham was so angry about this tentativeness that he batted with a kind of reckless fury himself.' England lost the match by 138 runs and never recovered, being beaten in the remaining two Tests as well.

England must have approached their tour of the Caribbean the following winter with a similar sense of trepidation. They had spent the summer in a home series against West Indies struggling to come to terms with the hostility of Holding, Roberts, Garner and Croft. (Especially Croft. Perhaps the most unsavoury sight of the summer had been Croft at Headingley bowling five successive bouncers from round the wicket at Boycott, the fifth of them cutting away from a batsman intent only on self-preservation to produce a catch at slip and the laconic remark from Jim Laker, commentating on television, that 'it's little short of murder what's going on out there'.) If they were outgunned on the slow English pitches, how were they going to cope in the West Indies?

Botham, the England captain, tried to talk a confident game after West Indies had scored 426 in the first Test at Port of Spain by saying that heads would roll if the match was not saved, but he had underestimated what the West Indies fast bowlers could achieve on what was an unusually slow pitch. When England did indeed lose – partly because Botham himself played an irresponsible shot against the part-time bowling of Richards – their confidence quickly ebbed away. (Their morale was not helped by events which had nothing to do with the cricket: the second Test in Georgetown was cancelled when the Guyana government refused a visitor's permit to Robin Jackman because of his sporting contacts with South Africa, and Ken Barrington, England's assistant manager, died of a heart attack during the third Test in Barbados.)

Botham, in particular, became increasingly perplexed by his side's inadequacies. He was profoundly affected by Holding's celebrated first over at Bridgetown, in which the sixth ball beat the still-raised bat of Boycott and sent the off-stump cartwheeling twenty yards. All of Holding's deliveries, Botham said, were like 'lightning flashes'; Boycott 'jumped and parried and danced as if he were standing on hot embers'. Later the same day, Botham went in. For some reason – 'I don't know what came over me' – he launched into the bowling, hitting Garner for four and shouting, in his usual fashion, 'Fetch that!' The next ball was the fastest Botham can ever remember facing: it almost took his head off, did remove his helmet and certainly

wiped the smile from his face. Confronted by Holding, he
became even more rattled. He hurled down his bat in disgust
after one bouncer and when, two balls later, he was caught
behind he kicked the pitch before departing. On reaching the
dressing room he startled his players by declaring; 'I'm sorry, I
can't play against that sort of thing.' Thanks, skip.

England returned home a shell-shocked side. Only Gooch,
who gave Croft a fearful drubbing at Kingston, and Gower,
who displayed a new maturity of approach in batting almost
eight hours for 154 not out to save the final Test, and Willey
could look back with much pride. Brian Rose came back before
the third Test because of eye trouble but was nevertheless
psychologically affected by what had happened. He described
the West Indies fast bowlers as 'the most ferocious and
intimidating fast men on earth'. 'They were,' he added, 'after
your blood ... you had to dominate your own fear before
you could go out there.' Botham, too, took a while to get the
experience out of his system. Shortly after his return, he came
up against Holding in a county match at Old Trafford and made
little secret of the fact that he didn't expect to last long. (He
was quite right: Holding got him for a duck.) He did not, in fact,
rediscover his self-belief until he resigned the England captaincy
almost two months later: only then did he do to Lillee and
Lawson what he would have liked to do to Holding.

Botham was not the only captain to reach for the revolver
after a tour of the Caribbean. Kim Hughes did the same,
although his finger loitered on the trigger longer. Hughes's
Australia would have lost all five Tests in the Caribbean early
in 1984 had not rain curtailed the matches in Guyana and
Trinidad. Depleted by injuries (three of their batsmen were
incapacitated) and the recent retirement of Greg Chappell,
Dennis Lillee and Rod Marsh (it's odd, isn't it, how many
players retire directly before a potentially difficult series?),
Australia showed little inclination to fight. Only Border, who
averaged 74.42 in the Tests, almost three times that of any of
his colleagues, displayed the necessary resolve. Hughes, who

did not score more than 33 during the entire series, described the West Indies as 'the strongest, most professional and most disciplined' team he had ever met; but these things are all relative: Marshall reckoned Australia was the poorest team to tour the Caribbean during this period.

Hughes hung on to take Australia into their next series, at home to the West Indies six months later, but resigned after losing the first two Tests. His tearful walkout midway through his resignation press conference seemed only to confirm the suspicions of some Australian officials and former players (Greg Chappell, Marsh and Lillee cosily among them) that he was not the man to maintain their team's fighting reputation. Hughes remained as a batsman, hoping to play on for Australia for three more years but scores of nought, two, nought and nought in the next two Tests quickly put an end to that idea. Hughes was succeeded as captain by Border, but even he could not prevent West Indies comfortably winning their first full Test series in Australia since the drubbing of 1975–6. It was an outcome that brought a fitting end to Clive Lloyd's Test career. At last, he – and his players – had sated themselves on the carcass of Australian cricket.

Neither Botham nor Hughes, though, saw the morale of their side sink as low as that of Geoff Howarth's New Zealand in the Caribbean in 1985. We have already heard how demoralized Hadlee became during this tour; the other members of the party were no different. When Coney had his arm broken by Garner the rest of the team envied him for having escaped the line of fire and Marshall said he never saw a batsman more scared of him than Ian Smith during this series. Howarth was unable to arrest this collapse in spirit. When he won the toss in the final Test at Kingston, he selected to field first in order to postpone the ordeal with the fast men, although by that stage of the series he was so disheartened himself that his attitude to batting was, according to Hadlee, 'The sooner I get in, the sooner it will all be over.' Ironically, in his last innings of the series, Howarth redeemed himself in a way Botham and Hughes were unable to do. With New Zealand following on 225 behind, he gave a pugnacious display and frustrated the West Indies pacemen for five hours in scoring 84. Even so, he was gone as captain by the time New Zealand next played an international match.

Which brings us to *the* tour. The tour after which tours were never the same again, at least for England cricketers. Many of the seeds of disaster for England's trip to the Caribbean in 1986 were sown long before the Test matches even began. For a start, there was the choice of captain. Gower was not a conventional leader. He was all for each man doing his own thing. If you did not want to train, you did not have to; if you did not want a net, you did not have to have a net. Gower did not give a fig for the fact that before play the West Indians – a demonstrably successful outfit – would go through rigorous workouts together. *His* players would do what suited them best. So it was that Gooch went on his own training runs; so it was that Lamb spent countless hours alone in the nets with a bowling machine; so it was that Gower and Botham rarely trained and rarely practised; so it was that the pair of them went sailing off St Vincent on the second day of the first match of the tour. This approach was all very well when you were winning – and Gower had just won impressive series victories over India and Australia, inspiring him to suggest, Greig-like, that West Indies would be 'quaking in their boots' at the prospect of meeting England – but once you started losing (as England were about to) it created all sorts of problems. OK, so you avoided the conventional siege mentality of sitting around the hotels making each other catatonic with fear about what Garner and Marshall were going to do to you in the morning, but you replaced it with a far more terrifying private hell of your own, in which you did not even have graveyard humour for company. At least Denness and his boys had their joke about the condemned cell.

When you started losing under Gower, you really went down the pan. This had been illustrated eighteen months earlier, when he led England in a home series against West Indies and lost 5–0. Pat Pocock, who joined the team for the fourth Test of that series, was shocked by the morale of the side: 'I had never known a more shoddy and apparently uncaring attitude in a Test team.' He even confronted Gower with his concern about his team-mates. 'Cricket is their last consideration,' said Pocock to him. 'Nobody even talks about the game. We're three Tests down, we're being stuffed out of sight and some of them don't seem to care about it.' He was particularly concerned about the influence that Botham's light-hearted approach was having on the younger members of the team: 'I was very disappointed by his attitude.'

To be fair, Gower's side had several pieces of bad luck in the Caribbean. One was to come up against opponents fresh and eager for battle, opponents who had scarcely played in the four months before the tour began. This was unusual: before their two previous home Test series West Indies had undergone strenuous overseas tours, and in 1982–3, two of their fast bowlers, Holding and Garner, had come straight from a Sheffield Shield season in Australia and were so jaded that they proceeded to take just 19 wickets between them in the Tests with India at the moderate rate of one every 86 balls. Partly as a result (and partly because of rain in Guyana and benign pitches in Trinidad and Antigua), India had escaped with three draws.

Gower's side had no such fortune. In fact, they experienced tortures enough for fourteen weeks in just their first four. All their matches before the first Test in Kingston were played on substandard pitches (a common problem in the Caribbean); they came up against some aggressive fast bowlers gunning for places in the Tests, notably the Jamaican pair of Courtney Walsh and Patrick Patterson; Gatting received his horrific injury in the first one-day international; and then there was the Kingston Test itself, played on a pitch like corrugated iron and completed inside three days. The injury to Gatting, Gower's vice-captain, was distressing not only for himself but also for his team-mates. Botham accompanied him to the hospital, where Gatting was stitched up and had x-rays to check that fragments of bone had not been driven back in his head (they had not), and several colleagues had the unnerving experience later that day and during the first two days of the first Test of being waved off from the pavilion by a man with a smashed nose and black eyes, a salutory reminder of the sort of thing that awaited them in the middle. Gatting then returned to England for further surgery (he could no longer breathe through his nose) but he returned three weeks later only to have a thumb broken by Vibert Greene, of Barbados, in his first match back.

The Kingston Test of 1986 was like Brisbane 1974: England were surprised by the liveliness of the pitch and the speed of a wild and largely unknown 24-year-old fast bowler. Patterson's speed was even compared with that of Thomson at his height and he was certainly as well suited to Sabina Park as Thomson had been to the Gabba. Patterson had recently helped destroy both Guyana (41 and 202) and Leeward Islands (77 and 162) there, his strike-rate in 40.4 overs being fourteen wickets and six injuries. Now, his seven wickets in 21.5 overs contributed to England's demolition for 159 and 152 and although no one was badly hurt it was a close-run thing: Willey's arm would probably have been broken had he not been wearing a guard and Edmonds, they say, owed his life to his chest protector. The main difference between Brisbane 1974 and Kingston 1986 was that survival at Sabina Park was the more precarious business, partly because the ball came through at a variety of heights, but also because of the refusal of the Jamaican Cricket Association to raise the height of one of its sightscreens, which was adequate only for bowlers no taller than 6 foot. Patterson, who possessed the sprinting run-up of Holding and the menacing grin of Oddjob, was a powerfully built 6 foot 2 inches and claimed all seven of his wickets at the End With No Sightscreen. He just banged the ball in and waited for things to happen.

Most of the England players admitted they had never known anything like it. It was not simply that they had come across one of the fastest bowlers and most dangerous pitches they had ever seen. They had looked into the eyes of the beast itself: fear.

Even the only two England players to score half-centuries in the match virtually conceded as much. Graham Gooch said there was a 'whiff of real danger'; Peter Willey that it was the 'only time I started to think about my little daughter and wonder what the hell I was doing there'. They all had good reason to be afraid. Phil Edmonds received five successive bouncers from Patterson and was then struck over the heart by the next ball, an attempted yorker which ended up as a beamer. Edmonds staggered into his wicket but the umpires rejected West Indian appeals for hit wicket, not because of any thought of the intimidation law but because the beamer is an illegal delivery. Lamb, the only England batsman to go into the match in any sort of form, was subjected to an even more ferocious cannonade. When he returned to the dressing room for lunch on the first day he was white and shaking: 'He looked,' Edmonds said, 'like people do when they have just been in a car crash.' Even for West Indies, this was no ordinary situation. Haynes, who spent the match fielding at bat-pad, said: 'When Patterson ran in, the fear in the English batsmen's eyes was a frightening sight in itself.'

Kingston well and truly knocked the stuffing out of Gower and his men. Patterson, in fact, was never the same threat elsewhere as he was there, but it was too late, the collective will to fight had gone. Thereafter several England players – Gower and Botham principally among them – adopted the attitude that the unplayable ball (or 'death ball', as Gower called it) was just around the corner and that, in that case, you might as well play your shots while you could. 'We said to ourselves that if there was half a sniff of something to hit we had to have a go at it,' Gower said. 'If you've batted for three hours and got twenty it's no insurance against a ball that can get you out at any time. You can seldom say you've played yourself in so you might as well have a go.'

You might as well have a go. Approached in a calculated fashion, the idea might have had merit – Lamb, who hit three centuries in the 1984 series with West Indies, and Gooch had demonstrated what could be achieved by measured aggression – but like so much else on this tour it was pursued half-heartedly. Gower batted with some success in the remaining four Tests, passing 40 four times, but few others prospered. And not all the players agreed with the plan. When Botham 'had a go' without success in both innings at Bridgetown, and then had the nerve to return to the dressing room on the second occasion and protest, 'How can you play that stuff on these bad wickets?', he was rounded on by Gatting for his irresponsibility. The strategy certainly made no material difference to England's performance: not even Peter May, the chairman of selectors, demanding during the third Test that the team 'stop the rot', or Gower, realizing he had lost control of his players and blowing up before the fourth Test, could do that. England kept on losing wickets (on average every 39.15 balls, the fastest rate in any modern Test series) and kept on losing matches. In fact, as they slid to their second successive Blackwash, *you might as well have a go* began to sound awfully like *we might as well give up*.

Everyone knew what they were letting themselves in for, of course. If you were going to play a series in Australia or the West Indies you knew you would encounter some of the world's fastest bowlers on some of the world's fastest and hardest pitches. Which is why everyone was armed and ready – not for a physical pounding (although they were ready for that as well), but for taking advantage of these conditions themselves. If you had a couple of likely assassins of your own, Australia and the West Indies were the places to play them. You wouldn't necessarily give as good as you got, but you could give it a bloody good go. It was called fighting fire with fire.

England were great advocates of this theory. They have a poor record of producing fast bowlers but they are well aware that those they have produced have invariably done well given the right conditions: Harold Larwood and Frank Tyson are both best remembered for what they did in Australia, John

Snow for what he did in Australia and the West Indies, while Bob Willis established himself in the Ashes series of 1974–5. On this principle, they took Graham Dilley to Australia in 1979–80 when he was only twenty years of age and had just one full county season behind him. The decision was thoroughly justified: although his Test returns were only modest he generated enough pace to surprise Border at Perth, gashing him nastily above the left eye and forcing him to return wearing a helmet, and to suggest that he was as fast as anyone on either side (and Lillee, Thomson, Pascoe and Willis all played in that series). It was a similar story the following winter in the West Indies: he didn't exactly pull up any palm trees but he was lively enough to make life uncomfortable for batsmen, and it was nice for a change to have him go round the wicket to *their* guys. Unfortunately, Dilley's subsequent international career rarely lived up to the early promise: he was hampered by injuries but even when fit was not often as hostile or as fast as one might have expected. He was on the winning side just twice in his 41 Tests: at Headingley in 1981, when his chief contribution was with the bat, and at Brisbane in 1986, when he took six wickets in the match. It is noticeable that the most successful Test series of his career was his second tour of Australia.

The same reasoning inspired England to take Norman Cowans to Australia in 1982–3 and Greg Thomas to the Caribbean three years later. Again, it worked up to a point. Cowans, with the ability to produce the occasional very fast delivery, turned in a match-winning performance in the Melbourne Test and Thomas, without doing anything startling, gave Gower's otherwise pedestrian attack an aggressive edge. Both, though, seemed to lack the temperament for long-term success and in the case of Thomas, who had an appalling record of taking wickets throughout his career, nine days was too long for the wonder. It was not until Devon Malcolm was taken to the West Indies as a 'wild card' selection in 1989–90 before he had played even one full county season that the England selectors received a reaffirmation of their policy. Malcolm took fifteen wickets in the first two Tests of the series and arguably bowled at a speed not seen from an England bowler since Tyson. Even the West Indies said they would have been proud to have had him in their side (which they might well have done: Malcolm was born in Kingston, Jamaica).

Pakistan had an even poorer tradition of fast bowling than England, but it was their man, Imran Khan, who – on that sensational occasion in Sydney – first successfully challenged the supremacy of Australia under Lillee and Thomson. He also bowled superbly when Pakistan toured Australia in 1981–2 – he took sixteen wickets and conceded only 312 runs from 150.2 overs in the three Tests and many critics reckoned he bowled better than any of the leading Australians and West Indians on show that season – but when they next toured there two years later he was unable to bowl because of a stress fracture to his left shin. Pakistan's selectors compounded the problem by leaving Sarfraz Nawaz out of the original tour party (he had been banned from playing for six months after criticizing them for omitting him from a recent tour of India) but when Pakistan were outplayed in Perth and Brisbane they realized their error, hastily lifted the ban and flew him out. Unfortunately it was too late: Sarfraz had missed the two surfaces most likely to help him and in three remaining Tests he took only eight wickets at over fifty runs apiece.

These were just minor skirmishes away from the main fields of conflict: Australia versus West Indies. Most of the times these countries met, they did so on pitches favouring fast bowling, battles royal from Perth to Kingston, from Brisbane to Bridge-town. Australia quickly got a hang-up about these occasions. They may have won emphatically in 1975–6, but they rarely won after that. They may have had Lillee and Thomson, but West Indies had Roberts and Holding, then Croft and Garner, then Marshall and Patterson. They were being outgunned and they knew it. That was clear from the time in 1979–80 when they went into the series in Australia with Lillee, Thomson and Hogg and still came off a poor second (Thomson and Hogg, admittedly, were not fully fit). For the next few years Australia had to content themselves – as England were already doing – with terrorizing the little guys. And in those situations, Australia's pace attack was still devastatingly effective. In six home Tests in 1980–1, Lillee, Pascoe and Hogg claimed 79 wickets between them as India and New Zealand were overwhelmed, three of the matches finishing in three days. (Five years later, Australia tried to administer the same punishment to the same sides but the pitches were different and Hadlee, concentrating on line and length, turned the tables spectacularly.)

You could tell Australia were desperate when Rod Marsh made an impassioned statement before the start of the 1984–5 series that the time had come to 'fight fire with fire'. The phrase was familiar on the lips of others but not on those of one of Ian Chappell's principal cohorts. He also said that the time had come to 'crack a few skulls', which was, at least, Chappell-speak. Ian Chappell, in fact, was not in favour of Marsh's tactics, because he felt that a bumper war would be resolved by a battle of wills between the two sides' fast bowlers and that Australia's bowlers would have less stomach for the fight. Nevertheless, Marsh's call was answered, even if it made no difference to the overall result. In the first Test of the series at Perth – when both sides fielded four fast bowlers and Australia were rattled out for 76 (you could see why they'd kept West Indies away from the place since they won there in 1975–6) – Hogg hit Gomes in the face and Alderman struck Dujon on the head. What is more, Australia incensed their opponents by not going to the aid of the stricken batsmen. If this wasn't fighting fire with fire, I don't know what is. Nor was it a one-off. In the second Test at Brisbane, Geoff Lawson needled Desmond Haynes into a public two-fingered gesture, an incident that earned Haynes a severe reprimand and Lawson a two-grand fine. For the remainder of the series, and the two that followed in Australia in 1988–9 and the Caribbean in 1991, relations between the sides were as sour as they can get.

Australia had decided that if they were going to lose it was not going to be for the want of being trying.

Lawson, in fact, was an arch wind-up merchant. Haynes said he was 'always chatting, saying abusive things'. Like Pascoe before him and Merv Hughes afterwards, he was good enough in his early days to earn the 'new Lillee' tag, but not quite good enough to overcome spending the rest of his days trying to live up to it. The end product was the same: all three bowlers expended too much energy issuing threats and not enough carrying them out. For a trained ophthalmologist, Lawson had a real problem keeping things in focus. When he first came up against an England touring side, at Sydney in November 1978, he was so pumped up he managed to get warned for intimidation during an England second innings that lasted only five balls (they had been left two runs to win). At Headingley in 1981, he bowled two successive beamers at Botham: his apology for the first was accepted but not that for his second. There was no question, though, that Lawson could bowl at high speed – Clive Lloyd described him in 1984 as the fastest white bowler in the world – and he developed into a more complete and sophisticated bowler than Pascoe ever was. He was Australia's leading wicket-taker in five successive series between 1982 and 1985.

Then, in the fourth Test of the series, Australia introduced a bowler even more capable than Lawson of fighting fire with fire: Craig McDermott. McDermott was something of a prodigy. Even as a teenager he was physically mature: tall, strong and extremely athletic. He first played for Queensland at eighteen and for Australia at nineteen: he was the youngest Australian Test cricketer for over thirty years. Even then he was extremely fast. When he took six for 45 against Tasmania at Launceston to effectively earn his first Test cap, he generated such pace – admittedly with the help of a strong breeze – that the wicketkeeper and slips stood back two lengths of the pitch. Allan Border, the Queensland captain, had no hesitation afterwards in describing McDermott as the fastest bowler in

Australia. 'He had quite a breeze at his back,' Border said, 'but I haven't seen the keeper or slips stand as far for a long time – probably not since Jeff Thomson's heyday.' McDermott also injured two of the Tasmanian batsmen: Danny Buckingham was hit a nasty blow in the throat and Brian Davison had his left forearm broken. Davison, who had been in the first-class game seventeen years, later said: 'I rate McDermott one of the quickest, if not the quickest, I've faced in my career, and I've just about faced them all.'

The West Indies, too, found him quick and when they got him in their own back yard – which was not for another six years – they paid him the compliment of singling him out for a special diet of short-pitched stuff. 'I can remember only one ball being pitched up to me in the whole series,' McDermott said. Welcome to the real world.

The West Indies started to feel victimized, started to feel *intimidated*. In 1984 they had won eleven successive Test matches against their two main rivals, Australia and England. They were indisputably the best team in the world and yet the more they won the more they were criticized. The noise was becoming deafening. It was louder than the steel bands and trumpets at Sabina Park.

People kept making these very public protests, especially when they came to the Caribbean. There was the Indian manager and captain complaining after the Bridgetown Test of 1983 of intimidatory bowling. There was Rodney Hogg bowling twelve bouncers in two overs during the Kingston Test of 1984, just to show what the West Indian umpires were prepared to tolerate. And then there was Richard Hadlee on the same ground a year later, making a similar point, only more pointedly, by giving Garner five bouncers in an over (he felt that Garner, after the way *he* had bowled earlier in the series, deserved to be on the receiving end). Hadlee's fusillade had naturally prompted Garner and Marshall to flame-grill the New Zealand batsmen later in the day. That in itself had caused an outcry. At the post-match press conference, Wes Hall, the manager, had had to make a defence of West Indies' tactics: not only for the boys returning Hadlee's fire, not only for the way they had bowled earlier in the series, but for the way they had bowled over the previous few years. 'Who started all this?' they had demanded.

It was not only that. There was also a lively old debate – a real old tea-party – going on in cricketing circles about whether the rules should be changed to stop all this intimidation. What they meant, but didn't say, was *to stop the West Indies winning*. It would not be the first time. They did it in the fifties with Ramadhin and Valentine with the front-foot leg-before rule. They did it in the sixties with Hall and Griffith and the front-foot bowling rule. Now this. There were all sorts of whacky ideas doing the rounds: a line across the middle of the pitch to decide which balls were and which were not too short (as though every batsman, every bowler and every 'bouncer' was the same height); lengthening the pitch from 22 yards to 22 metres; catches being allowed only off the bat rather than also off the gloves and wrists; and, of course, limiting bouncers to one per over. With typical missionary zeal, the English had even given the one-bouncer plan a trial in their domestic cricket but, with few other countries prepared to play ball, the experiment had achieved little other than to make their own batsmen less adept at playing the short ball and had ended after five years in 1983. But even in announcing its demise, the English authorities had managed to blame the predominance of short-pitched bowling in Australia and the West Indies for its failure. Anything, as Viv would say, to break up 'our beautiful team'.

There were other critics too. At about the time of Hadlee's protest, John Woodcock had more or less written in his editorial notes to the latest edition of *Wisden* that the bouncer was destroying the modern game and that West Indies were chiefly responsible for this. 'Their presence,' he wrote of the Caribbean fast bowlers, 'has brought a new and, dare I say it, chilling dimension to the game. Batsmen, however heavily protected, face them at their peril and . . . that is only partly to the bowlers' and their captain's credit.' He recalled a passage of play during the Oval Test of 1984 in which Marshall had repeatedly bowled short to Pat Pocock, who had acted as nightwatchman the previous evening: 'It was a woeful piece of cricket, entirely lacking in chivalry.'

Chivalry? Where have these English guys been living, the stone age? This isn't about nostalgia for a lost Empire, this is about claiming what is *ours*; this isn't about the past sixty years, it's about the future – starting with the next 0.44 seconds.

The problem with most of these guys is that they no longer believe in the assistance of the Greatest Player of Them All. That is, Him, not Viv; I mean the maker of lives, not bats; the keeper of souls, not wickets. He is batting for West Indies now. In the dressing room before play begins, they offer prayers to Him for a good performance. The only thing the English players seem to worship is the pub; that is the only thing *they* dedicate themselves to. These days, there is only one team which plays with a missionary zeal – and it's not the English.

7

The Nature of the Beast

There is this wonderful image of the fast bowler as an unbridled force, uncontrolled and uncontrollable. He is a brute, a Caliban of the cricket field, possessing little self-knowledge, responding only to the most primal of impulses, his one distinguishing feature the ability to bowl a ball at exceptional speed. He is immensely strong, so strong in fact that he skirts the boundary between human force and a force of nature. Once he arrives on the scene – and he often seems to come out of nowhere – nothing stands in his way: batsmen and umpires, trees and powerlines, are swept from his path. He is a whirlwind, a typhoon, a tornado.

The Untamed Force. It is an image that stretches back from the present day into the mists of antiquity: Merv Hughes – Merv the Mouth, Merv the Boorish Ocker – unleashing his highly charged verbal assaults; Dennis Lillee and Ian Botham smashing up the dressing room in Launceston; Roy Gilchrist letting slip so many bouncers and beamers in India in 1958–9 that he was sent home; Fred Trueman being left out of two England tours for being unable to hold his tongue before authority; Peter Heine telling Trevor Bailey he wanted to hit him over the heart; Leslie Hylton being hanged for the murder of his wife; and so on, to the great Spofforth, who withdrew from the first-ever Test match because they would not give him the wicketkeeper he asked for. *This is what happens. This is the way they are.*

The public privately thrills to hear of such inflammability. It is part of the pleasure of watching fast bowlers at work: you're never quite sure what they're going to do next. These men are governed by blood rushes. The public thrills to hear stories that suggest bowlers might mow down women as readily as they do wickets; thrills at the idea that they rail at the authority of umpires and administrators; thrills at the idea that they consume alcohol with the thirst of fire eaters. These are failings to which many people can fall prey. The public is captivated by stories of Andy Roberts's quick bouncer; of Croft staring at his wounded victims and of Willis walking away from his; of Clarke bowling from wide of the crease to minimize the batsman's escape; of the West Indies quicks making their Fury-like pursuit of men such as Amarnath, whom they rendered practically runless only a few months after he had been such a thorn in their side. Cruelty and vengeance are also common failings. Fast bowlers are emotional characters.

They are not so much forgiven as excused. If you're a fast bowler, people don't expect you to be a saint; it doesn't go with the job. Similarly, many people wouldn't bat an eyelid if they were to hear that such-and-such a fast bowler had been certified a homicidal maniac. They would say simply: 'Oh well, it's only to be expected, I suppose. He was a fast bowler, you know. He's been doing it all his life.' It is the undercurrent of violence that every successful fast bowler betrays that was being exploited when Hughes was photographed during the 1993 tour of England in Mad Max garb: astride a supercharged motorbike, sporting black leathers and sun shades, a cartridge belt over one shoulder and a pump-action shotgun in his hand.

It is even more tempting to look on the fast bowler as a wilfully malign force, a *satanic* force. This, too, is an age-old image: the destroyer with the supernatural powers of speed. Spofforth, after all, was nicknamed the Demon, and numerous fast bowlers since have conjured up similar notions of devilry, right down to Holding with his Dracula-like incisors and Lillee with his Mephistophelian moustache. Such a view has the advantage of reducing proceedings to the straightforward terms of a medieval morality play, batsman versus bowler as Good versus Evil. In this way, the batsman takes on the role of Peter Pilgrim, with the odds stacked impossibly against him – which just about sums up the situation if the man charging in at him is in a mean mood and has a fair breeze at his back.

Batsman versus bowler, Good versus Evil: it is an attractive idea. Pat Pocock recalls going out to bat in a Test match in the Caribbean in 1968 and finding himself facing the fearsome Wes Hall. As a batsman of limited abilities, Pocock was terrified at the prospect. Then a miracle happened. As Hall thundered in, the crucifix he wore around his neck, which often danced menacingly in the sunlight, flew up and caught him painfully in the eye. Hall had to stop in his tracks and was in so much pain that he had to leave the field for treatment. Pocock had been saved by the crucifix.

So perhaps it is true then. Perhaps God *did* invent cricket and the very Devil fast bowlers.

The fast bowler as Untamed Force: it's a nice idea, but it really won't hold. A lot of it – not *all* of it, but a lot of it – is illusion. Among his many characteristics, the fast bowler is an actor. He is playing out a role that everyone wants to believe in: he wants you to be scared of him. He wants you to believe he is six sticks of dynamite on the end of a very short fuse. But he is a fraud: the more he stares, the more he snarls, the more he hates, the more he reveals that what he really wants is wickets. What he wants to do is break your nerve, not your bones. In some ways, this applies not only to his behaviour towards batsmen, but also towards umpires.

Aggression is simply part of the fast bowler's armoury, perhaps the most important part. To be successful, he has *got* to maintain the psychological ascendancy, and inspiring fear is the surest way to do so, whether through war-mongering, like Hughes, or warpaint, like McDermott. This is not often a problem, as the stakes are usually high enough that both batsman and bowler know that it is a one-on-one, him-or-me situation, and the adrenaline is inevitably pumping. The fast bowler's greatest foe is familiarity. He cannot afford – even occasionally – to lapse into friendliness: it would break the illusion of the Untamed Force. Thus, he treats batsmen and umpires with cursory civility and is constantly wary of losing sight of this behaviourial benchmark: Larwood would remind himself that the batsman was there to take centuries and double-centuries off him; Lillee would work up a hatred of the batsman he was about to bowl to.

This is also why fast bowlers are often at their deadliest when they first burst on to the scene: there has been no time to shatter the illusion of the Untamed Force. They know they've got a head start: the batsman's imagination as to what this new guy might do to him is running riot. Once the illusion is shattered, it is desperately hard to repair. Ask Rodney Hogg. By the sixth Test of the 1978–9 series, he was so frustrated by his previous exchanges with Derek Randall that he was driven to greeting the final appearance at the crease of the jack rabbit himself with an artificial snake.

The friendly fast bowler is a contradiction in terms. There is a psychological war going on out there and it is no place for half measures.

Those who reckon that fast bowling is a crude art – and there are plenty of them – simply don't know the half of it. They'll demand to know what is subtle about four fast bowlers operating off long run-ups and rotating for hour after hour; they'll say it has all the sophistication of trench warfare. But in reality it is just about as subtle as the most excruciating of tortures; Graham Gooch compared the effects of just such an attack to water dripping away at a stone, and that is anything but crude. Each batsman has his own ideas of fear and it is the job of the fast bowlers to discover what those fears are and to keep them alive and well. It may be that the batsman is worried that he is not scoring fast enough, or that he feels he has a weakness outside off-stump, or that he is afraid he will not be able to resist the impulse to hook. One of the easiest fears to identify, of course, is fear of the short-pitched ball: the batsman will step away, take his eyes off the ball, jump in the air. 'His body language always betrays him,' Craig McDermott said. 'Once a bowler spots a first back-foot movement towards or, even worse, outside leg stump,' Botham said, 'he will exploit the weakness unmercifully . . . Once a flincher, always a flincher.' Whatever the anxiety, the fast bowler must rough-prod it into life at regular intervals.

This is why the fast bowler gets especially angry if the batsman hooks him to the boundary, or starts to signal his own fours, or talks back, or is unfazed by being hit. The batsman has shown himself to be at ease, and a fast bowler dislikes nothing more than a batsman at ease. Bowlers may be part acting, but they are the type who'll fight back if they are attacked. If a fast bowler is hooked by a batsman for four, you know, you simply *know*, that the next ball he bowls to that batsman will be a bouncer, and that it will probably be greeted by mock 'Oohs' from the crowd in recognition of the fast bowler trying to reassert his authority. If the batsman goes one step further and starts to take the bowler's cooperation for granted, things can get very nasty. In January 1993, Australia were comfortably placed in a World Series Cup match against West Indies in Sydney when Dean Jones asked Curtly Ambrose to remove his wristbands as they were proving a distraction. It was like wiggling a stick in a hornet's nest. Ambrose was so incensed at the presumption that he racked up his pace a couple of notches and ripped out five wickets in 9.3 overs to sweep his side to a 25-run victory.

Similarly, Lillee was at his most demonstrative during the 1974–5 series with England not because his side were not winning (they were) but because he was being overshadowed by another fast bowler (Thomson) in a way he had never been before (or would be since). Lillee did not take more than two wickets in an innings until the fifth match of the series but he made up for his lack of heroics with a surfeit of histrionics.

And it worked. The crowd was on his side even more than it was on Thomson's. Lillee had realized that the illusion could no longer be maintained by his bowling alone and that he would have to resort to other means to sustain it. Alongside Thomson's near-perfect impersonation of the Untamed Force he was in danger of fading into oblivion, of experiencing the thing the fast bowler fears above all else: people saying he is no longer up to it. Every fast bowler knows that his greatest gift – the ability to bowl fast – is a fleeting one; that few of his type are able to defy the years sufficiently to take wickets through pace alone long past their thirty-second birthdays. They either adapt into a skilful fast–medium bowler – as Lillee did so superbly – or die. No wonder they are all so highly strung.

Of course, some bowlers are better students of the vituperative arts than others, and some batsmen more easily impressed. As a rule, Australians and South Africans are more aggressive than English county players, even their club cricketers, partly because fast bowling is a more accepted part of the game there. The gulf is certainly vast. As Allan Border observed disparagingly during the 1993 tour of England, 'Your idea of sledging is to stare at one another.' Wherever the bowler comes from though, the best batsmen tend to look down their noses at their antics and dismiss them as childish and pointless. 'Fast bowlers are bullies,' Viv Richards said. The best way to deal with a bully is to ignore him until he goes away and picks on someone his own size (preferably another fast bowler). Desmond Haynes described how during his youth the fastest bowler in his school once threatened to knock his head off if Haynes didn't share his lunch with him. Haynes was confident enough in his own abilities to refuse. 'I didn't let him worry me,' he said.

Some batsmen take it on themselves to trade verbal abuse with the fast bowler in the hope of either disrupting his concentration or at least showing him they are not scared. Randall did this to good effect with Lillee in the Centenary Test, as did Javed Miandad at Perth in 1981, although with Miandad things went further than perhaps even he intended when Lillee became so riled that he aimed a kick at the Pakistan captain. Others prefer more gentle baiting, such as Michael Atherton, who rebuked Merv Hughes in England in 1993 for failing to think up any new ways to insult him. If a batsman hits on the right response, there is no doubt that he can explode a bowler's puffed-up pride in an instant, even if he is not bowling at the time. Once, during a Benson and Hedges Cup tie at Lord's in 1980, Mike Brearley intervened as he heard Imran Khan, who was batting, complaining to the umpire that Daniel was bowling too many bouncers. 'They weren't bouncers, they were below shoulder level,' Brearley threw in. 'And, anyway, you tried to get it up but couldn't.' Brearley swore he was only talking about Imran's bowling, but Imran was not so sure.

Lesser batsmen are more easily cowed. 'With batsmen of lesser fibre,' Lillee once said, 'you can make considerable ground by using tactics of outward aggression. Experienced batsmen are not usually intimidated by your words and actions but some do get a little irate at your effronteries and start to act rashly.' The problem is that once you start talking big you've got to be prepared to carry out your threats. Sometimes this means trying to knock off someone's head, even though you know that this will not in itself bring you his wicket. This is something that the majority of fast bowlers are well aware of, even though you sometimes might not think it. Lillee once said: 'Fast bowling by its nature is an aggressive act and it's up to you to carry that fire through.' Des Hoare, who belonged to the previous generation of Western Australia fast bowlers to Lillee, confirmed the sentiments: 'Fast bowling is not a gentle game. Any fast bowler worth his salt must sometimes play the game very hard indeed and must be prepared to shoulder the results of having an aggressive attitude.'

The intelligent fast bowler also knows the advantage of being inwardly calm. Creating an impression of untamed force is one thing, retaining mental control another. 'The ultimate greatness of a bowler,' C.L.R. James once wrote, 'is in his head.' Opponents were amazed when they first came up against Jeff

Thomson to find that, whatever he may have said off the field, he directed not one word at them while he was on it. The only cursing he ever did on the pitch was in self-admonishment. Other top-class performers could be similarly disciplined and Hadlee and Willis were two who were so determined to block out any external distraction that they would often appear remote even to their own team-mates. As every fast bowler can testify, allowing yourself to become genuinely riled or angry only serves to impair your judgement and effectiveness. Basically, if you lose your rag, you're gone. And often, those bowlers who appeared to be genuinely nasty on the field – men such as Pascoe and Patterson – were not always the most effective. Too much intimidation, not enough ingenuity.

So, if fast bowlers are part actors, what are they really like when they are not on stage? Many of them – incredibly – are kind and gentle; some of them – more incredibly still – are kind and gentle to the point of docility. In fact, people who meet these men off the field often cannot believe they are talking to the same characters who display such vicious hostility on it. Wayne Daniel and Merv Hughes, for example, are reportedly charming men without a ball in their hands, and Roland Butcher has said of Michael Holding that he was 'too nice a fellow to be a fast bowler ... he would not harm a fly'. Some fast bowlers, also, pursue the gentlest of lives when not in whites. John Snow, a clergyman's son, spent his spare time writing poetry; Andy Roberts never touched alcohol or tobacco and possessed a passion for nothing racier than fruit juice; Curtly Ambrose likes to sing and strum a guitar. More unlikely still, Thomson was not only quiet, he liked growing orchids, and in retirement went into the landscape-gardening business. Nor was he the only one to have green fingers: Spofforth, in later life, used to enjoy showing chrysanthemums. They spend their playing days trying to knock the heads off opposing batsmen and then get protective about the tops of small plants!

Nor are all of them the butchers on the field they would have you believe. Rumesh Ratnayake, the Sri Lanka fast bowler, once fainted in a Test match after catching sight of the bloody nose he had given John Wright, and Malcolm Marshall said that he almost passed out when he hit Mike Gatting. This raises an interesting point: if batsmen who can't handle short-pitched bowling shouldn't be playing international cricket – as West Indies keep telling us – then should bowlers who can't stand the sight of blood be allowed to play it either?

This is not to say that all fast bowlers are pussy cats. They're not. Many of the worst excesses you hear about are true – but a lot of it is, well, play-acting.

The point is this. As a fast bowler you have to be like a tornado. On the outside you create destruction, on the inside you are dead calm. When the storm subsides everyone stares at you in wonder, everyone treats you with the most touching reverence, everyone admires your breezes into humour ('Oh yes, Sylvester . . . Nice one. Ha, ha, ha . . .'). Of course you're sometimes kind and gentle to the point of docility. With a power like yours you hardly need to go around demonstrating it every minute of every day. You're so powerful you're virtually omnipotent . . . you're there reaching up out of the eye of the tornado, right up into the heavens, drawing your strength from the very fingertips of God Himself.

So why are England unable to produce quality fast bowlers? Why is it that over the past twenty years only two genuine speed merchants – Bob Willis and Devon Malcolm – have proved themselves capable of winning England more than one Test match?

Well, we could talk about the lifeless quality of many English tracks; talk about the string of flat-pudding pitches that were produced in the eighties to avoid a repeat of what had happened at the hands of Lillee and Thomson, and Holding and Roberts, in the mid-seventies; talk about the emergence of seamers' paradises in the late eighties on which any old medium-pace trundler could skittle out a county side by putting the ball on the spot and letting it swing and seam – just as long as he didn't bowl too fast (and on which batsmen could only survive by the forward push – excellent preparation for Test cricket!); talk about why the Test and County Cricket Board's chief inspector of pitches, Harry Brind, could produce a square of genuine pace and bounce at the Oval but was not required to do so elsewhere. If you're an evil bowler and you die, they'll send you to the equivalent of Dante's seventh level of Hell, where you will be shown a typical English pitch and then told to bowl flat out on it in purgatory's first Timeless Test match (and this one *won't* be called off after ten days).

We could talk about the coaches and their absurd obsession with line and length bowling; about how these coaches have distracted a generation of fast bowlers from their principal task of getting right their rhythm and action by talking to them about bowling down corridors of uncertainty when they possessed the speed to blow any number of batsmen clean out of the window (the Australians did not make this mistake with Thomson: Greg Chappell knew that his ability to terrify was far more important than his inability to pitch the ball on a sixpence). We could talk more widely about the negativity of English cricket, about all the white-hot talent it has quenched in the icy waters of defence and technical correctness; about the need for batsmen to learn to hit the ball again and for fast bowlers to once again revel in what Frank Tyson called the 'glad animal action'. Ask Clive Lloyd or Ian Chappell. They'll tell you. English cricket is capable of complicating the simplest things.

We could talk about the need for the fast bowlers themselves to become more professional, to set themselves rigorous training and dietary routines, to treat themselves like athletes. We could talk about the way the Australians, West Indians and South Africans prepare: about how they are aware of the need for proteins and carbohydrates in their diet and don't eat junk food like fish and chips and hamburgers; about how they train like fury by working with weights in the gym and running at least two nights a week; about how the Australians, if they don't do that, won't even get picked for a club match. 'Most English fast

bowlers,' Michael Holding said, 'don't have muscles in proportion to their bodies: you can't see where their biceps begin
and end.' You can be sure that this isn't the case with any
self-respecting fast man in the southern hemisphere: Craig
McDermott even used to train with Trevor Hendy, a world
iron-man champion. Imagine an English player doing the same!
Do they want to bowl fast or don't they?

We could talk about all these things, but it still would not
take us to the root of the problem.

You see, it is more fundamental than that. The whole
structure, the whole tottering, preposterous ziggurat of English cricket, is wrong. It works to the disadvantage of the
English cricketer, especially works to the disadvantage of
the English fast bowler. Nobody can play effectively for six or
seven days a week, for twenty successive weeks; nobody, certainly, can *bowl fast* effectively for six or seven days a week,
for twenty successive weeks. Ever since the introduction of
limited-overs cricket in 1963, ever since it began its poison-ivied
ascent of the tower, the English county cricketer has been
sapped of his strength. Before the transition to four-day championship matches was completed in 1993, the budding English
fast bowler could anticipate taking the new ball anything up to
five times a week, for each of those twenty successive weeks.
Each time, taking the red cherry, marking out your run, being
implored by your hand-clapping captain, your wicketkeeper and
your slips to give it all you've got: to make the early breakthrough. It was absurd. Not only could no young modern English bowler do it, nor could any superfast overseas superstar.
The only reason Willis (and Snow, for that matter) bowled
fast for England was because he unashamedly throttled back in
county matches, and the only reason Malcolm did so was
because Derbyshire had the sanity not to expect him to play in
all their matches. It was absurd then and it is absurd now,
because the change from 22 three-day to 17 four-day championship matches and the modest reduction in the amount of
one-day cricket being played has made precious little difference

to the workload. A stone removed here, a stone removed there
... it all makes little difference when what is required is that
the entire ancient and absurd structure be ripped down.

If you try to bowl flat out over an extended period what
happens is that you will eventually break down, especially if
you are young and not physically mature enough to stand the
strain. Neil Foster and Tony Pigott both had to have pins
inserted in their backs shortly after entering county cricket and
Waqar Younis, Ian Bishop and Martin McCague also sustained
stress fractures of the back early in their county careers. None
of these five had reached the age of twenty-five when he broke
down. Nor had Dennis Lillee when he required back surgery
following a prolonged period of top-level cricket in the early
seventies. Many other county bowlers have been under the surgeon's knife or have cortisone in their joints. England's problem
is that by the time their fast bowlers reach the age of twenty-five
most of them have had not only their backs broken but their
spirits also and have settled for life in a slower lane. Overwork
is so commonplace that few notice it is even going on. Brearley
overbowled Botham during his spells as England captain
between 1977 and 1981 (something that must have contributed
to the back problems Botham suffered from around the end of
that period), just as Gooch later did with Malcolm during the
tour of Australia in 1990–1. It's all so obvious when you think
about it. It's just another example of English cricket making a
simple thing complicated.

For years the counties' overseas players – who had been
brought up to play eight matches a year rather than eight days
a week (you'd let it go if you only got the chance to let rip once
a fortnight!) – had been telling them to reduce the amount of
cricket they played and allow their fast bowlers, in particular,
more rest. Many of these overseas players were, of course, fast
bowlers themselves and knew that the English system would
not get the best out of them until it changed. Many of them
coped only by either not bowling flat out every day (instead
developing their use of the leg- and off-cutter which English

conditions so favoured), refusing to bowl anything longer than four- or five-over spells, or demanding contracts which gave them scope to miss certain matches, as Imran did in his later years with Sussex. Others gave up in despair, like Roberts, who walked out on Hampshire in 1978 claiming he had been over-bowled.

Of all the overseas fast bowlers of modern times, probably only Marshall and Hadlee bowled at anything like a sustained pace throughout their county careers, and they managed it only because their technique relied to an unusual extent on their rhythm. For this reason – and despite the recent 'refinements' of the system – other countries remain reluctant to let their fast bowlers pound the county beat. In 1992, Craig McDermott withdrew from his contract to play for Yorkshire following a warning of the dangers from Bob Simpson; he gave as his reason the need to undergo a groin operation, but then continued to play for Australia in the World Cup. A year later, Imran advised Wasim Akram and Waqar Younis to follow his example and cut down on the amount of county cricket they were playing. 'Too much county cricket is useless,' he said, 'since it puts undue stress on fast bowlers. It is a serious threat to a long career.'

It is not simply a matter of reducing the workload though, it is also a matter of helping the best players find a route to the top. Willis, for one, is absolutely clear about this. And as an English fast bowler who managed to climb the ziggurat, he ought to know. The English professional circuit is choked with 400 players, 360 of whom are not good enough to go any higher. Why not face up to this fact and return them to the amateur ranks which they should never have left? Do, in fact, what they do in Australia? 'In Australia,' Willis said, 'they play ten first-class matches. That is forty days' cricket, twenty of which are on Saturdays and Sundays. If you take twenty days off work you can play first-class cricket. You can do that and do your job as well. It would only be if you kept scoring hundreds or taking five wickets for London, Surrey or Middlesex – or whoever they happened to be called – that you'd eventually get asked to play for England, and you might then have to make a decision as to whether you can continue with your job. Not until you get into the international scene would you become professional. At the moment, blokes have to make the decision, "Right, I'm seventeen years old, I'm going to be a professional sportsman." Anybody with parents with half a brain will tell them, "No you're not, you're going to get a degree and get a proper job." So we lose most of the intelligent sportsmen at that age because they go on to become lawyers, doctors, accountants, journalists instead.'

But then there *is* the poison ivy. 'One-day cricket does not encourage bowlers to take wickets,' he added. 'It's a complete myth that one-day cricket is an attacking game. It's a purely defensive game. On good pitches, where everything's in favour of the batsman, you're trying to stop them scoring runs, not get them out, and that's not what a fast bowler's job is. In the last Test at the Oval in 1993, Devon Malcolm's overs might have been quite expensive but it doesn't matter, to win a Test match you've got to get the opposition out twice. Under the Gooch—Stewart regime, most of the time we had medium-pace bowlers bowling who weren't conceding many runs but never looked like getting anybody out.'

Imran agrees with Willis that the English structure must be changed. He has played domestic cricket in both England and Australia, and is adamant as to which system he prefers. 'Seven-day cricket was like work,' he said. 'I couldn't think of it like that. To me, it had to be fun. English cricketers are under stress and the administrators haven't realized it. You need enthusiasm to compete. I once played a season of Sheffield Shield cricket with New South Wales and it was incredible, each match was like a Test match to those guys, they had been looking forward to it for ages. In Australia it takes them three and a half years to play the amount of cricket they would get through in a season of county cricket. English cricketers actually decline as time goes on. In the end I got bored, turning up each day, going into the dressing room and seeing all those weary faces, seeing those

Letting Rip

guys slowly pulling off their ties, slowly pulling off their shirts. Another day at the office . . .' Imran, though, was fortunate: he was intelligent enough to know when he was bored, and wealthy enough not to have to play county cricket if he didn't want to.

English cricket needs to rediscover its enthusiasm, needs to find out that the game can still be fun. Stress, boredom and fatigue have never been a winning formula.

Jeff Thomson was never bored, he never lost his enthusiasm. He was in love with the thrill of speed. He couldn't get enough of it. In the late seventies, when he was somewhere near the height of his cricketing fame, Thomson bought himself a Ferrari and used to like to take it out on to the wide, open roads of the Queensland countryside, underneath the vast blue skies, and let rip. The car's top speed was about twice that of his bowling. In such moments, as he once again created a blur down a fast track, with the wind rushing through his mane, you can imagine that Thomson must have been in a state of complete happiness.

Once again, he was back in the eye of the tornado.

8

Keeping it Down

Fast bowlers possess an unfair advantage. What they *do* is unfair. If things are in their favour, if their rhythm is right, if the pitch has pace and bounce, they can bowl, some of them, at speeds that will defeat even the best batsmen. Even the finest batsman in the world can be beaten for pace, especially early on, before he has got his eye in. Is there a batsman alive who can honestly say that he would have been confident of making runs against Thomson in 1974, Roberts in 1975, Holding in 1978, le Roux in 1979, Marshall in 1982, Patterson in 1985, Wasim Akram or Donald in 1990? At those dates each of those men was twenty-four years old, physically mature and probably bowling at something like his top speed (if not yet at his most cunning). And it is the speed that is the dangerous thing. That is what is so unfair. 'Speed,' to reiterate John Snow's famous remark, 'defeats reactions.'

Imagine what it must be like to be a batsman – a specialist batsman, say, someone with some pretensions to the art – facing one of these 24-year-old slips of wind for the first time. You have been playing the game for several years – years of practice, years of playing, years of crafting a technique that gives you a fighting chance of surviving every type of situation you can envisage and then along comes a tornado in Brisbane, or a typhoon in Bridgetown, or whatever, and changes everything. You'll get up the next morning and face yourself in the shaving mirror and know that you've been found out, know that you'll never master the guy who practically tore your face off with that ball you nicked to the keeper, know you'll never fully have his measure. Your eyes look sunken, your face has a grey hue and if you don't pull yourself together quickly ... you'll be getting another nick very shortly.

After such an experience, how do you pick yourself up?

A player of ordinary ability will probably react by changing his methods in an attempt to prevent a repetition – and thus only create further difficulties for himself. What he will do is over-react. What a really top-class player must do – probably will do – is accept that there was nothing he could have done: that batting against a top-class quick is a hit-and-miss affair, that now and again it will be the bowler's day, and that he must not let the dismissal prey on his mind but resolve to make his adversary pay the next time they meet. Coming to terms with the vulnerability of their existence is one of the hardest things a batsman has to do.

A mutual awareness of this vulnerability forms one of the many sub-plots of any contest between a batsman and a top-class fast bowler. The batsman can play any number of devastating shots, hit the ball to the boundary any number of times, and still he – and the fast bowler – knows that the next ball could leave him helpless. Against some bowlers, against some attacks, the batsman is never safe. One ball is enough to change everything.

Each ball is another drop of water hitting the stone.

Talk of a batsman's fear in relation to fast bowling and you are really talking of two things: his fear of failure and his fear of injury. It is next to impossible to separate the two. His fear can, though, manifest itself in several ways. Sometimes it acts as a positive influence, sharpening his concentration to such a degree that he is actually a better player than when confronted by a less physically threatening opponent. Robin Smith, for example, often responds in this way. At other times it acts as a negative influence, freezing the mental and physical responses so that the batsman is unable to function in a normal way and his performance is seriously undermined as a result. This in itself can either be a temporary state of affairs or something more permanent. Fear can sneak up on a batsman one day, tap him on the shoulder and say, 'I'm here, you know,' and then not return for a long time; or it can find him and stalk him for days, weeks or months until he is technically and psychologically wrecked. It can happen to even the most able and courageous of players: you get blown away – or hit – once; you start to think it can happen again; soon you come to expect it. This is the sort of thing that happened to Tony Greig over several weeks against West Indies in 1976 and to Dennis Amiss over several months against Australia in 1974 and 1975. No one likes fast bowling; people just react to it in different ways.

Many of the bravest players find the element of physical danger to be a spur. They will seemingly play whole innings – match-saving, match-winning, heroic innings – on nothing more than the rush of adrenaline. Some of them bat with bravado, others try to grit it out. But once they have left the field of battle they will rarely admit that fear was ever a factor. Just as a fast bowler must be aggressive, so a batsman must say he is not afraid of fast bowling. He says it partly to reassure himself and partly to reassure the rest of the world, including the fast bowler himself (who, remember, hates nothing more than an assured batsman). There is another reason: he is also thinking about what will happen when *it* occurs, when he does, eventually, get hit. 'You have to understand,' Viv Richards once said, 'that if you play long enough you will get hurt. The acid test is how you come back after injury.' Acting tough is one way of easing the rehabilitation process.

Some batsmen have taken this toughness to extremes. Brian Close was one. He would have died rather than lose his wicket and he went to extraordinary lengths to demonstrate his bravery. One of his most famous remarks was that 'a cricket ball can't hurt you because it's only on you a second'. And then there he was, at Old Trafford in 1976 at the age of forty-five, taking blow after blow on the body and returning to the dressing room to reveal a torso so mottled with bruises that it looked like somebody had pushed marbles under his skin, a torso so bruised that he was unable to sleep. Did those deliveries hurt? Not as far as Close was concerned. He was too busy hurtling down the motorway to Edgbaston to take on Willis and show how fearless he still was.

Mike Gatting is another. He has sustained several severe injuries but would never admit to having been afraid. Long before Marshall smashed him in the face, he had taken a battering at the hands of Daniel and been hit on the head by Imran and Clarke, not to mention once risking life and limb taking on Croft in fading light in a county match at Lord's in 1982. Then, when he was hit by Marshall, he showed just how deep ran his bulldog spirit by first asking to be allowed to resume his innings – before it was explained to him that the ball had, after crushing his nose, dropped into the stumps – and then three weeks later returning to the Caribbean after surgery in England only to have his thumb broken within twenty hours of his arrival.

Not that extreme bravery is necessarily a sign of being in command. Close was an effective batsman against pace but never established a regular England place (his longest unbroken run was his seven matches as captain), while Gatting, although a masterly player of spin, reached fifty only once in nine Tests against the pace-dominated West Indies. It could, perhaps, be argued that both were brave only in the sense that they were less worried about being hit than they were about failing. Gatting, for instance, was so terrified of the unplayable ball during his one appearance against West Indies in 1984 that he was leg-before playing no stroke in both innings. At a lower level, Roy Dexter, the Nottinghamshire batsman, drew the admiration of Len Pascoe for not flinching after being hit by the Australian at Trent Bridge in 1980. 'Top guts, mate,' Pascoe whispered, 'top guts.' Dexter may have been able to stomach the pain, but he couldn't take the pace. Shortly after the incident, he fell for three successive ducks to Malcolm Marshall and Hartley Alleyne, and by the end of the next season had disappeared from the county game.

Other players, while equally aware of the importance of not allowing an injury to undermine their confidence, will at least admit that on certain occasions they may feel a degree of apprehension at facing the quicks. Few of them are actually prepared to get their tongues around the words 'fear' and 'scared', but the message is usually clear. They are the sort who would share the old pro's gritted-teeth confession about fast bowling: 'None of us likes it, but some of us show it more than others.'

Allan Border has probably taken more flak from the fast men than any other player in modern times but he has nevertheless proved astonishingly durable. Despite having played at international level for over fifteen years, he has never missed a Test match through injury and – apart from being pinned by Dilley at Perth in 1979 – has rarely been badly hurt. Even when he broke a finger taking a catch at Old Trafford in 1981 he scored an unbeaten century later in the same match. The worst injury he ever experienced occurred in a county match at Edgbaston in 1988 when he was struck over the ear by a ball from Tony Merrick and had to have twenty stitches inserted in the wound, but he promptly eased a helmet over his blood-soaked bandages (Van Gogh, the Essex boys called him) and resumed his innings. Just occasionally, though, you knew Border had had his cage rattled. He admitted the tour to the West Indies in 1984 was a traumatic experience. Not only was it his first of the Caribbean, he also fought several lone battles against the pacemen, including batting ten and a half hours for unbeaten innings of 98 and 100 to save the Test in Trinidad. 'I thought I was going through purgatory,' he said. He could never admit, though, to having been scared by fast bowling. Acknowledging that Marshall was the bowler most batsmen were afraid of, he said: 'I think apprehensive is the best word to describe the way I feel about facing him ... apprehensive about him sending down some rocket well enough to get me out.'

Robin Smith, too, is proud of his record against pace, especially about the fact he has been injured so few times. He had his right index finger broken by Walsh on the first day of the Antigua Test in 1990 but felt that it might not have happened had the match not followed so quickly upon the previous, exhausting, Test in Bridgetown, where he had batted almost ten hours. The same finger was then badly bruised at Southampton in June 1991 by a high full toss from Ambrose, but on each of these occasions Smith did not allow the break to prevent him playing on: he batted in the second innings at Antigua (before another blow to the finger forced him finally to retire hurt), and played in the Trent Bridge Test only five days after the Southampton incident. 'I don't really mind if I get hit by the ball,' he has said. 'Of course it stings for a while if you get hit on the inside of the thigh or on the chest, but I've found that I can switch off my mind to the pain ... I've been hit on the helmet twice and have had my right index finger broken, but I don't think these blows have had any effect on the way I bat.' He actually regards his most memorable piece of batting as the four or five overs he survived from Ian Bishop before lunch on the fourth day of the 1990 Antigua Test, when he reckons he received thirteen bouncers in fourteen balls. 'I got hit on the body a few times, but it was unbelievably exhilarating.'

Possibly the only time Smith has been afraid was towards the end of the 1992 season, when he was struggling to maintain his enthusiasm for county cricket. In the match against Essex at Chelmsford, he attempted to sharpen his concentration by batting without a helmet, only to find that Mark Ilott took offence at the implied insult and noticeably raised his pace. 'He can be quite difficult to pick,' Smith recalled in his autobiography, 'because he's got the left-armer's ability to deliver a short ball with a flick of the wrist rather than a coil of the body, and he let go a bouncer that I shaped to pull, missed, and the ball shot past my head. I knew that it had been a close call because I had heard the air whistle as the ball went by ... I should have called for a helmet after that but I had far too much pride.'

The incident did nothing to lessen Smith's appetite for battle; he remains happier against pace than spin. The following winter, when he was confronted by an India side containing three spinners, he readily declared, 'Give me Ambrose on a fast, bouncy pitch any day to these guys.'

Graham Gooch has insisted on several occasions that he is not afraid of even the most hostile fast bowling and has demonstrated his equanimity on countless occasions. His record against West Indies, for instance, is second to none among players of the modern era. He has rarely been hurt and when he has it has been nothing more serious than hand injuries, most notably the double-fracture he sustained during the 1990 tour of the Caribbean which kept him out of two Tests. Even so, he concedes that there have been occasions when he did not feel comfortable. He has admitted that at Trent Bridge in 1980 – his first Test against West Indies – he felt 'confused and apprehensive' during a period in which Holding was bowling very fast. 'For some reason I just didn't feel right. My feet were not moving as quickly or as accurately as they should have been and it was in my mind that he could hit me if I did not sharpen up.' He also admits there was a 'whiff of real danger' at Kingston in 1986, when he also thought he might be hurt. Perhaps, though, Gooch was happy to play the fast men partly because he knew he had difficulties with bowlers who swung the ball at slightly below top speed: he had a tendency to play round his front leg and across the line of the ball which made him vulnerable to medium-pacers who swung the ball, and gave him good reason to prefer the ball that came on to the bat. Did Gooch not, after all, find Marshall at his most difficult not when he was bowling flat out but when he decided, in 1988, to reduce his pace and concentrate on swinging and seaming the ball?

David Boon also prefers the apprehensive-rather-than-scared line: 'I personally don't like the word scared because if you're scared you're gone, but if there's not a little apprehension about the possibility of being hurt, that's not a good attitude for a batsman.'

Few batsmen of the modern era, though, have looked at such ease against pace as Sunil Gavaskar and David Gower. Both were ice cool, Gavaskar particularly so when you remember that he played for a country that had little firepower of its own and little chance to retaliate against aggressors. He was a master at swaying and ducking out of the way of the bouncer, his eye always on the ball, and in 125 Test matches he was never badly hurt. 'I always believed in giving the first half-hour to the bowler – the next five were mine. That was my maxim for being an opening bat . . . There was no fear when playing the West Indies pacemen. Apprehension yes, because in the first few overs you wonder whether you can cope with the bounce and speed. When the bowlers are fresh and the ball's moving about, you want to feel that your feet are moving too.' Gavaskar went to great lengths to keep opposing fast bowlers happy, once naming both Lillee and Roberts as the finest bowler in the world rather than offend one of them. Only occasionally did the veneer crack: in the aftermath of the Battle of Kingston, when he described the West Indies bowling as 'barbaric'; at Faisalabad in October 1978, when he could take no more from Sarfraz and Imran and called for Bedi's assistance; and at Melbourne in January 1981, when he was so angry at being given out leg-before to Lillee that he attempted to take Chauhan, his partner, with him from the field.

He rarely wavered in his belief in his own abilities: he felt his height (5 foot 4¾ inches) was an advantage against pace, because it meant the bowler had to pitch the ball on a good length to trouble him, and there were few bowlers he confessed to disliking. 'Andy Roberts was the number one. You could never relax, even if you'd scored a hundred and fifty . . . With most of the others you'd get past thirty and feel you were ninety-nine per cent in charge. Not with Roberts. He put so much into his deliveries he had to put the brakes on to avoid bumping into you. Malcolm Marshall was the nearest thing to Roberts. I was never completely at ease with him, nor with Imran in the early 1980s.' One of his few recurring problems was a vulnerability early in his innings on the bouncier pitches of Australia and the Caribbean, where, in three tours between 1977 and 1983, he averaged only 35 and passed fifty just five times, all but once in the second innings when the life in the pitch had died down.

Gower was also rarely hit. He says the only time he was badly hurt was when he top-edged a pull into his face during a Sunday league match at Luton in 1977, although he also needed medical attention after ducking into a bouncer from Hadlee during the Trent Bridge Test of 1983, and had a thumbnail ripped off by a ball from Clarke at the Oval the following year (which was, he said, the fastest bowling he ever faced). He went through an anxious period on the tour of Australia in 1978–9 when he saw several players suffer nasty injuries and was first prompted to wear a helmet, and did not like it when the likes of Hogg or Holding went round the wicket to bowl short and cut off his off-side strokes, but it was almost impossible to ruffle his feathers (after being hit by Hadlee, he still refused to don a helmet and even risked a couple of hair-raising half-hooks at the New Zealander later in the innings). He claims to have never been 'frozen with fear' and one can well believe it, for even in his darkest hour – the tour of the West Indies in 1986 – his fear that the 'death ball' was just around the corner clearly related only to his fear of failure and not to any thoughts that he might be hurt.

When it came to survival, Gower was always one step ahead. He raised his game according to the challenge he was presented with. He loved facing the great fast bowlers, it brought out the best in him. For a player who often struggled to motivate himself (county cricket was *certainly* not made for him), here was something, he felt, worth playing for. 'Whenever I come up against a bowler that I particularly admire and rate highly,' he said, 'there is the challenge of playing well against him. I loved playing against Dennis Lillee, and the gladiatorial nature of the combat appealed to me ... there is both one's reputation at stake and the fear that if you don't motivate yourself you will get hit.' But if he was worried about getting hit, it never showed. 'Gower bats,' Lillee said, 'as though he has never known fear and rarely experienced uncertainty. At times, Gower's approach is not altogether technically correct, but he more than atones for that with his wonderful eye and superb timing. Gower's attitude was amazing – he sort of bubbles forth. Even in moments of greatest stress he seemed to be playing village green cricket, so relaxed was he.'

However they rationalized it – whether it was that a cricket ball couldn't hurt; that they were not scared, only apprehensive; or that they knew they had never been frozen with fear – these players worked out a way of conquering the unconquerable. All of them though, I suspect, knew occasions when the mental defences they had so carefully erected were breached. Whatever Close may say about Old Trafford 1976, whatever Border may say about the Caribbean in 1984, or Gooch about Trent Bridge 1980 and Kingston 1986, it was there that they felt the hand of fear on their shoulder. It may have been only a fleeting thing but it was something they would never forget, something they would wish never to go through again. It was the remembrance of it that partly drove them on.

Others have gone through similar experiences. Willey and Lamb did so on the same occasion as Gooch, at Kingston in 1986, when Phil Edmonds recalled that Lamb returned to the dressing room after his first innings white and shaking. Chris Tavaré, usually as unflappable, in his own way, as Gower ever was, once returned from a brush with Garner on a fresh pitch at Taunton in 1979 looking more than a touch chastened.

Imran Khan, another cool customer, has never forgotten a ball he received from Roberts during the fifth Test at Kingston in 1977. Imran went in to bat with Roberts in the middle of a fast spell and the pair of them had been exchanging bouncers all series, so he knew what was coming, but the fourth ball still shook him to the quick. It was, he said, 'one of the fastest deliveries I have ever faced', and had passed the wicketkeeper by the time he was halfway through with his shot. Imran recalls the delivery with awe: 'Before I could notice anything it had kissed my cap, just touched Deryck Murray's gloves and gone for byes. An inch closer and it would probably have ended my career. After this experience I had no hesitation in donning a helmet the moment they came into use.'

Martin Crowe, too, had a harrowing experience against Roberts in a county championship match at Taunton in 1984 but he found that far from destroying his confidence it actually helped prepare him for a tour of the Caribbean New Zealand made early the next year. Roberts, who had returned to county cricket with Leicestershire on a part-time basis in 1981, was disappointed not to have been chosen by West Indies for their tour of England in 1984 and only too keen to show he still knew how to bowl with fire when injuries led the county to ask him to return to help them in June and July. Despite being thirty-three years of age, he bowled magnificently. 'I took a few on the shoulder,' Crowe said in *Declarations*, 'a couple in the guts and he whizzed a few past my nose. In between all that, he was bowling beautiful outswingers. It was classic stuff.' Crowe survived but Roberts was taking wickets at the other end. 'Towards the end of our innings,' Crowe continued, 'he started bowling short at me again, and when he came into bowl I ducked before he delivered the ball. He knew that I knew that he was going to bowl me a bouncer. Then he bowled me another bouncer and I ducked out of the way again. I thought, Next one he'll pitch up at me, he can't keep bowling short. By that stage I had made three or four strides down the pitch and hit him back over his head. You can imagine the next two balls – they just flew past my ear. He was now trying to pin me, and I got very pumped up. He soon wrapped up the innings, and I walked off, shaking and white. Roberts had really got to me and I had lost control . . .' Crowe was left unbeaten on 70 and returned to the dressing room to reveal a chest that looked like tenderized meat. In the second innings, in which Roberts finished wicketless, he scored 190. Not bad for a kid who left the field shaking and white!

So what are the signs of a player who is experiencing long-term psychological problems with fast bowling, someone who is really spooked? How can you tell?

It's not easy. For a start, the signs are often confusing. There are those who will confidently assert that Boycott was afraid of fast bowling, that he spent three years out of the England team in the mid-seventies for the express purpose (excuse the pun) of avoiding Lillee and Thomson, Holding and Roberts, and the rest. Everyone knew that he had been having problems with fast bowling at about the time of his withdrawal from the 1974—5 tour of Australia — his stated reason was that if he went he 'wouldn't be able to do justice to myself' — and it seemed the most natural conclusion in the world. He had had his arm broken by Garth McKenzie in Australia in 1970—1, had a finger smashed by Willis in 1972, and had been given several rough rides by Lillee. On the tour of the West Indies in 1974, he had gone through a crisis over his technique in handling new-ball bouncers and had been dropped down the order for the third Test at Bridgetown, an extraordinary experience for the world's leading opening batsman.

But the facts don't bear out the case. Boycott's self-imposed exile was unfortunately timed. He was not to know that the Australia tour would prove a watershed in the game's history, was not to know that Lillee would complete a successful comeback from injury, was not to know that Australia had a terror called Thomson. But those who went on the tour nevertheless found it hard to forgive his absence. Greig was fined, suspended and stripped of the Sussex captaincy for stating in a newspaper column in 1977 that Boycott's ability to be where the fast bowlers were not was well known, and another of England's batsmen on the tour recalls, 'Boycott was frightened to death . . . he missed out on Lillee and Thomson because he knew they were going to hit him. He was very clever.' But Boycott returned to Test cricket and, despite the accusations that he had been avoiding Lillee for seven years and hiding from the West Indians, despite being battered by Hadlee, Hurst, Hogg, Croft and Lillee among others, despite supporting calls to limit bouncers to one an over, despite sporting more body armour than a medieval knight, he worked out a way of staying in the middle longer than any other England batsman of the period, of eking out runs, of being the scalp these hunters he was supposedly scared of still prized more than any other.

Many of those who played with Boycott for England would defend him from the charge that he was ever scared – or that his exile had anything to do with fast bowling. 'The finger was pointed at him but nobody knew anything about Jeff Thomson at the time of the 1974–5 tour,' Willis said, 'so it can't really be said he didn't go because of the quick bowlers. Geoffrey's been in the hottest kitchens around so I don't go along with that. He was just having some mental problems about himself and England and the Yorkshire captaincy that got on top of him. If you were to ask him, I think you would find that he regrets not playing for England during that time.' Gooch said: 'He was one of the most courageous and skilful players of fast bowling I have ever seen at close quarters . . . He never shirked the fight – ignore the rumour that Boycott didn't like fast bowling.' Since retiring as a player, Boycott has written and spoken graphically about what it is like batting against extreme pace: about how the new ball sounds like a fire cracker as it rips past, about the 'common dread' all players have of speed, about the overriding need for courage. In some ways he may be conceding that he felt vulnerable when he was in the middle, but in another he is perhaps simply being honest about the matter. *This is what it is like.*

Then there are those who would assert that Botham was among the bravest players ever to step on to a cricket field (Don Mosey once said of him that he was 'devoid of any sense of physical danger and would die rather than display fear'). But it all depends what you mean by bravery. Botham often succeeded in moments of great danger: such as when he survived a blow in the mouth by a ball from Roberts to play a match-winning innings as an eighteen-year-old, or hooked balls from Lillee off his eyebrows for six. But he also shrank in defeat at such times: such as when he admitted to being shell-shocked after the tour of the Caribbean in 1981 or to having little chance of surviving against Holding in a county match a few weeks later, or when he backed away towards square leg against Cowans at Weston-super-Mare in 1982. He may have said he was afraid only once (against Mike Procter, Bristol, 1974) but he made some remarks which suggested the dangers were often uppermost in his mind, especially against West Indies. 'Few men are prepared to get killed on the cricket field,' he once said, 'yet that is the risk you take every time you step out to bat against these fellows. Every ball could remove your teeth. Cricket is a physical game, a game of danger ... At the start of our series against the West Indies in 1984 the press asked if I was going to wear a helmet. I said, Yes. They said, Why? I said, Because I'm twenty-eight and I've got a family and I want to see tomorrow.' Geoff Lawson said of Botham, 'I don't think he actually relishes the real bouncer as much as he thinks he does.'

Mike Brearley, who was supposed to know better than any-one else what made Botham tick, defends him from the accusa-tion that his supercharged self-confidence was a cover for his true feeling, that fear of physical harm was ever his inspiration, even on his troubled tours of the West Indies. 'I doubt if that was physical fear, at least not primarily. I think that was much more a case of the bowling being too difficult to play – fear of failure rather than fear of physical harm. That's a big factor. It's so public, so miserable ... I do think, though, that there's a few of them who, against the West Indies in the early eighties, took the sort of attitude that we'd better get some runs off them before they get us, and they would therefore play a lot of shots and they'd pick people who were strokeplayers. There was one batting line-up [at Bridgetown in 1981] that had Gooch – who in those days was much more of an attacking player than he became later on – Gatting, Gower, Butcher and Botham, and I think they all got into a frame of mind, admirable in a sense, of being too attacking. I'm not sure that was out of fear but out of a sense of: they'll get you sooner or later so you might as well pick up a few runs in the mean time.' (This philosophy did not reach its defining moment, of course, until Gower's tour five years later.) Perhaps in the case of Botham, as Peter Roebuck once said, he was simply too much of a crackpot to be a coward.

Not even their most hostile critics, though, would claim that Botham or Boycott was ever mentally destroyed by pace. They may have had their problems but they never walked out to the middle a broken man, as Amiss did, or went to get their eyes tested or sought out a psychologist because they no longer trusted their own physical and mental powers to get them through.

Which brings me to Greg Chappell and Graeme Hick. Here are two guys who really know what it is like to suffer, who have had their weaknesses pushed and prodded until they thought their heads would burst. Two guys who have been all the way to Room 101.

Both had a history of trouble against pace, both after all were basically front-foot players (front-foot, face-first, it's much the same thing). For a long time Chappell's problems lay dormant, and during this period he established himself as one of the greatest batsmen ever produced by Australia (Hadlee still reckons Chappell is the finest batsman he ever bowled to), but the clues were there for anyone who cared to look for them, clues as to his real feelings about fast bowling. He had been through a nasty experience in 1968, his first season of county cricket, when he was 'sweded' by John Snow, an attempted hook on a damp pitch at Hove cannoning the ball into his right eye and leaving him with splits above and below the socket which it took fifteen stitches to put right. When he returned, at Chelmsford a week later, he went out to bat in poor light and the first ball he received was a Keith Boyce beamer which he only just fended off from his face. One cannot help but suspect that he never quite forgot this incident. It was not simply that he was so obviously pleased when he knew he would never again have to face Thomson; it was that everyone in the game seemed to know that one of their best chances of unsettling Chappell was to slip him a judicious bouncer. Peter Lever was not the only one to discover that.

But it was not until Packer started up that Chappell hit trouble. There, as a member of the Australia XI, he was in the front line. All their matches were against either the West Indies XI or the World XI and both were packed with fast bowlers. For Chappell, the best batsman in his side, there was simply no respite; of all Packer's much-punished batsmen, he probably suffered the most. He faced some terrifying deliveries, a few of which he has not forgotten, like the one from Holding that flew past his nose at VFL Park after it hit the ridge in the pitch; or the one from Roberts that he gloved off his face on a lightning quick surface at the Sydney Show Ground ('His colour just drained,' Knott said, and he was out next ball). By the second season of Packer he was shell-shocked and wracked by self-doubt. The incessant bouncers and the balls coming into his ribs from round the wicket were forcing him to go on to the back foot, but he was reluctant to do so and his footwork had gone to pieces. He kept on getting rapped on the shins (remember his outburst at Garner?), kept on getting out leg-before. He showed his class by recovering sufficiently to score three successive centuries when Packer lifted camp to the Caribbean early in 1979, but his problems were far from over yet.

Things really fell apart not the following winter – when Chappell returned to Test cricket with masterly innings of 74 and 124 against West Indies at Brisbane – but two years after that, when West Indies paid another visit in 1981–2 and his game collapsed almost completely. A double-century in the second Test against Pakistan seemed to refute suggestions that he was still having technical problems, but a fortnight later at Melbourne – on a pitch he described as 'a disgrace and an embarrassment to Australian cricket' – Chappell began an appalling sequence of performances in internationals. In 18 innings (four against Pakistan, 14 against West Indies), he made seven ducks and six scores between one and 12. His other innings were 35, 59, 36, 61 and 61. During this spell, Chappell had a couple of heated disputes with officials which may, or may not, have had something to do with the personal crisis he was going through. The first was during a one-day international on what Chappell considered to be the substandard surface at Melbourne: during the game, he confronted Bob Parish, the chairman of the Australian Cricket Board, and told him to call off the match there and then before someone got hurt (Parish refused). The second occurred at Adelaide in the last Test of the season, before which match Chappell, disbelieving at his failures, had gone to have his eyes tested. Ironically Chappell rediscovered his form in the first innings, scoring 61, but he was peppered with so many bouncers – Croft gave him five an over for three overs and he had his knuckle broken – that for much of the time he was engaged in a running battle with umpire Bailhache over the official's interpretation of the intimidation law.

Chappell never fully recovered from this episode. He played Test cricket for two more, largely untroubled, years – although England fitfully exploited his insecurity against the short ball when they toured in 1982–3 – but his decision to retire directly before Australia left for a tour of the Caribbean can have surprised few insiders.

The clues as to what might happen to Hick were even more apparent from his early career than they were with Chappell. Hick's trepidation at facing speed emerges clearly from his account of his formative years, *My Early Life*, which was published in 1991, when he completed his seven-year qualification period for England (he had been born in Zimbabwe). As an invitation to intimidate, it is hard to beat. It is littered with references to alarming encounters with well known and, in many cases, still active fast men.

It is true that Hick was relatively young when these incidents took place, but there is nothing like giving the game away. In 1982–3 he played against Mike Whitney as a sixteen-year-old: 'He was like greased lightning ... I wore all the protective equipment I could find ... I was nervous and felt out of my depth for the first time.' In 1983 he was a member of Zimbabwe's World Cup squad but did not play in any of their matches, thus avoiding the need to face the likes of Lillee, Thomson, Holding, Marshall and Garner: 'Before each World Cup match, we'd gather for a team meeting the night before and I'd sit there, thinking, Please don't pick me, they're too quick for me.' In 1983–4 he played in a one-day game against a Young West Indies side: 'I closed my eyes to one delivery off Rod Estwick and just swung hopefully at it. As I opened my eyes, I saw the ball soaring over mid-wicket ... That was the first time I had tried the pull shot in any class of cricket; before, there wasn't much need because I could get on to the front foot against most of the bowlers in Zimbabwe. The fast, short stuff only really came at me when the Australians or West Indians were touring.' In 1984 he made his first-class debut for Worcestershire against Surrey, whose attack included Sylvester Clarke: 'Sylvester was a nasty prospect, with his steep bounce and the habit of hitting batsmen rather painfully. He was easily the fastest I had faced at that time and as I sat with my pads on, I kept telling myself, Stay side-on; if he squares me up, he's got more of a target to hit.' So you don't like the fast men, then, Graeme?

Perhaps the most surprising thing is that, despite these and other similar experiences and despite the warnings of those such as Imran, who predicted that he might prove to be another Zaheer, Hick did not do more to prepare for the short-pitched bombardments of Test cricket. It was understandable that he should place great faith in the front-foot methods that had made him such a devastating force in county cricket but they were going to be of only limited use against a modern Test attack. Hick seems to have been aware of this – in 1990 he asked Basil d'Oliveira, the Worcestershire coach, whether he should not start to play more off the back foot and was told to carry on playing the way he always had – but was slow to act on his own initiative. Robin Smith has described how, before one of their early Test match appearances together, he found himself in the nets alongside Hick: while Smith was practising bobbing and weaving against bouncers, Hick, he noticed, was polishing up his cover drives. What did he think it was? Christmas?

But whatever Hick did, life at Test level was never going to be easy for him. By the time he qualified for England, his first-class centuries totalled 57, his career average was over 60 and public expectations were infinite. His own success was the most intimidating thing he ever had to face. Because of it opponents were prepared to give him nothing: nothing, that is, except four balls an over around his head or into his ribs. And not many of the bowlers he faced in his first fifteen months were pushovers: Ambrose, Marshall, Walsh, Wasim and Waqar knew how to make a batsman hop after all. And, my God, did Hick hop. If no batsman ever suffered the way Chappell did in Packer, no batsman has ever had to put up with the things Hick has in Test cricket. And if Chappell, with all his knowledge and experience, could not prevent his footwork going to pieces, could not prevent the walls caving in, why should Hick? Would Compton or Bradman have fared any better? Ranji or W.G.? Was it really a surprise that by the end of 1992 Hick was not thumbing his way through *Wisden* in search of more batting records to shatter, as some people had anticipated, but through the telephone directory in search of a good psychologist?

Hick is no more vulnerable than many other modern batsmen, it is just that he has attracted special treatment. Does he close his eyes against the fast men more often than Mark Greatbatch, or dislike the rising ball into his ribs more than Steve Waugh? And what of the silent majority, those four hundred county professionals? How many of them also hide behind thigh pads, arm protectors and helmets? How many of them are scared of failure or injury? How would they like to receive the attentions of a hit squad?

As everyone keeps on saying, the ones you've got to feel sorry for are the tailenders. As things have got rougher, they have become more and more involved. Once, they were regarded as deserving of special treatment; now, after the open warfare of Packer, after the advances in protective equipment, after the rise of limited-overs cricket and the greater demands it has made on the batting skills of all players, they are seen as fair game. Whereas once they were just rabbits, now they are rabbits in the headlights – and the headlights belong to vehicles too fast and ferocious to avoid the odd mark on the road.

This is not to say that the standard of batsmanship among tailenders hasn't improved. It has. Look at Richard Hadlee. In his early years, he could hardly be described as brave or technically correct: against pace he'd often just give it a go, or not move his feet and hang out his bat. Most opponents had him worked out, none more so than Brearley's England side in 1978, who realized that they could render him virtually runless by bowling leg-stump bouncers. But the introduction of the helmet brought about a change in Hadlee. It steeled his courage sufficiently to enable him to stay in line instead of backing off towards square leg. In 1978 he was batting number ten for New Zealand; by 1984, he was batting number six for Nottinghamshire and capable enough to become the first player for seventeen years to complete the double of 1,000 runs and 100 wickets.

But not everyone improved to such an extent. Some did not find the helmet such a comfort: Rodney Hogg, for instance, was so alarmed by the incident in which Rick Darling's heart stopped after he was hit by Willis that when it was his turn to bat he went out wearing not only a helmet but also a couple of yards of chest protection. 'He could probably have survived a rifle bullet at twenty-two yards,' Boycott said. Others found that their protective equipment served only to create the impression – for opponents and umpires in particular – that they were a safe target, while technically they were no safer than they had ever been. Peter Lee, the Lancashire fast-medium bowler, whose batting skills rarely took him higher than number ten, found this out to his cost in a tense, low-scoring match at Old Trafford in 1981 when he was hit on the helmet by Garner and had to be led away with blood dripping from his ear.

Others still imagined that they were safe targets, only to find out the hard way that they were not. Craig McDermott was wearing a helmet and a visor when he attempted to hook Walsh at Kingston in February 1991 – he was in good form with the bat at the time – and was hit over the right eye. The blow resulted in ten stitches and so badly affected his confidence against pace that for a long time he backed away and tried to steer the ball over gulley, a method which, when he was playing West Indies, led to shouts of 'fucking white coward'. And for years Geoff Lawson fancied himself as a half-decent batsman, happily exchanging verbal fire with the opposition however strong their fast bowling attack, for years playing the short-pitched ball badly, often turning his head away, often getting thumped, but never being seriously hurt. Then, one day at Perth in December 1988, in a Test match against West Indies, he lost sight of a lifting ball from Curtly Ambrose and – because he had not taken the precaution of attaching a visor to his helmet – was smashed on the chin. His jaw was fractured in several places and he had to be stretchered from the field, which was funny really because he had always wanted to be a proper batsman and here he was being carted off – just as they used to do with Rick Darling.

Despite all the protective equipment, you can still get hurt in all sorts of ways. There must be lots of tailenders whose principal worry when they face fast bowling is not that they might get hit on the head or over the heart (although I bet that crosses their minds) but that they might get struck on the hand or foot and receive a broken bone that will keep them out of action for several weeks. That is probably the sort of thing uppermost in the minds of Devon Malcolm and Phil Tufnell when they make their tours of the crease as the ball is delivered.

Don't you go believing there are no cowards any more. And don't listen to those who tell you that fear isn't what it used to be.

9
Gloves Off

If you really want to know about fear, look no further than Vivian Richards. It was not that he was afraid, of course; far from it. The words afraid and Vivian Richards do not sit happily together. It was just that Richards demonstrated what you had to be like to survive in cricket's most violent and dangerous era. He had this incredible mental strength. He was unbreakable. Have you ever seen a close-up photograph of his face and studied the eyes? They look like they have been burnt. They have: from the inside.

It's difficult to talk about Richards without descending into psychobabble. People are only too keen to discuss his Black Power politics, but this was not the thing that drew him to cricket in the first place. His love of sport did that. Who's to say what it was that drove him on so relentlessly? All that one can say with certainty is that as a cricketer he was driven, that he was able to expel from his mind many of the emotions – fear among them – that occasionally weakened the resolve of even the hardiest of other batsmen. Not only that. Once he scented a challenge, Richards pursued it with obvious relish: any opportunity to demonstrate his bravery and superiority was welcomed. They used to say on the county circuit that when Richards was really steaming – when he was in that so-you-think-you-know-how-to-get-me-out mood or did his it's-time-these-guys-were-taught-a-lesson routine – there was practically nothing you could do about it. He was going to achieve what he set out to achieve and that was often the end of it. Let's face it, he was not known as Smokey – after Smokin' Joe Frazier – for nothing. They both knew a thing or two about steaming into an opponent.

Richards had a great passion for boxing. In his teens, during a period when he was banned from cricket for having publicly disputed an umpiring decision, he had even ventured into the ring. In many ways, perhaps he was temperamentally more suited to boxing than to cricket, for he certainly displayed many attributes of the pugilist around the popping crease. He prepared himself mentally and physically for each contest with all the fanaticism of a fighter (his physical strength was the source of many of his runs). His entrances into the ring had all the timing and assurance of a heavyweight confident of his prize. And, perhaps most significantly of all, for physical protection he never had more than cricket's equivalent of a pair of boxing gloves. During an age in which most batsmen willingly encumbered themselves not only with the traditional pads, gloves and boxes but also with protection for their toes, thighs, arms, chests and heads, Richards made do with just pads, box, thigh pad and a two pound seven ounce bat. He had good reasons for adopting this spartan approach: he felt it allowed him to continue to rely on his natural senses, something he had done ever since learning the game on the unreliable, hard pitches of Antigua, where the ball could bounce in any direction and where he had acquired 'a certain respect for the fundamentals of the game'. Playing under the leadership of Brian Close once he reached England only reinforced many of his own heartfelt principles. When helmets came in, he instinctively knew that he could not wear one because he had long ago decided that: 'I would be on my own out there. I would not hide behind anything.'

And once he was out in the middle, he even behaved like a boxer. He was under no illusion that cricket was anything other than a one-on-one fists-raised affair – between batsman and bowler – and this suited him fine. He focused all his attention

on the bowler, channelled all his energies into destroying the
mind of this one opponent. He used various ploys to achieve
this. One was the chewing gum. No cricketer has ever chewed
gum with such sinister intent as Richards. Another was the
Stare. No cricketer – not even Lillee and Thomson, who taught
him the trick, or one of the many other fast bowlers who
have used it as their trademark – has used the Stare against an
opponent to such devastating effect ('When I get on that
field,' Richards said, 'and look in the eyes of that guy opposite and suss out whether he has it or not . . . that is what
the game is really about'). Then there was the way he would
hit the ball so ferociously hard . . . and the way he would run
past the stumps at the bowler's end after hitting a boundary
just so he could turn and again catch the guy's eyes and
see how confident he was looking then . . . and the way he
would shout, as he lifted the ball back over the bowler's head,
'Shit ball, man!' If someone didn't step in to stop it – in other
words, if the opposing captain didn't pull his man out of the
attack – Richards was liable to do a bowler serious psychological damage.

The fast bowler, of course, had a special place in all this for
Richards. He provided the most exhilarating test. He had the
ability to defeat a batsman at any time and was himself interested in destroying minds. Richards could accept that occasionally the fast bowler might defeat his reactions but would not
accept that he could break his mind: 'I never let the fast bowlers
get to me. On their day they can turn me over, but not frighten
me.' Nevertheless he loved the duel: 'I love the drama of facing
a fast bowler. I love the way such a bowler will try to bully you,
by shouting, snarling, glaring . . . any method of intimidation he
can think of. It is all an attempt to unsettle the mind of a
batsman and dent that all-important confidence.' It was, as he
put it on another occasion, 'the survival of the psychologically
strongest'. When Richards was engaged in one of these
struggles, you could almost feel the crackle of electricity in the
air, the steely mind defying the lightning bolts, but if Richards

The eye of the tornado: Jeff Thomson prepares to create havoc twenty yards away.

The greatest attack of all time? Joel Garner, Colin Croft, Andy Roberts and Michael Holding prepare to put Australia through the mill at Adelaide in 1980.

Richard Hadlee bends the mind of another batsman at the Oval in 1983. 'There is no skill,' he said, 'in banging the ball in half way down the track.'

Patrick Patterson acquaints England's batsmen with fear in the Caribbean in 1986.

Imran Khan in the Headingley Test of 1987, when he gave an outstanding exhibition of pace and swing bowling to return match figures of ten wickets for 77 runs.

Local boy made good: Devon Malcolm returns to his home town to help England win their first Test match against West Indies for sixteen years in Kingston, Jamaica, 1990.

Back-foot blues: Waqar Younis beats David Gower with late swing in the Oval Test of 1992. It was Gower's last ball in Test cricket.

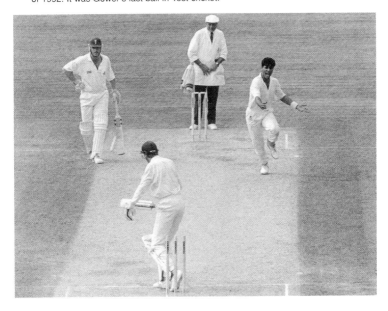

Allan Donald's speed encouraged South Africa to rely on pace when they returned to Test cricket in 1992.

Riding the roller-coaster: Mohinder Amarnath hooks Sarfraz Nawaz at Lahore in 1978. Amarnath was hit in the face by a ball from Imran during this match but returned to carry on undaunted.

In the crucible: Vivian Richards takes on Jeff Thomson at Perth in 1975 during a series in which he learned some lessons he was never to forget.

Robin Smith, a fearless player against pace, gets into line behind a ball from Ian Bishop in Antigua in 1990.

Graham Gooch sways out of the way of a Merv Hughes bouncer at Trent Bridge in 1993.

had not been confident that he was the psychologically strong-est, he would surely not have loved it so much.

Just occasionally, the immense demands he made of himself took their toll on Richards and he started to act like it was he that was the Untamed Force. Why else did he demolish a dressing-room door at Delhi in 1983 after disagreeing with a leg-before decision? Why else did he smash his bat to smither-eens after Somerset had missed out on their second one-day competition in two days in 1978? Who needs boxing when you can go several rounds with a piece of willow?

Richards may have given up boxing but he resolved to make himself the undisputed heavyweight champion of cricket. No one was going to intimidate him, no one was going to hurt him, no one was going to stop him. Least of all some burly-looking bloke with a ball in his hand. And if necessary he was prepared to smash him out of the ground to prove it.

Now who was it who once said that fast bowlers are basically bullies?

From the start, Richards the cricketer was not prepared to be pushed around. Even as a teenager, he knew the importance of playing his shots and refusing to buckle. This approach may have often got him out, but he worked on the principle that his confidence would worry bowlers and win him important psychological battles. Time and again he was proved right.

It took him seven days as a county cricketer with Somerset – as a 22-year-old in 1974 – to provide a dramatic demon-stration of his methods. It was his third match for the county, a Benson and Hedges Cup tie against Gloucestershire at Taunton. 'When I first played against Mike Procter in England,' he said, 'I had had a bellyful from the senior Somerset players about his fast bowling – all they could talk about was the way he swung the ball at speed off the wrong foot. They made him out to be a world beater and some of our batsmen were beaten before they faced a ball. Soon after I walked out to face Procter, I went down the pitch and hit him over the top. It felt marvellous. I had backed my ability and ignored Procter's reputation. I got away with it that day because I would not be overawed.' Richards actually took fifteen runs off his first over from Procter, including successive cover drives to the boundary and a hook in front of square for four. Just to underline the point, three weeks later Richards scored his maiden first-class century against Procter in a championship match at Bristol – the match, in fact, in which Botham admits he was afraid.

It was not long before Richards's Somerset colleagues were also being astounded by his fearless hooking of Andy Roberts. Roberts, an old friend who had shared a flat with Richards when they first came to England, was – alongside Procter – the fastest and most feared bowler on the county circuit in 1974. During his early years on the county circuit, Richards used to tease rival teams by reminding them of the destructive power of Hampshire's strike bowler ('And here is the news...' he used to say, 'another ambulance was sent for at Southampton...') but when he himself faced Roberts it was never anything less than the most cutthroat duel. 'When Andy Roberts used to bowl to him,' Geoff Boycott said, 'it was like a bout between knuckle-fighters; Roberts had to bounce him and Richards just had to take him on. A challenge match with no holds barred.'

It was not until 1976, however, when Richards established himself as the world's leading batsmen by breaking the record for Test runs in a calendar year, that the fast bowlers started to search him out. Once this happened, the nature of Richards's existence as a batsman changed. Every fast bowler was looking to make an impression on him, every one of them was looking for a short-cut to fame, and with each passing year more of them gathered on his tail. Before, he used his confidence as a psychological weapon of attack; now, he needed it to keep the hounds at bay. It was not long, though, before he became men-tally hardened to his special position, particularly after his two years in the pace-dominated world of Packer.

Imran Khan was one of those who tried in vain to make his

mark. He came up against Richards in the Caribbean in early 1977, at a time when he was not at his fastest but possessed some useful variations in pace. 'He played me almost as if I were a spinner,' Imran recalled. 'To block my inswing he would put his front foot down and across the wicket. I would continue at medium pace and then try to surprise him with a bouncer: although he was on the front foot he would merely lean back and hit the ball over mid-wicket.' Len Pascoe was another. During a Packer match at Sydney, he gave Richards successive bouncers that were top-edged to the boundary; he gave him a third, which put Richards on his back. Pascoe started blowing and snorting and snarled at Richards: 'Next ball you're in hospital, you . . .' Richards said nothing, just gave him the Stare. Pascoe's next ball was, as it happens, a perfectly respectable, good-length ball but it was picked up off the back foot and driven straight back over his head and into the stands. 'After that,' Richards said matter-of-factly, 'Pascoe was finished against me.'

As far as Richards was concerned, it was either him or them. There could be no in-between. He sought to destroy fast bowlers before they destroyed him. This was partly an individual approach, but it was also the way West Indies approached their cricket in general. As a team, they liked to focus on a particular batsman or bowler, perhaps someone who posed a particular threat, and attempt to break him. 'That is their tactic,' Bob Willis said. 'They have destroyed bowlers – particularly spinners – by literally flogging them in the first couple of overs to get rid of the close fielders and then played in a completely different way once the field has been spread out. They'd play some very optimistic heave against Emburey and he'd go for eight an over for two overs and then he'd get very frustrated, take the short legs away, and then be milked at three or four an over and be totally ineffective.'

Richards took it upon himself to take on the fast bowlers in this way and over the years he broke countless hearts and ruined many reputations. In 1979–80, for example, he shattered the confidence of Rodney Hogg, who had entered the season on a high after his successes against England a year earlier. One passage of play during the Melbourne Test was particularly significant, Richards rallying from a painful blow in the face by Hogg to hit his next ball high into the stands for six and continue mauling him so savagely that Hogg later hobbled from the field with a back injury and figures that read 6–0–59–0. Hogg did not play international cricket again for almost a year. Richards meted out similar treatment to Bob Willis, with whom he had had a memorable first encounter while playing early in his career for Leeward Islands during England's 1974 tour of West Indies. Richards often saved his most blistering strokeplay for Willis and things came to a head during West Indies' tour of England in 1980, when Willis almost bowled England to victory in the first Test at Trent Bridge and had begun to pose a serious threat as a strike bowler. Richards chose to strike during the third Test match at Old Trafford, his determination doubtless steeled by recent newspaper reports of a feud between the two players, and that England reckoned they knew a way to keep him quiet. He not only launched a devastating attack on Willis's bowling but pointedly reserved almost all his aggression for these deliveries: 53 of his 65 runs, and twelve of his thirteen boundaries, came off Willis. Four years later, when they next met in a Test series, Richards was instrumental in seeing that Willis ended his distinguished England career in an undignified fashion, with 367 runs and only six wickets coming from his last 85 Test overs.

If there was one thing that Richards couldn't stand, though, it was a bowler who thought he had got his number. If he ever got to hear of such a thing, his response was always swift and devastating. A classic example of this was his treatment of Devon Malcolm during England's tour of the Caribbean in 1990. Malcolm dismissed Richards in each innings of the first Test at Kingston and was later quoted in the press as saying that he reckoned he knew how to get Richards out. They did not meet again until the fourth Test at Bridgetown but Richards had not forgotten what had happened. He went straight after Malcolm, hooking his first ball for six (it smashed into the face of the scoreboard) and taking 18 runs off his first over. Three overs later Malcolm, who had taken fifteen wickets in his two previous Tests, was withdrawn from the attack and was ineffective for the remainder of the match.

Perhaps the most devastating put-down Richards ever delivered was to Greg Thomas during a county match at Taunton in 1986. Richards had only just come in, and Thomas had his tail up, having just taken a wicket, and for a while the West Indian played and missed. Thomas could not resist a little self-satisfied dig. 'Hey, Viv!' he shouted by way of assistance, 'it's red and it's round!' The next ball Richards did not miss: it was dispatched back over Thomas's head and out of the ground. Richards fixed him with his stare: 'You know what it looks like, man. You go and fetch it.' That was the first of six sixes and twelve fours Richards hit in a 48-ball century and Thomas finished the Somerset innings with an analysis that was both red-faced and rounded: 17.2−1−100−1.

Nor did Richards spare his fellow West Indians the punishment. He particularly relished his duels with Roberts, Croft, Daniel, Holding, Marshall, Patterson and the like, partly because he did not get many opportunities to pit his wits against them and partly because they were among the most dangerous bowlers in the world and offered a natural challenge to a man who prided himself on his position in the game. The prospect of facing them must have enlivened what might otherwise have been a routine and mundane county or island match. He enjoyed a special rivalry with Marshall, the pair of them constantly teasing each other about what would happen the next time they met in opposition. 'Viv is always telling me how he is going to take me apart,' Marshall said, 'and I'm always telling him how I'm going to destroy a legend.' In fact, neither could claim to have gained an ascendancy over the years, but Richards enjoyed one spectacular success when he fetched Marshall for fourteen runs from the last scheduled over to win a championship match at Southampton in 1990. After the game, Marshall told Richards that the six he had hit him for in that final over was the biggest there had ever been off his bowling.

Richards's desire to impose himself on bowlers from the outset often got him into trouble and often brought about his early downfall, but it was a risk he was always prepared to take. Some people may have reckoned that he could be lured into a false hook stroke and a loose swish outside the off-stump before he had got his eye in, but his aggressive methods were part and parcel of his strategy. OK, so he sometimes steamed in a little too early, sometimes he was so pumped up he'd go reaching for a bouncer he just *had* to smash into the outer – as he did when he was caught off Dilley at Antigua in 1981 – or sometimes he'd get carried away by his own success – as he did shortly after taking five boundaries off his first seven balls from Hadlee in the Christchurch Test of 1987. But this was the way Richards reckoned it had to be. There was, for him, no other way to play the white-hot stuff. And who's to say he is wrong?

There was only one time Richards will concede he came off second best to the fast men over an extended period and that was to Lillee and Thomson during the 1975–6 series in Australia. 'That was,' he said, 'murder . . . we were bumped all over the place.' Thomson not only smashed his box, he also hit him a painful blow on the jaw, which swelled up 'as if I had the mumps'. In eleven innings, during the course of which he scored 426 runs at an average of 38, Richards fell five times to Lillee and three times to Thomson. He attempted to play his shots against them, and enjoyed some unforgettably satisfying moments when these attempts came off, but he came to realize that it was almost impossible to pursue this policy with any consistent success when the pair of them were fresh and bowling to attacking fields.

Needless to say, Richards wanted revenge for his – and his side's – failures during this series, but unfortunately he got only a handful of bona fide opportunities to take on Lillee and Thomson in unison and never before Thomson's action had been irreparably damaged by his shoulder injury. In these encounters – they comprised five Packer Supertests and three establishment Test matches – he did at least have the satisfaction of improving on his record against them. In thirteen innings – in which he again fell five times to Lillee and three times to Thomson – he scored 601 runs at an average of 50 and was especially destructive in his next Test matches against them back in Australia: his only innings in the 1979–80 series were 140, 96, 76 and 74.

Perhaps more telling than even these statistics was Richards's behaviour when he next came up against Lillee and Thomson after that first series in Australia. His meeting with Lillee was in a Packer Supertest at the VFL Stadium, Melbourne, in December 1977. In the first innings Richards scored a brilliant 79 and its most dazzling period was a spell in which he hooked Lillee for six just in front of square, drove him off the back foot for four and then square-cut him for another four. In the second innings he made 56 and Lillee finished the match without Richards's wicket and with 36 overs having cost him 177 runs, leaving no one in any doubt as to who had won the exchange.

Three months later Richards caught up with Thomson. He would probably have gone after him at the first opportunity, during the first Test match in Port of Spain, but for the fact that before he could get to the wicket Haynes had already launched an explosive counterattack against Thomson – the one in which he took twenty runs off an over – and had effectively stolen his thunder. Richards therefore delayed his assault until the second Test match in Bridgetown a fortnight later, when conditions, as it happened, were far more favourable to Thomson than they had been in Trinidad. The pitch was faster and bouncier and Australia's batsmen had given him more of a total to bowl at (250 as against 90). West Indies began their innings seventy minutes before stumps on the first day and Richards came to the wicket in the third over after Thomson, who was putting in a tremendous effort knowing that everything rested on him, had had Greenidge caught off a glove in the slips. 'Thommo was very, very sharp,' recalled Haynes, who batted throughout the seventy minutes. 'He was putting so much into it that his perspiration was splashing over me when I was the non-striker. He had no support from the other end. Although it was the quickest bowling I'd ever seen, he used the bouncer sparingly because it tended to soar straight over your head. He just concentrated on the ball that was fractionally short of a good length. You'd be looking to hit it off the back foot and it would whizz past your chin.'

With Thomson having claimed an early victim and bowling so ferociously, Richards might have been expected to forsake all risks and wait for the storm to blow over, hope that the morning might find him in less hostile mood. Not a bit of it: Richards could not wait until the morning. He had to take on Thomson now. So, even though Thomson beat him for pace and almost had him leg-before in his first over at the crease; even though Thomson induced him, still before he had scored, to mistime a hook which was dropped behind square leg; even though Thomson struck him on the body with a steeply rising ball; even though Thomson did all this, Richards was still determined to take him on. And he produced some streaks of pure gold: he drove Thomson off the back foot over mid-off for four; hooked him for six through mid-wicket; hooked him for four; lifted him overhead for another four. It became difficult to tell which of the two was most panicked: Richards was trying to smash everything out of sight, Thomson started to bowl no-balls. Then, off the last delivery of a nine-ball over which had cost 19 runs, Richards top-edged another wild hook and was brilliantly caught by Wayne Clark down by his ankles at long leg. His dismissal for 23 exposed Kallicharran to Thomson, who duly had him caught at backward short-leg off the last ball of the day, but, as with Lillee at the VFL, Richards was paying no heed to the match situation. For him, on these occasions, there was no match, only his private duel. He had his man in the ring and all he wanted was to finish him as soon as possible. With Lillee it worked, with Thomson it didn't.

Was this the most dramatic encounter between a batsman and fast bowler of modern times? Show me one better!

So am I saying that the rules which apply to most batsmen faced with top-class fast bowling did not apply in the case of Viv Richards? That he was so mentally tough and possessed such extraordinary gifts of coordination and eye that except for a few early skirmishes with Lillee and Thomson he did not know what it was to be afraid, or what it was like to take a shuddering and painful blow, or what it was like to find his reactions unequal to the challenge of speed?

Well, no, I am not saying that. Richards's refusal to admit publicly that fear was something to which he was susceptible did not mean that privately it did not exist. He was not so supreme that he was not once deceived by a ball from Greg Chappell and hit between the eyes; or so disciplined that he did not once drink too much the night before a match, thereby dulling his reactions so much that he was hit on the head by David Colley, who, like Chappell, was scarcely of the highest pace. Nor was he so infallible during his heyday that he was incapable of being dismissed for nought in Test cricket by Lillee, Dilley, Lawson and McDermott. Nor were his eyes so perfect that his habit of playing across the line did not lead him into such difficulties in Packer Supertests in 1979–80 that he reached fifty only once in fourteen innings. Perhaps, also, like many West Indies Test batsmen, he would not have looked so good if he had had to regularly face his own fast bowlers. Richards likes to dismiss such an observation as 'stupid', pointing out that they face their own bowling all the time in inter-island matches in the Caribbean. But what he fails to state clearly is that his record against some of the other islands – those with the pace batteries, in fact – is decidedly modest. From 1979 his first-class scores against Barbados, whose attacks included Clarke, Garner, Daniel, Marshall, Alleyne, Moseley, Stephenson, Estwick and Cummins, were 0, 3, 4, 13, 4, 46, 0, 45, 16, 70, 25 not out, 19 and 7; against Jamaica, whose attack included Holding,

Patterson and Walsh, 1, 0, 106, 73, 50, 2, 5, 42, 16, 16, 17, 112 and 8 not out. Richards was not infallible, but he is the nearest thing there has been to an infallible batsman during an era in which the existence of batsmen has rarely if ever been so physically vulnerable.

Richards may have been mentally the toughest cricketer of modern times but he did make one serious error of judgement. He went on too long. He had always said that the day the fast bowlers started to worry him would be the day he quit. 'No one is going to hurt me or make me look ill-at-ease at the crease,' he said, 'and if it ever came about that I was worried about my personal safety, I would pack it in.' But he didn't pack it in. Like so many heavyweights, he kept hanging on and tried to challenge the advancing years. Four years too many, Viv.

Had he retired from the game at the age of thirty-seven after the triumphant tour of Australia in 1988–9 – an appropriate enough place to wind it all up, after all – then he might now be able to look back on his career with even more satisfaction than he undoubtedly already can. Instead, he played on for two more years at international level – averaging fewer than thirty in three of his four Test series – and for two more years after that at county level. With each passing year his batting became more frenetic and less effective. He seemed to want to hit each ball for four. It was like the January sales: everything had to go.

He was battling with his waning powers and he knew it. The less he was able to defend his pride with strokeplay, the more he became inclined to do so with spleen; the less capable he became as a pugilist of the popping crease, the keener he was to be one around the pavilion. It was as though the incredible mental demands he had made of himself for over ten years had finally taken their toll: the vast surges of electricity through his steel-hard brain had finally started to short this most sophisticated piece of machinery, causing it to behave in all sorts of bizarre ways.

Did Richards really mean to do some of the things he did? In the field he started to go in for histrionic appeals (as when Rob Bailey was given out by umpire Barker at Bridgetown in 1990) and at the crease to dispute his own dismissals (as he did at Kingston in 1989, sparking a crowd riot). He started to talk about himself in the third person. And, of course, the gloves finally came off: at Bridgetown in 1988, after a leg-before decision against him had been turned down, he allegedly invited the bowler, Wasim Akram, to see him outside the ground after play so that they could settle their differences there; at Antigua in 1990, rather than lead his team out on to the field, he entered the press box and threatened to 'whack' an English journalist who had written a piece critical of him; and, on the same ground twelve months later, he allegedly threatened to 'fix' Craig McDermott behind the grandstand after the Australian had returned some verbal abuse.

In the case of his exchanges with Wasim and McDermott, Richards's behaviour may have had not a little to do with it having become fairly clear that he was no longer able to tackle their bowling head-on: he had given up attempting to hook Wasim's faster ball and McDermott had further exposed his increasing vulnerability against the short ball. He definitely came off worst in the altercation with McDermott. His remarks so fired up the fast bowler that when Richards went out to bat later that day in what was his final Test match in the Caribbean, he found McDermott couldn't wait to get at him: 'The crowd was wild with excitement and expectation as he walked out to bat,' McDermott said in his autobiography. 'The spectators realized this was a historic occasion – one of the all-time great cricket careers was coming to an end – and they were obviously hoping Richards would mark the occasion by doing something special. I am sure this is what Richards himself intended. He walked past me on his way to the crease and, in his usual manner, he gave me a cold, hard look. If this was meant to intimidate, it had the opposite effect. Before he had scored, I bowled him an off-cutter which pitched just outside off-stump and moved in. Richards tried to play it, but he barely moved his feet and the ball hit his pads right in front of the stumps. I roared an appeal, and so did all the Australians behind the wicket. At first the umpire seemed unimpressed and began moving away from the stumps. In that fraction of a second I thought to myself, I can't believe this is happening – he can't turn this appeal down! But after he had taken about two paces to the side, the umpire raised his finger. It was a brave decision, because the entire crowd was willing him to rule against the appeal. Viv Richards was out leg-before-wicket for a duck.

'After all that happened, I was delighted to claim his wicket, but I made no remark of any kind to him as he walked out. I did not have to.'

Frankly, I just don't understand what all the fuss was about with Richards. I reckon I could have got him out even when he was at his height. First of all, I'd have tested him out with a few early bouncers, just in case he wasn't seeing the ball right. If that didn't come off, I would have worked on this weakness to the ball outside off-stump that was moving away. He just couldn't resist having a go and would have been bound to give a catch to the slips, gully or cover sooner or later.

Hey, only-kidding, Viv. You were the greatest, man. You were the greatest of them all. You really were.

10

Breaking Diamonds

Clive Lloyd and Viv Richards reckoned the West Indies could not be beaten in a full Test series. They believed they had found the most efficient way to play and they stuck to it religiously. They had built their team around a four-man pace attack but the key to its success was not the destructive powers of the attack but a collective discipline: the discipline of the captain, the discipline of the batsmen, the discipline of the bowlers. They had become the most stupendous big-match players.

Lloyd had wanted to turn the West Indies into a team of grit-hard professionals and he got his way. Gordon Greenidge and Desmond Haynes matured into awesomely efficient run-scorers and Lloyd himself was almost as adept as Richards at putting a dangerous bowler to the sword. When Croft, Roberts, Holding and Garner departed the scene, there were other fast men who were, if not all as imaginative or as gifted as those who had encouraged them, equally dedicated to the cause of defending Caribbean pride. Courtney Walsh, who first played Test cricket in November 1984, eleven months after Roberts's last match, may have bowled more bouncers and not been of quite the same pace, but he was just as silent and as selfless, and once said with pride, 'I would never lose my temper on the field.' Curtly Ambrose, who first played a Test in April 1988, five months after Garner announced his retirement, was one inch shorter but more predatory and even more accurate and was described by Richards as having 'the biggest heart of any bowler I've known'. 'We share,' Marshall said, 'a common ambition to be top of the world and there is not one ego which has ever been allowed to intrude in our shared aim. Not even Viv himself is bigger than the team and he would be the first not only to acknowledge it but also to encourage the rest of us to look upon ourselves as equals.'

Confidence has so much to do with success and failure in sport that this single-minded determination not to be broken was the ace in the pack for the West Indies. When opponents came to understand that they were unbreakable, so they themselves began to break. Without any apparent weaknesses to exploit, they had nothing to feed off, nothing on which to nurture their hopes, and they shrank when they realized this. This process took longer on some occasions than on others but the effect was almost always the same. In the 24 series West Indies played under Lloyd and Richards after Packer, they were rarely beaten after the opening match. Of the first Tests, West Indies won nine, their opponents seven. Subsequently, as they asserted their psychological hold, they won 42 and lost only six. Of these six defeats, three occurred when the series was already won, the other three when the series could not be lost. Their most serious blemish was their failure to draw level in New Zealand in 1980 after losing the first Test at Dunedin by one wicket, but even then there were extenuating circumstances: the absence of Richards and the controversial umpiring.

So, in a way, Lloyd and Richards were right: once West Indies were up and running and the series was at stake, they were unbeatable (and for them not being beaten, as opposed to winning themselves, was the overriding concern: Richards was chaired from the field by his players at Edgbaston in 1991 not because the rubber had been won but because it could no longer be lost). And the longer the series, the more formidable they were. Seven of the 24 series under Lloyd and Richards were of three matches in length: one was won, five were drawn and one lost; 17 of them were of four or more matches: of these, 15 were won, two were drawn and not one was lost.

Opponents literally could not stand the pace. While the West Indies themselves would usually choose from a select core of men throughout a series, their opponents were often forced to search out replacements for players physically or mentally scarred long before it reached its end. In four series in England between 1980 and 1991, West Indies relied on no more than 14 players each time; their hosts never called on fewer than 18. The West Indians liked nothing more than to see an opposing camp in disarray: it was like a wolf catching scent of its prey. 'When I watch them practise,' Haynes once said of West Indies' opponents, 'they sometimes look as if they feel they have no chance of winning, that we are too good for them. It's a great feeling.' Even batsmen who achieved some measure of success against their fast bowlers, even those who avoided being injured, were rarely able to sustain their momentum throughout a long series. Dilip Vengsarkar, who began the 1983–4 series with innings of 14, 65, 159, 63 and 100, finished with scores of 23, 1 and a first-ball duck; Allan Lamb ended the 1984 series, in which he hit centuries in three successive Tests, with scores of 9, 12 and 1.

Long before Richards retired in 1991 there was not an opposition team in the world who had yet to get the message.

OK, guys! Enough's enough! We promise not to try to make you grovel, we promise not to give you any abuse (well not much, anyway). We know you're no longer a soft touch. Just ease off, OK?

But, of course, most people had long since realized they were never going to let up (why give up something you're so good at?). And gradually it dawned on a few people that something would have to be done.

Someone was going to have to get a grip.

By the mid-eighties the question that was exercising everybody's mind was: how could the West Indies be beaten? How could you beat them even once, let alone over an entire series? By the end of 1986 the West Indies had lost only three Tests in the previous seven years and they had, in Richards, a captain who had made it clear that he intended to carry on exactly where Lloyd had left off. The home defeats of New Zealand in 1985 and England in 1986 that he supervised were as ruthlessly efficient as any in living memory. Opponents seemed to be as far away as ever from toppling the champions of the world.

Funnily enough, it was out of England's crushing defeat in the Caribbean under Gower that part of the answer came. No one, of course, discovered the holy grail of how to beat the West Indies over five matches or anything like that, but there was undoubtedly a subsequent change of approach among their opponents that was to reap its own modest rewards. In the five years from 1987 until Richards's retirement in 1991, West Indies lost ten times in Test matches, which almost made it a common occurrence, even if some of these defeats did take place towards the end of series West Indies could no longer lose.

What Gower's tour did was to show everyone what not to do. His acceptance that the West Indies fast bowlers were so good that they were inevitably going to take wickets at regular intervals and that all you could do was score as many runs as possible before they got you out was as unacceptable to most observers as it was to some members of Gower's own team. It went against one of the first tenets of captaincy, which is that you make life as difficult for your opponents as possible. Even if you cannot alter the outcome of the match, you should at least make them fight for their runs and wickets, at least let them know they had been in a match. More specifically, with West Indies it became clear that you should at least try to disrupt their practice of working over one or two key individuals – usually the leading batsman and captain – to psychologically destroy the rest.

Once Gower reminded people of these basic aims, it was a small step to the realization that you had to select men with the courage to achieve them. You did not want batsmen who would flinch in the line of fire, or captains who were incapable of doing the things they had to demand of their players. You did not want batsmen who were going to hook themselves into oblivion, or captains who went sailing on tour. Strokemakers were out. And so were captains who burst into tears. What you wanted were men who would try to break diamonds with their teeth if you asked them to.

This was a huge change of outlook and it took time to complete but the result was a fairly spectacular clear-out of 'Gower-types' among several Test teams. Australia, who in any case had not won a Test series for three years, got rid of a whole handful after failing to regain the Ashes in 1986–7. Greg Ritchie, Greg Matthews, Tim Zoehrer and, a year later, Craig McDermott (who was then less 'committed' than he later became) were all dropped in favour of the sort of streetfighter who had been a hallmark of Ian Chappell's Australia sides. Although Allan Border, the captain, stayed on, he too started to cultivate a tougher image. On the 1985 tour of England he had been communicative and friendly towards his opponents; by the time of his next visit, in 1989, all that had changed. 'I became a harder sort of bloke,' he said, 'more ruthless, less sociable.'

The sort of henchman Border now surrounded himself with was typified by the hard-working and aggressive Merv Hughes, whom Bob Simpson would describe as the 'spirit of Australian cricket'. No task was too great for Hughes: he established himself with a heroic performance at Perth in 1988, when Lawson was out of action with a broken jaw and Hughes bowled 73.1 overs and took thirteen wickets, and he was still performing heroics five years later in England, when McDermott fell ill and he bowled 296.2 overs and took 31 wickets in six Tests. And the changes worked: Australia started winning again. They won the one-day World Cup in November 1987, comfortably recovered the Ashes in 1989 and eighteen months after that even gave West Indies a run for their money in the Caribbean. ('There were a lot of things said during that series,' Richards said. 'Nasty things. Just like it was, way back, when I first played against them. Their players like to ride that hype. They like to believe they are the nastiest, meanest team in the world.')

Pakistan, who were the first country to face West Indies in a Test series after the Gower tour, were already committed to rebuilding their side after the retirement of the brilliant but individualistic stars who had studded their side in the seventies. Imran Khan, the captain and only survivor of that generation, was well aware that players were now needed who were less mentally brittle than those who had gone before and was keen to instil the message into his young players before the visit of Richards's side late in 1986. For many of them the first Test in Faisalabad was their first taste of Test cricket against this most fearsome of opponent.

'I had told the batsmen that I didn't mind if they failed,' Imran wrote in his autobiography, 'but they would have to fight all the way, and I would not tolerate any lack of courage. On the first day of the series, the West Indian fast bowlers overawed our top order, and I came in to bat with the scoreboard reading 37 for five. The very first ball I received from Marshall was a quick, sharply rearing delivery which hit me on the shoulder. Very soon my shoulder swelled up and became stiff. I realised that, if I went off, the team would be bowled out immediately and the match virtually over. Salim Malik and I were steadying the innings somewhat when a ball from Walsh broke Salim's arm. Qadir lasted for a while, as did Tauseef. I was the last to go, after making 61 from a total of 159.' It was only a modest total but the bravery of Imran and Salim (who batted again in the second innings despite his injury) had turned the match. Pakistan went on to win by 186 runs and take a share of the series, and Imran was able to proudly declare that his players had 'withstood the pressure'.

A little over a year later, when he took a side to the Caribbean, Imran again showed that he knew what was required. He took many of the players who had acquitted themselves so well at home – although there was an important addition in Shoaib Mohammad, a superb attritional batsman – but the side suffered some early setbacks: several players, including Imran himself, were not fully fit and all five of the one-day internationals were lost. Intikhab Alam, the team manager, suggested, Gower-like, that the players might benefit from some time off before the Test series began. Imran refused, choosing instead to put them through some rigorous training sessions – which included batting practice against tennis balls thrown from eighteen yards to familiarize them with the short-pitched delivery – and to issue them with a chilling ultimatum: 'The first one of you I see flinch will be on the next plane home.' This, too, worked. Pakistan fought tooth and nail throughout the three-match series and emerged with a 1–1 draw, although their victory in the Test at Georgetown – set up by the first of two centuries in the series by Javed Miandad, and the first time West Indies had been beaten at home for ten years – was greatly assisted by the absence of Richards and Marshall, both injured. Imran's contribution with the bat was modest but his 23 wickets made him the most influential bowler on either side.

After Kapil Dev's dismissal as captain following the 1987 World Cup, India sought to rally their players behind a similarly resilient and accomplished player in Dilip Vengsarkar, indisputably their best batsman against fast bowling. Unfortunately, although Vengsarkar surrounded himself with brave foot-soldiers such as Sanjay Manjrekar and Mohinder Amarnath (before the latter fell out with the selectors), his leadership skills were not as finely tuned as Imran's and he was unable to inspire by example in the same way. His fine batsmanship in his first series in charge – at home to West Indies – could not hide his tactical errors and when he himself lost form in the Caribbean in 1989 he had little to offer except accusations of cowardice against his fellow batsmen.

The most spectacular clear-out occurred in the England camp. Gower was quickly replaced as captain and Bob Willis, who had been assistant manager on the Caribbean tour and responsible for organizing practice (what practice?), was overlooked for any future England posts. In their place were brought in two British bulldogs in Mike Gatting, Gower's vice-captain in the West Indies, and Micky Stewart, who succeeded to Willis's position on the tour of Australia the following winter and subsequently became England's first full-time manager. This pair brought a more professional approach to preparation and playing, a process which was continued when Gooch assumed the captaincy in 1989.

Gooch was nothing if not professional. He loved training in the way Australia, South Africa and West Indies loved training. In the winter, before a tour, he would organize his own nets and join the West Ham United football squad in their training sessions. Once on tour, he would go on ludicrously long jogs at ludicrously early hours in the morning. And, having witnessed at first hand the way England had been outclassed in the West Indies in 1981 and 1986, he became a great admirer of the 'perfect' West Indies system: the closely knit squad of élite players, who trained and practised rigorously together and who went on to the field totally committed to the cause of winning. And the only thing Gooch loved more than training was winning. The 1986 West Indies tour did for him what the 1976 Australia tour did for Clive Lloyd: it made him determined to stop the rot, to stop the world regarding his team as a soft touch. Even before he became captain Gooch had had some success in this regard: it was his rearguard action at Trent Bridge in 1988, when he batted almost ten hours for 73 and 146, that had ended England's sequence of ten successive defeats at the hands of West Indies. And once he became captain he was determined to foster a collective desire to win. He had a catchphrase, which was not 'nice guys never win', but which had the same sentiment: 'If you fail to prepare, you prepare to fail.'

When Gooch took a side to the West Indies in 1990 he and Stewart made them prepare as they had never prepared before. Before leaving, they spent six weeks undergoing special training exercises and special coaching designed to help them combat the sort of things that the West Indies fast bowlers, in particular, would put them through. Only those players who were sympathetic to such regimes were chosen for the tour: thus Wayne Larkins, who had not played Test cricket for more than eight years but was known as a staunch batsman against fast bowling, was selected, but Gower and Botham were not. Gooch also decided to return to a policy of playing six specialist batsmen rather than five. After three series in which England had failed to pass 205 twenty times in thirty innings against West Indies, it was time to start doing what Woolmer and Tavaré had been doing when they were dropped in 1980: occupying the crease.

The strategy worked. In the first three Tests in the Caribbean, England built competitive first-innings totals through century stands between Smith and Lamb in Jamaica and Barbados (Lamb scoring a hundred on each occasion) and between Gooch and Larkins in Trinidad. The Test in Jamaica was won, the one in Trinidad would have been had not rain intervened on the final day, and the Test in Barbados was lost only after a devastating spell of bowling by Ambrose, who took five wickets in five overs, induced an old-fashioned collapse in the final session of the match. In the end, England lost the series as much through battle fatigue as any technical failings; they returned home with three of their specialist batsmen (including Gooch and Smith) carrying broken bones in their hands. Gooch and Smith recovered to continue their resistance in the series between the countries in 1991 and were instrumental in England gaining a 2–2 draw and becoming the first team to beat West Indies twice in a series since – well, since Australia in 1975–6. Gooch batted almost 24 hours for 480 runs, Smith, who missed the Edgbaston Test through injury, 20½ hours for 416 runs.

What Gooch, Smith and Lamb succeeded in doing was coming to terms with the special demands of facing an all-pace attack. They accepted that the rate at which they received deliveries would be slow and that they would be unable to score off many of the balls they did face. By approaching the task in a scientific manner, they were able to reduce their feelings of danger and frustration. 'It can be a continuous bombardment at the head,' Smith once said. 'If they bowl fourteen overs an hour and you face your share, you get forty-two deliveries, of which maybe twenty go over your head and a dozen may be wide of off-stump or going down the leg side. It leaves only ten balls an hour from which to score . . . For my part I don't mind if they bowl at my head because there is less chance of getting out.' One of the main difficulties was remaining positive enough to make the most of the opportunities they did get to score. Smith got badly bogged down at times in the Caribbean in 1990, partly because he had cut out several scoring shots that he had come to regard as risky. Lamb, who always liked to score quickly, looked to take singles wherever possible, partly to keep the scoreboard moving but also to relieve the pressure of long spells on strike. Gooch was the same. He preferred playing a shot at the ball to evading it altogether and became adept at working it off his body. He admits that when he carried his bat through the England second innings at Headingley in 1991 for what proved to be a match-winning 154, he rarely hit the ball in the middle of the bat.

It was not simply the batsmen, of course, who enabled England to defeat West Indies three times in nine Tests in 1990 and 1991. Gooch also demanded disciplined performances from his bowlers, and they too had more success against West Indies than anyone since 1976. It was their ability to deny the West Indies batsmen the chance to play their shots – doing, in fact, what Greig's bowlers had failed to do in 1976 – that kept England in matches that might otherwise have got away from them. In the West Indies, the accuracy of Small and Fraser acted as the perfect foil to the raw pace of Malcolm; in England, where the pitches were better suited to fast-medium swing bowling, it was simply the unrelentingly tight line of DeFreitas and Pringle. In the West Indies in 1990, Gooch said, 'The general feeling was that the West Indies batsmen love fast bowling and they like to play it off their legs . . . So we decided to bowl just outside the off-stump, a nagging line at fast-medium pace. We hoped that after a time, they'd get impatient, play a loose shot and get caught in the slips or drag one into their stumps. That's

exactly what happened several times in Jamaica and in Trinidad
... Tight attritional bowling is the method against them, not
meeting fire with fire.'

Gooch's bowlers effectively signalled the end for the
let's-fight-fire-with-fire brigade. It had never really been very
effective as a tactic, certainly not with West Indies who, between
1979 and 1991, played 101 Test matches and lost only six
directly because their fast bowlers were outperformed: at
Dunedin in February 1980 (by Hadlee), at Melbourne in
December 1981 (by Lillee), at Christchurch in March 1987
(again by Hadlee), at Georgetown in April 1988 (by Imran
Khan), at Karachi in November 1990 (by Wasim Akram and
Waqar Younis) and at Antigua in May 1991 (by McDermott
and Hughes). By comparison, West Indies won 51 of these
matches, all of them the result of the work done by their fast
bowlers. 'The one thing you mustn't try and do,' Mike Brearley
observed, 'is copy them.' In fact, those most in favour of the
idea of fighting fire with fire were often not the ones who would
have had to carry it out: it was the last refuge of the former
player who felt that today's cricketers didn't have as much
spunk in them as they used to in his day. Few active players
were ever keen on the idea. Rather ironically, after England
announced their party to tour the Caribbean in 1990, Ted
Dexter, now chairman of selectors and still pursuing his Campaign for Real England Fast Bowlers, predicted that they would
be going there to fight fire with fire. Nothing was farther from
the captain's mind.

By the time Gooch demonstrated one way to attack West
Indies, another was already well established. This pursued the
theory that if your fast bowlers could not outperform theirs,
your spin bowlers could. Given the right conditions, this could
produce sensational results, particularly for the spinner who
turned the ball away from the bat of the right-hander. In the
Caribbean, fast bowling so dominated the game that few batsmen there encountered high-quality spin during their formative
years and the game internationally had so neglected the art

since the early seventies that even when these batsmen ventured abroad their ability to play spin was rarely tested to the full. Everybody was so preoccupied with pace that few countries bothered to prepare pitches that would turn.

Things had started to change in November 1984, when a pair of New South Wales spinners, Bob Holland (leg-breaks and googlies) and Murray Bennett (slow left-arm), inflicted on West Indies their first defeat in a first-class match outside a Test for four years. The match was played at Sydney, on a pitch that responded to spin throughout, and Holland and Bennett took fifteen wickets between them in 77.3 overs. The only West Indies player to score more than 40 in either innings was Lloyd (64 not out and 47), who was the one player whose mature experiences went back to a time when the ball was as likely to rip around your feet as it was around your ears. The significance of this result, coming as it did just a week after the West Indies' pace battery had administered another hiding in the first Test match at Perth, was not lost on Australia, who played both Holland and Bennett in the fifth Test at Sydney six weeks later. Once again the pitch turned and once again West Indies succumbed. Once again Holland and Bennett took fifteen wickets and once again Lloyd, who was playing in his last Test match, coped better than any of his colleagues. Australia won by an innings and 55 runs, the first Test defeat in three years for West Indies, who had ignored the signs so badly – the Sydney pitch had been turning all season – that they went into the match without a spinner themselves.

After that, Australia could not wait to get West Indies back to Sydney. Whenever they did, they made sure they had spinners to hand and over the next few years they enjoyed several further successes. During the limited-overs World Series Cup competitions in 1986–7 and 1988–9 they won three of their six encounters there with West Indies and each time spinners played prominent roles: in the first and second wins, two more New South Welshmen, Greg Matthews and Peter Taylor; in the third, Taylor and Allan Border, who only rarely unfurled his gentle slow left-arm. Border was sufficiently encouraged by his performance to bring himself on at an early stage when the sides met a fortnight later in the Sydney Test of January 1989 and promptly took seven for 46 from 26 overs as West Indies collapsed to 224 all out on the first day. Border took a further four wickets in the second innings, enabling Australia to repeat their triumph at the ground of four years earlier, and although West Indies were better prepared this time – they had one specialist spinner in Roger Harper and two part-time practitioners in Hooper and Richards – they came in a poor second to Border, Taylor and Trevor Hohns, a leg-spinner. The three Australians took eighteen wickets for 370 from 157 overs; the three West Indians two for 262 from 122.3 overs.

The problem for Australia was that they had few other opportunities apart from Sydney to capitalize on their spin advantage. Most of their other home venues were more suited to pace than spin and since the square at Port of Spain had been relaid in 1980 they could not be sure of seeing the ball turn regularly anywhere in the Caribbean. Short of instructing their groundsmen to dig up the squares at Perth, Brisbane and Melbourne, where the West Indies fast men usually thrived, and prepare slow turners, there was little that could be done. They might even have been tempted to follow that course – despite their own predilection for pace – had it not been for the fact that their specialist spinners were neither of the highest class nor in the first flushes of youth. After Sydney 1985, Bennett quickly faded from the international scene and Holland, who was thirty-eight, played on for only two more years; after Sydney 1989, Hohns, who was thirty-five, had to have his arm twisted to play even one more full Australian season, while Taylor was unable to command a regular Test place. Matthews was far too much of an individualist for anyone to dare plan anything long-term around him. So Australia were forced to listen in silence while West Indies openly dismissed their Test defeats in Sydney as an irrelevance. It was impossible to argue, for they were right. At the time that each match took place, the West Indies were already three up and had the series won.

Others, having noted the events at Sydney in 1984–5 with interest, were to encounter similar problems. Pakistan, who possessed perhaps the best leg-spin bowler in the world in Abdul Qadir, had to wait twenty-one months for the chance to unleash him in a Test match against West Indies, at Faisalabad in October 1986, but it proved well worth the wait. His devastating spell of six wickets for 16 in 57 balls helped complete a rout – begun by Imran Khan – in which West Indies were dismissed for 53, their lowest-ever Test total, after they had been left 240 to win. During the remaining two Tests of the series and the one that followed eighteen months later in the Caribbean, Qadir made several other important contributions, most notably to the victory in Georgetown inspired by Imran's fast bowling. With both these series ending in one-all draws, Pakistan had high hopes of overall victory when the sides met again on their soil late in 1990 and pitches were allegedly tailored to their spinners. Unfortunately, by the time the Test series began, the bowlers on whom they had been banking – Qadir and Mushtaq Ahmed, a leg-spinner – had lost their edge and badly let them down. Pakistan, like Australia before them, were left with West Indies indifference ringing in their ears. 'One beautiful day,' Richards had said after the humiliation of Faisalabad, 'does not make a summer.'

India had to wait almost three years for their chance, but when it came they had home advantage and played three spinners throughout the series. It was not until the fourth and final match, though, on what *Wisden* described as a 'deplorably underprepared pitch' at Madras in January 1988, that they saw any return on the policy. There they introduced Narendra Hirwani, a leg-spinner of only nineteen years of age, for his first Test match and on a pitch that turned from the start he proceeded to expose West Indies' vulnerability to leg-spin to an even greater degree than Qadir or any of the Australians had done. He created such panic among the batsmen that they were heaving the bat wildly long before the end, which came with a day to spare after West Indies had been skittled out for only 184 and 160. Hirwani's sensational performance – he took sixteen wickets for 136 in just 203 deliveries – gave India an easy victory and a share of the series, and raised the possibility of them making a serious challenge in the Caribbean a year later.

Unfortunately, Hirwani was unable to repeat his triumph, taking only six wickets in the first three Tests before missing the fourth through injury, and it was not until Phil Tufnell (slow left-arm) captured six wickets in 33 balls at the Oval in August 1991 – Richards's last Test, in fact – that the West Indies batsmen were seen to panic again. Both Hirwani and Tufnell might have benefited from more sympathetic handling by their captains: Vengsarkar seemed unsure how to set Hirwani's fields in the Caribbean and Gooch was reluctant even to select Tufnell. Not only was the game waiting for a spin bowler good enough to topple the champions of the world, it was also searching for a captain with the skills to give one the chance.

The problem for West Indies as the game entered the nineties was that they had done nothing new for years. They had been bowling fast for years, intimidating opposing batsmen for years, scraping together sufficient runs for years, been mentally more resilient for years, been winning for years. Their cricket was based on a negative philosophy rather than a positive one: that of avoiding defeat. In the all-pace bowling attack, they believed they had discovered a strategy which would enable them to achieve their aim for years to come.

They pursued the policy with little imagination. Some of the bowlers they chose were poor imitations of the masters of the fast-bowling arts who had graced the team a decade earlier. Even Ambrose, the new leader of the pack and an indisputably fine bowler, did not display great variety or innovation. He stuck to a few basic principles with awesome single-mindedness and great success: he bowled beautifully straight and with a lot

of bounce, letting the ball fly around off the seam and forcing
batsmen to play the type of deliveries they would far rather
have left alone. He didn't actually swing the ball much but
because of his great height batsmen found it difficult to pick up
the length and line of the ball, just as they had against Garner.
When he first entered the game, Ambrose seemed to possess an
original weapon in his command of the devastating yorker (in
those days he loved to see the stumps cartwheeling out of the
ground) but he lost control of it and instead developed a pride
in his ability to keep the runs down, a strange thing for a fast
bowler to do. If someone took him on, he could be roused into
a ferocious bout of wicket-taking; but as long as he was not
proving expensive he could be inclined to let things drift.

And while West Indies continued to play the same way, other
things had changed. For one thing, pitches – especially those
outside the Caribbean – were favouring pace less than they used
to. This may have had something to do with the surfaces having
been covered for several years; or with teams trying to nullify
the advantage of opponents (West Indies in particular) who they
regarded as possessing stronger hands in fast bowling than
themselves; or with sponsors and television companies wanting
matches to go the distance; but whatever the cause, it was unde-
niably the case. For another, batsmen generally had become
more skilful at coping with the short-pitched ball. They had
had to, to survive. Collectively, their defences were sounder;
they felt better protected and less afraid; they thought twice
before venturing on to the front foot and knew what they were
doing on the back foot. As Richardson himself said, 'People
have been afraid of us, but now I don't think they are as afraid
as they used to be.' Another, slightly disturbing, development
was the diminishing enthusiasm among the Caribbean public
for a team that had possibly been triumphing for too long in
the same win-at-all-costs way.

Despite all these things, though, West Indies continued to survive, continued to avoid defeat. Even after Richards retired, they
remained as diamond-hard as ever. Richardson, his successor

as captain, was less of a zealot but fought for the same cause and was prepared to play by the same uncompromising rules (he, like Richards, refused to don a helmet, even after suffering a confidence-fracturing blow on the head by a ball from Danny Morrison in March 1987). Indeed, under Richardson, West Indies pulled off some of their most remarkable victories, victories which owed much to their resilience and their sheer bloody-minded refusal to be beaten. At Bridgetown in April 1992, South Africa began the final day of the inaugural Test match between the teams needing 79 runs to win with eight wickets in hand. Ambrose and Walsh took those eight remaining wickets that morning for just 26 runs. At Adelaide in January 1993, Australia, with their last pair at the wicket, needed two runs to take a winning 2–0 lead in the five-match series. Walsh then had McDermott caught behind to win the match for West Indies and four days later in Perth Ambrose decided the series with a spell of seven wickets in 32 balls. And at Port of Spain in April 1993, Pakistan, who had been widely tipped to end the Caribbean hegemony, began their three-match Test tour by dismissing West Indies for 127. Ambrose, Walsh and Bishop responded by dismissing Pakistan themselves for 140, Haynes batted almost eight hours in the second innings for 143, and West Indies won the match – and ultimately the series – comfortably. And if anyone stood in their path, they were just as likely as before to get rough with them: witness how determinedly Walsh ended Malcolm's stay at the crease in February 1994.

But we are getting ahead of ourselves. By then, other things had changed as well.

11

Revolution in the Air

I think I've given the impression that Thomson got us into all these difficulties. That would not be strictly accurate. We should really go back further than him. Much further back: back into the mists of antiquity, back almost one hundred and seventy years, to the late 1820s. Then, there were people warning us that this sort of situation would arise.

There was a revolution going on in the cricket world then. It was to do with the way the ball ought to be delivered. During the game's early evolution in the eighteenth century, the ball was always bowled underarm. Then along came a man called John Willes, who, in 1807, began a long and solitary campaign to be allowed to deliver the ball with a round-arm action (that is, with the arm coming as high, but no higher, than the horizontal). Willes was an unpopular figure with the establishment and was no-balled when he tried to use his method of bowling at Lord's in 1822. A few years later his cause was taken up by two other professionals, William Lillywhite and James Broadbridge, who raised the controversy to new heights when they bowled Sussex to two victories over All England in 1827 and provoked an amateur, G.T. Knight, to successfully use the method against them in a third match the same year.

A great debate ensued before the gentlemen of the Marylebone Cricket Club, the guardian of the laws, accepted that the new method should be legalized, although their reluctance was manifest from the fact that at first, in 1828, they agreed to allow the bowling arm to be raised only as high as the elbow. Seven years later, they were forced to accept in law what was already accepted in practice, that the arm could be raised as high as the shoulder. Twenty-seven years after that William Lillywhite's son, John, provoked the law to be rewritten for a final time to permit the bowler to deliver the ball overarm when he no-balled Edgar Willsher, the best bowler in the land, in one of the most important matches of the season, for raising his arm too high. Willsher left the field in protest and took the other eight professionals in his team with him, but James Lillywhite had actually done him and his cause a favour: Willsher played on at the highest level for another decade and captained an English side to the United States in 1868.

The point about all this is that those who had been cautious about what was described as the 'march of intellect' bowling were right. They were afraid of what the consequences would be and they were right to have been so. Without strict controls who knew what devilry the bowler might devise? Deliberately bounce the ball out of the reach of the batsman, denying him the opportunity to score runs? Deliberately aim the ball at the batsman's body? Bounce the ball at the batsman's body? One sceptic, John Nyren, a retired player, feared that 'the elegant and scientific game of cricket will degenerate into a mere exhibition of rough, coarse, horseplay'; another, William Denison, a journalist by profession, claimed that round-arm bowling 'must lead to a dangerous pace, such as cannot be faced on hard grounds, save at the most imminent peril'. Is not that exactly the situation that existed by the 1980s, with teams using the fastest bowlers available to them to stifle and batter opponents into submission, unchecked by the regulations save for a law on intimidation so laden with subjective judgement (Was the bowler trying to intimidate? Was the ball likely to inflict physical injury? Was the batsman skilful enough to cope with the bowling?) that umpires were unwilling to enforce it? The more bowlers of dangerous pace you possessed, the more successful you were. It had become as simple as that.

By the mid-eighties pretty much everyone except the West Indies – the team with more bowlers of dangerous pace than anyone else – had come to the conclusion that something had to be done; that it was time to give the laws the backbone they so obviously needed and introduce an effective and universal limit on the number of bouncers bowled similar to the one that had been brought in to avoid negative tactics in limited-overs matches. The English authorities had long been sympathetic to the idea and the Australians became impatient for action after suffering two heavy series defeats at the hands of West Indies in 1984 and 1985 (by 1986 they were ready to outlaw the bouncer altogether). In 1989 – only a few months after one of West Indies' most relentless bombardments, against Australia at Melbourne – the New Zealanders agreed to a draft proposal by the Test and County Cricket Board for a worldwide limit of one bouncer per over and although the plan was narrowly rejected by the International Cricket Council that year and again in 1990, by 1991 it had gained majority approval. The limit was introduced to Test cricket for a three-year experimental period. A short-pitched ball was defined as a delivery which passed the batsman at shoulder height. Infringements of the rule would be penalized by, first, a no-ball; second, a caution; and third, a ban from bowling for the remainder of the innings. It was not insignificant that this legislation was brought to fruition by Sir Colin Cowdrey, who had seen the game undergo dramatic changes during his playing career and who had experienced at first hand what it was like to fall for Roberts's sucker punch and what it was like to be battered by Lillee and Thomson.

The West Indians and the Pakistanis, who stood most to lose and who had voted against the motion, were furious. Their players were unconcerned if the games they took part in were utterly physical and utterly relentless and that you might not see a cover drive executed all day. So what? Wasim Akram claimed that the new rules had been brought in only to protect Graeme Hick, whom he must have been looking forward to terrorizing in England in 1992. Viv Richards, the West Indies captain, muttered about racism and hypocrisy, and kept on about people wanting to ruin 'our beautiful team'. 'I know damn well,' he would say, 'that there are people at the top of the cricketing establishment who feel that the West Indies have been doing too well for too long.' Clyde Walcott, the president of the West Indies board, spoke of 'a fundamental and unnecessary change in the way the game is played'. And, of course, the West Indies players were very happy with the way the game had been played up to that point. Not only had their bowlers been able to terrify the opposition all day long; their batsmen had known that retaliation would be minimal and most of the deliveries they received would land in their half of the pitch. When West Indies played their last Test match before the new regulation came into force, at the Oval in August 1991, they seemed so preoccupied with exercising their right to overdo the short-pitched ball that they allowed England to score their first total of over 400 against them for fifteen years and go on to win the match.

Ironically, within two years it was clear that the rule was proving unsatisfactory and that it would have to be revised when its trial period came to an end. There had been objections that it made bowling tactics predictable and allowed the batsman an undue advantage once he had received his one bouncer for the over. In July 1994 the ICC revised the law to permit two bouncers per over, regardless of who was on strike, but asked umpires to take into account the relative skill of the batsman. There was no question of going back to the situation that had existed before. The days of the attack comprising what Sir Colin described as 'four killers' were still intended to be well and truly over.

Some people, though, already thought it no longer mattered how many bouncers you bowled. One an over, two, three, four . . . so what? That's no longer the way to win matches. They were convinced that the Velvet Revolution had arrived, and not before time. *You want to bowl bouncers, you go ahead!*

There were two principal reasons for this. One was that they thought they'd finally found a leg-spinner the cricket world could believe in. Here was someone, they said, capable of destroying the world's best batting sides on a consistent basis, playing under a captain who had invested time in him and knew how to handle him. Someone to provide the game with the subtlety that had been so absent for twenty years. Funnily enough, he came from the south-eastern corner of Australia, sported a bleached mane and loved the great outdoors: he was another Nature Boy, just like Thomson. OK, so he hailed from the outskirts of Melbourne rather than the outskirts of Sydney, but you get the drift. He, too, was going to launch the game into a new era!

Shane Warne had a few other things in common with Thomson. When he started playing for Australia he was very raw and it took him time to settle. For a while, some people thought he wasn't going to make it. Like Thomson, he made his Test debut at the age of twenty-two and, like Thomson, he was a disaster. Warne's first call came for the Sydney Test match against India in December 1991. Sydney should have been a pretty good place to start, but the pitch had been refurbished – it would remain a turner but it was still bedding down – and Warne's luck was definitely out. He took one wicket in 45 overs, dropped a return catch off Shastri, who went on to add another 140 runs, and India amassed 483. Warne failed to take a wicket in the next Test at Adelaide and was dropped for the Test after that at Perth. But Border persisted with him and took him on a tour of Sri Lanka a few months later. There, in the opening Test in Colombo, he first showed signs of his match-winning potential when the home side collapsed in panic against himself and Greg Matthews when they had been within 54 runs of victory with eight wickets standing (Warne took the last three wickets in eleven balls without conceding a run). But that was only Sri Lanka.

It was not until a few months after that, in December 1992, that people really started to take notice. Warne helped win another Test match, this time at Melbourne and this time against West Indies. Chasing 359 to win, they were 143 for one shortly before lunch on the last day, and thinking in terms of victory rather than defeat, when Warne bowled Richardson with his flipper. The collapse that followed was as spectacular, in its way, as any that West Indies had experienced against leg-spin in the previous eight years: subsiding to 219 all out, only two of their last eight batsmen reached double-figures. Warne's final spell was seven wickets for 21 runs. By now, Warne had gained the confidence to really give the ball a rip, and was willing to deploy the full range of weapons in his armoury. Although he did little in the remaining Tests against West Indies and Richardson dismissed him as a threat ('I don't think our batsmen are afraid of him, he's not a worry'), during 1993 as a whole Warne took 72 Test wickets at 23.56 each and played large parts in defeating New Zealand at Christchurch, Hobart and Brisbane and England at Old Trafford, Lord's and Edgbaston. In all of these victories he took at least six wickets.

The revolution appeared to be well and truly underway. Other Test teams were also showing faith in leg-spin: Pakistan had Mushtaq Ahmed, England had Ian Salisbury and India Anil Kumble. All were even younger than Warne and all had overcome similar early scepticism about their credentials: it was said that they couldn't turn the ball, got disheartened easily, were overweight or simply unfit. Salisbury and Mushtaq (who again failed to deliver against West Indies when Pakistan toured the Caribbean in 1993) enjoyed mixed fortunes in their early careers but Kumble proved almost as destructive as Warne. In twelve Test matches between October 1992 and August 1993, he claimed 63 wickets at an average of 24. He contributed six-wicket hauls to wins over England in Calcutta, Madras and Bombay, over Zimbabwe in Delhi and over Sri Lanka in Colombo. Although it is true that these sides could hardly be ranked among the strongest teams in the world at the time, Kumble also embarrassed South Africa's batsmen and when he got his chance against West Indies, in the final of a limited-overs tournament at Calcutta in November 1993, he took it so well that in 37 balls he had claimed six wickets for 12 runs and won the match. Not only were Warne and Kumble match-winners, they could also keep the runs down: both of them were going for barely two runs an over. Not like the wild men: they'd concede half a dozen boundaries before they even found their length. These guys could keep you quivering and quiet!

People started wondering whether the previous twenty years hadn't been some sort of historical aberration; whether cricket's chroniclers wouldn't simply look back on the period as a reign of fast-bowling terror dividing two greats eras of spin. Spin! What a test of skill it presented. What a cultured and civilized art. Do you remember how Barry Richards once said in the seventies (before Packer, admittedly) that he had never been afraid of any fast bowler and that the greatest challenges he had faced had all been from spinners. The things Bishen Bedi could do to your mind! And didn't Viv Richards once say that he had been 'terrified' of Chandrasekhar when he had first come into Test cricket. Imagine him saying that of any fast bowler! And now here we had Kepler Wessels admitting that Warne presented a challenge every bit as mentally taxing as the world's fastest bowlers and Robin Smith begging to be allowed to face Ambrose in Antigua rather than Kumble in Calcutta.

That should finally bring the ideological walls tumbling down. You don't need to threaten to knock someone's head off to get them out, you know. Just show him your wrong 'un!

For the second reason as to why people started to think that it would no longer matter how many bouncers you bowled, it might be best if we sent you back to the crease. No, don't worry. It won't be like the last time. Promise.

This time it's not the early eighties, it is the here and now. A Test match against Pakistan at Trent Bridge. You're an older and wiser head now, one of the senior batsmen in the England team. You've been in the side over ten years and you've seen a few things in your time. You've not faced Pakistan in a Test match before though. Your captain wins the toss, the pitch is excellent for batting – so flat and true that it occurs to you that even West Indies would have a job to bowl you out on it – and you are sent out to create the platform for a big total. Don't want to see you until the lunch interval, that sort of thing. Your opening partner is Graham Gooch, who is, incredibly, still playing. He seems to have been around for ever, ever since the mid-seventies. The era of Lillee and Thomson and all that. The age of the dinosaurs.

Rather impressively, you and Gooch do the job. You bat through to lunch unbeaten. You even pick up runs quite quickly, for the score at the interval is 98 for no wicket. These are untold riches. It's not at all like when you bat against West Indies.

It is not all plain sailing, however. Waqar Younis and Wasim Akram, Pakistan's opening bowlers, have given you some uncomfortable moments. The most striking thing about them is that they're always trying something different. They're not content just to bowl fast, or ping the ball around your head: they try to swing the ball and are capable of doing so both ways. Fortunately, neither has been able to settle during the morning session, otherwise they might have been a real handful. Waqar, remarkably, began by bowling at his top pace. He seemed to have no need to loosen up at all, he just started bowling fast from the outset. And he is capable of a distinctly lively pace: he had not been playing Test cricket a year, and was reportedly still in his teens, when Martin Crowe, the New Zealand captain, said late in 1990 that Waqar was the fastest bowler he had ever faced. Mercifully, here he has struggled to find his line and several times strayed down the leg side, giving away either byes or easy runs when either you or Gooch could get a bat to the ball. His methods seem touchingly naive: he charges in to bowl and hurls himself through his delivery with all the gung-ho enthusiasm of a new boy in the nets, and it seems what he would really like to do is to bowl fast, swinging yorkers every ball. What he often ends up doing though is serving up half volleys and full tosses that do not swing very much at all. Many of these you and Gooch have despatched to the boundary with scarcely disguised glee. He has really been quite expensive. Even so, he has resorted to surprisingly few bouncers. It's amazing, he seems to regard them as a waste of time.

Wasim is different. For one thing he is a left-armer. He is also 6 foot 3 inches, three inches taller than Waqar, and is five years older. He began in the Pakistan team in 1985, early enough to see at first hand Imran bowling at something like his best. Wasim has potentially more variety than Waqar, as he demonstrated by going round the wicket as well as over, of swinging the ball in as well as moving it away, of pitching it up as well as dropping it short, but he seemed preoccupied with trying to bounce you and Gooch out and spent a lot of deliveries to no great effect. He is always doing this. In his second Test match he put Lance Cairns, the New Zealand tailender, into hospital for several days with blurred vision, and he has had several run-ins with umpires over his fondness for the short-pitched ball. It's fairly obvious he doesn't like it when things don't go his way because he got very upset when neither you nor Gooch fell for his bouncer trap, but he'll have to try harder than that because both of you have been around long enough, and played West Indies enough times, not to succumb to that old trick. Perhaps he is so fond of the bouncer because he spent so much time under Imran's wing.

When the pair of them take a breather, they are succeeded by two bowlers of similar style, Ata-ur-Rehman and Aamir Nasir. They are relatively inexperienced and not too difficult to handle but they are clearly being moulded along the same lines. They too, like Wasim and Waqar, are from Imran's part of Pakistan, the hardier northern reaches around Lahore. To think that the country took so long to produce a fast bowler worthy of the name!

So what's the difference? What's the difference between this means of attack and that so beloved of the West Indies? OK, so these guys are always looking for wickets, but one of them keeps over-pitching and giving away easy runs and the other overdoes the bouncer. Whatever you say about West Indies, at least they don't give runs away. So what's new?

Well, the difference comes after the lunch interval, in this case about half an hour into the afternoon session. The ball is about forty overs old and Wasim and Waqar have come back. It all happens very quickly, like a great wave washing over you. You have made sure you are up at the non-striker's end for Wasim's first over back – you have not been around all these years for nothing – so you are able to watch him start by going round the wicket to Gooch. He starts by drilling a series of short-pitched balls into his ribs; they're not full-blown bouncers but they're enough to get Gooch firmly on to the back foot. Then, with the final ball of the over, he brings his arm over much faster – it's a sort of round-arm action, funnily enough, much rounder than when he goes over the wicket – and delivers a ball of fuller length which screams back in from outside off stump, following the line of his arm, and takes Gooch, who is far too late with his bat, plumb on the back pad right in front of the stumps. Salim Yousuf is already tearing up to congratulate Wasim before the umpire has even raised his finger.

You don't know how you survive the next over from Waqar. It may be his first of the spell but he again starts by bowling at his top pace and this time the ball, which is polished on one side and rough on the other, is really starting to swing. Two or three times Waqar beats you all ends up. The first time you are trying to remain positive after the loss of Gooch's wicket and you look to drive what appears to be another of his over-pitched wannabe yorkers, but it dips and swings late and would undoubtedly have taken your middle stump had you not got half a bat and half a pad to it (the audible snick does not stop the wicketkeeper and all the close fielders going up for the earth-shattering shout). Another late inswinger, fortunately one that was this time going well down the leg side, crunches you a painful blow – sorry, forgot about that one – on the side of the foot, and the outswinger with which Waqar finishes the over practically turns you inside out. By now, the atmosphere has definitely changed.

Wasim immediately decides to go over the wicket to Ramprakash. He gets in close to the stumps and starts bowling him a series of big inswingers and keeps committing him to playing a shot. Then he goes wider and sends down a yorker that looks for most of its flight – from where you're standing – like it's heading for first slip, before it swerves in over its last few yards of travel to neatly pluck out the off-stump. Ramprakash, who did not move his feet one inch, has gone without scoring.

For the next few overs you and Smith hang on. Smith even plunders a few boundaries off Waqar's more wayward deliveries and feels confident enough to come down the pitch and tell you that he's liking the way the ball is coming on to his bat. You don't feel so sanguine, however, and your fears are soon justified when Smith thrusts his front leg down the pitch in an attempt to pad away a wide ball from Waqar only for it to swing later than he expects and take him on the back pad in front of off-stump. Hick is in next. He survives his first two balls and looks like he is going to survive his third before it nips back and takes his glove on its way through to the wicketkeeper. Hussain does not even last that long. His first ball is another fast inswinging yorker – Waqar has really got this delivery going by now – which spreadeagles his stumps. In the space of eight overs you have gone from 114 for no wicket to 138 for five: two wickets for Wasim, three in five balls for Waqar, and not a bouncer in sight.

This sort of collapse against this pair of bowlers is not in fact anything new, particularly when they are operating with the old ball, which they swing far more readily than the new one. They have been accused by more than one set of opponents of using illegal means to achieve this movement – fingernails, bottle-tops and nails have all been suggested as implements with which one side of the ball is roughened – and some have even confessed to having tampered with the ball themselves in an attempt to show that the practice is widespread within the game. But what many people forget – even those who testified in defence of Allan Lamb when Sarfraz Nawaz took him to court in 1993 for alleging in a newspaper article that Sarfraz had shown him how to tamper with the ball – is that the ability to swing an old ball is neither new nor the preserve of Pakistan cricketers. Do you not remember the likes of Procter, Lillee, Botham (in his early days), Marshall and Hadlee all being capable of swinging the old ball?

What is different about Wasim and Waqar is their ability to swing the ball late in its flight. Geoff Arnold, Surrey's coach when Waqar first arrived at Surrey in 1990, identified this as Waqar's special gift when he said that year: 'He has greater ability to swing the ball late, and at a faster pace, than anyone I've seen.' But even this was not a new technique; as long ago as 1977, Lillee was writing in his *Art of Fast Bowling* that, 'Tests have shown that a cricket ball will not swing when it is travelling above a certain critical velocity and this may be why some fast bowlers have the ability to swing the ball very late in its trajectory.' It just depends on the precise speed of your bowling and how full a length you bowl – and, let's face it, how many fast bowlers of the past twenty years have pitched the ball up enough to see it swing late? What Wasim and Waqar have done is to demonstrate that Hadlee was right: there is not much science in banging in the ball half way down the pitch.

It's still 138 for five and you're on strike. Wasim's bowling and you take the whole over from him. He's going round the wicket again now, trying to swing one into you late and beat you for pace in the way he did with Gooch; he's also varying his pace by adjusting the speed of his arm, which is often, in any case, so fast that it's difficult to pick up the ball's flight. You know he's doing it, but it's one thing knowing it and another coping with it. Luckily, he hasn't quite got his line right and although he beats your bat a couple of times it only happens outside off-stump. By the end of his next over, though, which you also take, you think you've started to work out a way of playing him. The way he ambles up it's easy to think that he's not very fast when in fact he is, so what you start to do is get yourself ready two seconds before he delivers the ball. This helps your timing, you play a couple confidently out of the middle of the bat, and when Wasim attempts to ruffle you by dropping one short you pull him with certainty through mid-wicket for four.

You start to feel more comfortable. You go down the pitch to offer some words of encouragement to Russell, who has still not stopped looking ashen-faced. For goodness's sake . . . anyone would think they were going to hurt you. They're not going to take your head off, you know. This is the nineties!

Russell manages to squirt one wide of the slips for a single. This leaves you the rest of the over to face Waqar. The trouble is, you've got into a rhythm watching Wasim's delivery arm and that's no use against Waqar: he gets his variety in a more surreptitious way still, through minor adjustments of his grip. His first ball is a big swinging yorker into the block-hole: you're late on to it and only just manage to keep it out. You actually trap the ball between the base of your bat and the ground. Waqar, thinking at first he had bowled you, has to cut short his celebrations and you are so relieved at your escape that you have still not settled properly when he starts to charge in for his next delivery. What's he going to try next? What's the last thing you'd expect him to do? A bouncer. That's what he'll bowl now. A bouncer. But it isn't. It's another yorker, only this time it swings even later and more extravagantly. In your urgency to get your legs out of the way and make room for your bat, you virtually swing off your feet: when the ball thumps you on the right shin your legs are indeed knocked from under you. As the ball rebounds into the stumps, you stumble, drop your bat and finish scrabbling on your hands in the popping crease.

Your first feeling, as you pick up your bat, dust yourself down and troop off for the pavilion, is one of humiliation. You've never before been made to look so stupid! No wonder people harbour dark suspicions about these guys: you want to do the same. But almost immediately you forget your hurt pride and marvel at what has just happened. You're so astonished, you're not as disappointed at being out as you normally would be. This is the finest bowling you've ever faced. More destructive than West Indies, more devastating than any new-fangled leg-spinner. This is the real revolution! You shake your head in disbelief: fifty minutes ago the score was 114 for no wicket, now it is 145 for six. And the pitch is still perfect! West Indies may be more relentless and more disciplined, but these Pakistanis are unquestionably more sophisticated. A touch more steel and they might soon be the ones no one else can beat. Put it this way, if Ambrose could bowl like this, he would!

As you reach the pavilion gate, you still can't believe it. Wasim and Waqar have beaten you, all of you, through the air. Gooch leg-before, Ramprakash bowled, Smith leg-before, Hick caught behind, Hussain bowled ... you bowled ... they scarcely need any help from their fielders and none at all from the pitch. The pitch they just by-pass altogether. They maroon you on the back foot. How ironic. Just when you all thought how good you were getting on the back foot...

Then, as you sit down in the corner of the dressing room, a thought strikes you. Maybe that's it, maybe that's where you're now going wrong.

Maybe it's time to start getting back on to the front foot again ...

Postscript

Tuesday 29 March, 1994. Late afternoon on the fourth day of the third Test match between West Indies and England at Port of Spain, Trinidad. A young England side, beaten in all-too-familiar fashion in the previous two matches, are strongly placed to claw their way back into the series after dominating a low-scoring match on a seaming pitch. They have experienced a couple of setbacks on this fourth day – rain took ninety minutes out of the early afternoon and dropped catches have made the victory target of 194 at least fifty more than it need have been – but they remain confident of winning.

With fifteen overs left in the day, the England players, under the leadership of Michael Atherton, resolve between innings to concentrate on not losing more than one wicket that evening and to go in pursuit of whatever runs remain the next day. They know that the West Indies fast bowlers, and Curtly Ambrose in particular, will be striving for a breakthrough, and they know the light is becoming murky.

As Atherton and Stewart go out to start the innings the atmosphere in the ground is subdued. The crowd is not large, and seems even smaller in such a big ground as the Queen's Park Oval, and the match situation gives the majority little to shout about.

England's plans, and the onlookers' moods, change in an instant. The first ball of the innings is like a hammer-blow to all their expectations. It is delivered by Ambrose, whom Richie Richardson has come to trust in such tight situations. Without the luxury of a loosener, Ambrose deals Atherton a jagging inswinger that catches him strokeless, arms spread in involuntary, inevitable supplication, as the ball hits the front pad: Atherton's prayers are beaten to the heavens by the umpire's finger as the West Indies players enter a Bacchic dance. The noise the small crowd makes is fantastic, uncanny.

Four balls later, Mark Ramprakash hestitates fatally on a second run and is run out by half the length of the pitch. Pandemonium once more. In Ambrose's next over – by now Ambrose is really flying – Smith is comprehensively bowled; his leg-stump smashed out of the ground. England are five for three and already a target that was reasonable minutes earlier appears virtually impossible.

The eleven members of the England team, and their retinue, are plunged into various states of shock. They are grappling to come to terms with what has happened, what *is* happening, but it is happening too quickly. All they can think of is trying to hold out until the end of play, which suddenly seems an unbelievably long way off, and of limiting the damage so that they can remount that push for victory in the morning. They make no attempt to regain the initiative, there does not seem time for that. Too much time, too little time. They are trapped.

For a while – for seventeen minutes, in fact – Stewart and Hick do succeed in holding on. Then Hick plays a timid stroke against Ambrose, is caught at the wicket, and the haemorrhaging begins. Stewart, Salisbury, Russell and Thorpe fall in quick succession, each swept away in the irresistible flow, each one's hopes more fragile than the last.

By the mercy of stumps England, a laughable distance from being one wicket down, are staggering, reeling, tottering, call it what you will, at 40 for eight.

Ambrose, as pumped up and focused as he has ever been, has bowled a relentless, probing line, moving the ball around from just outside off-stump at a pace challenging enough in itself. He has delivered 47 balls and claimed six of the eight wickets: one leg-before, three bowled, one caught behind and one caught in the arc of slips and gulleys.

He had stirred up wild scenes of excitement among the crowd, but they were nothing compared to the frenzy that had been generated out in the middle. Four days later Smith described to a newspaper reporter what he remembered of his six minutes at the eye of this storm: 'Everything was happening so quickly it was like a dream – or rather a nightmare. We just couldn't believe what was going on. We were caught up in a whirlwind.

'When I got out to the middle I was amazed at how fired up the West Indies were. All I could hear was Richie Richardson shouting, "We want five tonight." I have no excuses nor has anyone. I didn't think it was possible for a Test match to change course so completely so quickly. It was heart-breaking having been on top for three days to lose the game in an hour.'

Smith would tell also of what it was like in the England dressing room at the close of play: the stunned silence, the utter desolation. There must have been something eerie, too, about Atherton, whose first-ball dismissal triggered the collapse. While the mayhem progressed he was in the shower and seemed strangely detached from the disaster. Even from the sanctuary of the shower, though, he knew well enough what was going on outside from the roars of the crowd that washed over him. He will still remember it as the worst hour of his cricketing life.

West Indies claimed the remaining two wickets the next morning at a cost of six runs to clinch the series. Both were taken by Walsh, leaving Ambrose with a return of six for 24. England's total of 46 was their second-lowest of all time and occupied just 116 balls – the shortest Test innings of modern times. At least it gave Englishmen something more recent to wring their hands over than Old Trafford 1976.

The most remarkable thing, though, about Port of Spain 1994 was that the England team bounced back to win the following Test in Bridgetown, Barbados, where West Indies had not tasted defeat in a Test match for fifty-nine years.

They did it in style too, by a margin of 208 runs. Moreover, Stewart, who batted over 13 hours in the match and hit a century in each innings, and Atherton began by scoring 171 for the first wicket, thus making light of putting a total of 46 in the shade. England's batsmen scored heavily both in this match and the following one at Antigua and made Ambrose look mortal again.

To recover in such a manner from such a humiliation was testimony to the strength of England's resolve and Atherton's leadership. It was a feat few sides of the recent past could have accomplished. Perhaps they would not have managed it had Atherton not been in the shower.

Nineteen ninety-four was a vintage year for fast bowlers, even by the high standards of the previous twenty years. Ambrose's performance may have been the most remarkable by one of their kind, but it was far from statistically the best: on Saturday 20 August, Devon Malcolm, so often mishandled and misunderstood by England, took nine South African second-innings wickets for 57 runs in 99 balls on a fast, hard pitch at the Oval. It was the best return by an out-and-out fast bowler in the history of Test cricket.

It is ironic that Ambrose and Malcolm, bowlers of essentially old-fashioned virtues (one committed to working off a faultless line, the other to ferocious pace), should prosper, because the rise of the New Wave fast bowler continued unabated.

Wasim Akram and Waqar Younis, the leading exponents of this style, were instrumental in Pakistan winning Test series in New Zealand, in Sri Lanka and at home to Australia. In the seven matches in which they played, they took 89 wickets between them at an average cost of 19.10 runs and at an average rate of a wicket every 37 balls. Their imitators flourished too, most notably perhaps a young Yorkshire bowler, Darren Gough, who entered the England team and showed an early command of the fast, late-swinging yorker.

Malcolm's day of destruction was a classic fast bowler's tale. A normally placid fellow, he was fired up by a series of slights to his pride. The first was his recent treatment by England. He had been injured during the tour of West Indies, had flown home to undergo surgery and returned to the Caribbean eager to play in Barbados and Antigua. Both times he was overlooked. Then, during the English season, he struggled to retain a regular Test place and was stung to be named in the party for the Lord's Test against New Zealand, only to be sent away the day before the match started.

That was one thing. Another was what happened towards the end of South Africa's first innings at the Oval, when Atherton had been furious with him for the way he had bowled to Donald, their number eleven. Malcolm had already knocked out Jonty Rhodes earlier in the day. Atherton was so angry, he stormed off the field at the close on the first day and proceeded to have a set-to with Malcolm in the dressing room. According to Atherton, 'the air was blue between us on the Thursday night'.

Then, on the Saturday morning, as England's own first innings was coming to a close, Malcolm was hit himself, struck on the helmet just above the eyes by a deadly first-ball bouncer from Fanie de Villiers. The blow damaged the helmet sufficiently for it to need replacing and it was during this process that Malcolm issued his now famous threat: 'You guys are history. You're going to pay for this'.

They paid promptly. With his first ten balls of the innings, Malcolm removed both South Africa's openers and Hansie Cronje, one of their most accomplished batsmen. The evergreen Kepler Wessels, who was nursing a suspected broken finger, then led a rearguard action worthy of Ali Bacher's claim that he was the 'most fiercely determined cricketer I have ever met', but Malcolm returned with decisive spells either side of tea. The second accounted for the last four wickets of the innings and South Africa, who were all out for 175, readily conceded that his was the fastest bowling they had faced since their return to Test cricket.

Ambrose and Malcolm had further cause for satisfaction. They were among the few bowlers to create difficulties for Brian Lara, who emerged as a batsman of extraordinary gifts during the first six months of the year, when he broke the record for the highest individual scores at Test and first-class level. Malcolm's pace caused him discomfort in the Jamaica Test in February and Ambrose exposed his weakness to the short ball pitched on leg-stump during an enthralling duel in a county match at Northampton in June.

Here was proof once more – as if proof were needed – that no batsman, however brilliant, can ever feel safe against a top-class fast bowler.

Statistical Appendix

HOW THE FAST BOWLERS TOOK THEIR TEST WICKETS

Qualification: 50 wickets between 1 October 1974 and 10 March, 1995

Bowler	Country	Career	Tests	Wkts	RPW	RPO	BPW
Waqar Younis	Pak	1989/90–94/5	33	190	19.16	3.18	36.09
M.D. Marshall	WI	1978/9–91	81	376	20.94	2.68	46.76
I.R. Bishop	WI	1988/9–92/3	18	83	20.45	2.60	47.13
C.E.H. Croft	WI	1976/7–81/2	27	125	23.30	2.83	49.32
J. Garner	WI	1976/7–86/7	58	259	20.97	2.47	50.84
R.J. Hadlee	NZ	1972/3–90	86	431	22.29	2.63	50.85
M.A. Holding	WI	1975/6–86/7	60	249	23.68	2.79	50.92
B.P. Patterson	WI	1985/6–92/3	28	93	30.90	3.57	51.92
D.K. Lillee	Aus	1970/1–83/4	70	355	23.92	2.75	52.01
J.R. Thomson	Aus	1972/3–85	51	200	28.00	3.18	52.67
A.A. Donald	SA	1991/2–94/5	19	84	26.50	3.01	52.82
L.S. Pascoe	Aus	1977–81/2	14	64	26.06	2.94	53.17
R.G.D. Willis	Eng	1970/1–84	90	325	25.20	2.83	53.40
Imran Khan	Pak	1971–91/2	88	362	22.81	2.54	53.75
Wasim Akram	Pak	1984/5–94/5	61	261	23.20	2.58	53.78
C.E.L. Ambrose	WI	1987/8–94/5	50	224	21.08	2.33	54.19
A.M.E. Roberts	WI	1973/4–83/4	47	202	25.61	2.78	55.12
C.A. Walsh	WI	1984/5–94/5	70	255	24.77	2.62	56.68
C.J. McDermott	Aus	1984/5–94/5	65	270	28.50	3.00	56.98
M.G. Hughes	Aus	1985/6–93/4	53	212	28.38	2.93	57.94
G.R. Dilley	Eng	1979/80–89	41	138	29.76	3.00	59.36
G.F. Lawson	Aus	1980/1–89/90	46	180	30.56	2.96	61.76
R.M. Hogg	Aus	1978/9–84/5	38	123	28.47	2.75	62.05
D.E. Malcolm	Eng	1989–94/5	32	111	36.27	3.31	65.55
N.G. Cowans	Eng	1982/3–85	19	51	39.27	3.48	67.68
Sarfraz Nawaz	Pak	1968/9–83/4	55	177	32.75	2.49	78.81

RPW: runs per wicket; RPO: runs per over; BPW: balls per wicket

As every fast bowler worth his salt will tell you, his first duty is to take wickets, not save runs. Thus his strike-rate (balls per wicket) is the most important fact about him, not his runs per wicket (the conventional way of measuring a bowler's performance) or his runs per over. Waqar Younis takes his Test wickets at a rate of one every six overs, an outstanding and unrivalled record in modern times, but in striving for the unplayable ball he often gives away runs, which is why his 'economy rate' (runs per over) is unusually high. The above table also illustrates how destructive fast bowlers are when they hunt in packs: the top half is dominated by West Indians and Australians who played regularly together.

The other important requirement of a fast bowler is to win matches. Of the above bowlers, Marshall (25 times) most often contributed six or more wickets to a winning cause. He is most closely followed by Lillee (20), Hadlee (18), Waqar Younis (13), Holding, Wasim Akram and Imran Khan (12 each), and Willis (11). By contrast, Dilley, Hogg and Pascoe did so only once each.

HOW THE FAST BOWLERS SURVIVED IN TEST CRICKET

Qualification: 50 wickets between 1 October 1974 and 10 March, 1995

Bowler	Country	Career	Age	Wickets taken at age −24	24–28	28–32	32+
Waqar Younis	Pak	1989/90–94/5	17–22	190	–	–	–
Wasim Akram	Pak	1984/5–94/5	18–28	111	111	39	–
C.J. McDermott	Aus	1984/5–94/5	19–29	80	118	72	–
M.A. Holding	WI	1975/6–86/7	21–33	57	82	110	–
I.R. Bishop	WI	1988/9–92/3	21–25	30	–	–	–
D.K. Lillee	Aus	1970/1–83/4	21–34	51	120	91	93
N.G. Cowans	Eng	1982/3–85	21–24	49	2	–	–
M.D. Marshall	WI	1978/9–91	20–33	47	168	114	47
G.R. Dilley	Eng	1979/80–89	20–30	45	40	53	–
A.M.E. Roberts	WI	1973/4–83/4	23–32	35	99	39	29
C.A. Walsh	WI	1984/5–94/5	22–32	23	111	88	33
R.J. Hadlee	NZ	1972/3–90	21–39	20	87	72	252
Imran Khan	Pak	1971–91/2	18–39	19	99	114	130
C.E.H. Croft	WI	1976/7–81/2	23–28	16	88	21	–
G.F. Lawson	Aus	1980/1–89/90	22–32	15	130	34	1
R.G.D. Willis	Eng	1970/1–84	21–35	14	64	120	127
J.R. Thomson	Aus	1972/3–85	22–35	–	145	27	28
C.E.L. Ambrose	WI	1987/8–94/5	24–30	–	140	58	–
J. Garner	WI	1976/7–86/7	24–34	–	94	109	56
B.P. Patterson	WI	1985/6–92/3	24–31	–	59	34	–
D.E. Malcolm	Eng	1989–94/5	26–31	–	58	53	–
M.G. Hughes	Aus	1985/6–93/4	24–32	–	54	154	4
A.A. Donald	SA	1991/2–94/5	25–28	–	75	9	–
Sarfraz Nawaz	Pak	1968/9–83/4	20–35	–	43	80	54
R.M. Hogg	Aus	1978/9–84/5	27–33	–	41	52	30
L.S. Pascoe	Aus	1977–81/2	27–31	–	13	51	–

The career of a successful fast bowler is not long, certainly shorter than that of the top-class batsman, wicketkeeper or slow bowler. The quality of many of the above bowlers was recognized at an early stage – the average starting age of their Test careers is twenty-one – but only a few of them had turned in a match-winning performance (six or more wickets towards a victory) by the age of twenty-three. Most had ceased to be successful by the age of thirty-three (which is the average retirement age of those of the above who have finished their Test careers). Hadlee's astonishing haul of wickets beyond the age of thirty-two is tribute to his decision in his late twenties to cut down his pace. Lillee's record is all the more remarkable when one considers that he bowled an average of 263 balls per match – more than any of his rivals. Waqar Younis's accepted date of birth is 1971, although there is evidence to suggest that it actually took place two years earlier.

THE BATSMEN WHO SURVIVED BEST IN TESTS AGAINST WEST INDIES

Between 1 October 1974 and 10 March 1995 (excluding three matches vs Australia in 1978 and six vs India in 1978–9 in which West Indies were without their Packer players). Qualification: 10 innings

Bowler	Country	Career	Tests	Inns	NO	Runs	HS	Avge	100	50
G.S. Chappell	Aus	1975/6–81/2	12	23	5	1058	182*	58.77	4	5
Wasim Raja	Pak	1974/5–80/1	11	21	5	919	117*	57.43	2	7
G.R. Viswanath	Ind	1974/5–75/6	9	16	1	823	139	54.86	2	4
I.R. Redpath	Aus	1975/6	6	11	0	575	103	52.27	3	2
M.E. Waugh	Aus	1990/1–92/3	10	17	2	707	139*	47.13	2	4
Salim Malik	Pak	1986/7–90/1	7	13	3	456	102	45.60	1	3
M.D. Crowe	NZ	1984/5–86/7	7	13	1	544	188	45.33	3	1
B.M. Laird	Aus	1979/80–81/2	6	12	0	540	92	45.00	0	6
G.A. Gooch	Eng	1980–91	26	51	2	2197	154*	44.83	5	13
R.A. Smith	Eng	1988–93/4	15	27	4	1028	175	44.69	3	6
K.C. Wessels	Aus/SA	1983/4–91/2	8	15	0	670	173	44.66	1	6
S.M. Gavaskar	Ind	1974/5–83/4	17	31	2	1243	236*	42.86	5	3
D.C. Boon	Aus	1984/5–92/3	18	34	4	1285	149	42.83	3	7
A.J. Stewart	Eng	1989/90–93/4	10	19	2	716	143	42.11	2	2
G. Boycott	Eng	1980–80/1	9	18	2	663	104*	41.43	1	4
D.B. Vengsarkar	Ind	1975/6–88/9	19	31	2	1179	159	40.65	4	6

* not out

Greg Chappell scored 702 runs in 11 innings (five not out) during the 1975–6 series in Australia when West Indies' bowling attack was not as powerful as it later became.

Gavaskar's innings of 236 not out at Madras in December 1983 is the highest played against West Indies during this period. Gooch is the only batsman since 1979–80 to score 150 runs in a day against West Indies, when he made 153 in 315 minutes on the first day at Kingston in 1980–1.

The Batsmen Who Failed to Survive Against the Fast Bowlers

Batsmen retired or absent hurt in Tests between 1 October 1974 and 10 March 1995

Batsman	Injury	Bowler	Venue	Season
vs AUSTRALIA				
D. Lloyd (E)	abdomen	J.R. Thomson	Perth	1974–5
J.H. Edrich (E)	ribs	D.K. Lillee	Sydney	1974–5
A.I. Kallicharran (WI)	broken nose	D.K. Lillee	Perth	1975–6
B.D. Julien (WI)	broken thumb	J.R. Thomson	Sydney	1975–6
C.H. Lloyd (WI)	jaw	J.R. Thomson	Sydney	1975–6
M.A. Holding (WI)	face		Sydney	1975–6
S.M. Patil (I)	unconscious	L.S. Pascoe	Sydney	1980–1
N.S. Yadav (I)	broken toe	L.S. Pascoe	Melbourne	1980–1
R.A. Woolmer (E)	bruised arm	G.F. Lawson	Lord's	1981
P.J.L. Dujon (WI)	blurred vision	T.M. Alderman	Perth	1984–5
S.M. Gavaskar (I)	elbow	C.J. McDermott	Adelaide	1985–6
M.D. Crowe (NZ)	chin	B.A. Reid	Christchurch	1985–6
C.G. Greenidge (WI)	eye	T.M. Alderman	Melbourne	1988–9
D.L. Haynes (WI)	toe	C.J. McDermott	Kingston	1990–1
A.L. Logie (WI)	forehead	C.J. McDermott	Kingston	1990–1
D.L. Haynes (WI)	cheekbone	J. Angel	Perth	1992–3
A.J. Stewart (E)	finger	C.J. McDermott	Melbourne	1994–5
vs ENGLAND				
E.J. Chatfield (NZ)	fractured skull	P. Lever	Auckland	1974–5
D.B. Vengsarkar (I)	hand	R.G.D. Willis	Madras	1976–7
M.G. Burgess (NZ)	elbow	R.G.D. Willis	Christchurch	1977–8
Iqbal Qasim (P)	mouth	R.G.D. Willis	Edgbaston	1978
G.P. Howarth (NZ)	head	I.T. Botham	Trent Bridge	1978
W.M. Darling (A)	heart	R.G.D. Willis	Adelaide	1978–9
A.R. Border (A)	forehead	G.R. Dilley	Perth	1979–80
D.B. Vengsarkar (I)	head	R.G.D. Willis	Madras	1981–2
J. Dyson (A)	shoulder	R.G.D. Willis	Brisbane	1982–3
B.A. Edgar (NZ)	hip	I.T. Botham	Headingley	1983
C.G. Greenidge (WI)	forehead	I.T. Botham	Kingston	1985–6
D.L. Haynes (WI)	finger	C.C. Lewis	Bridgetown	1993–4
J.N. Rhodes (SA)	unconscious	D.E. Malcolm	Oval	1994
vs INDIA				
R.W. Tolchard (E)	hand	M. Amarnath	Madras	1976–7
W.M. Darling (A)	head	Kapil Dev	Bombay	1979–80
M.W. Pringle (SA)	fractured eye socket	J. Srinath	Johannesburg	1991–2
vs NEW ZEALAND				
B.C. Rose (E)	bruised arm		Wellington	1977–8
G. Miller (E)	face	R.O. Collinge	Christchurch	1977–8
Mudassar Nazar (P)			Christchurch	1978–9
S.M.H. Kirmani (I)	jaw	R.J. Hadlee	Christchurch	1980–1

C.J. Tavaré (E)	mouth	R.J. Hadlee	Oval	1983
S. Wettimuny (SL)	groin	R.J. Hadlee	Colombo	1983–4
R.S. Madugalle (SL)	head	R.J. Hadlee	Colombo	1983–4
B.N. French (NZ)	head	R.J. Hadlee	Lord's	1986
N.S. Sidhu (I)	wrist	D.K. Morrison	Christchurch	1989–90

vs PAKISTAN

M. Amarnath (I)	face	Imran Khan	Lahore	1978–9
S.F.A. Bacchus (WI)	shoulder		Faisalabad	1980–1
D.B. Vengsarkar (I)	arm	Sarfraz Nawaz	Karachi	1982–3
R.W. Marsh (A)	fractured cheek	Azeem Hafeez	Adelaide	1983–4
J.F. Reid (NZ)	chin	Azeem Hafeez	Auckland	1984–5
B.L. Cairns (NZ)	fractured skull	Wasim Akram	Dunedin	1984–5
R.L. Dias (SL)	wrist	Mohsin Kamal	Sialkot	1985–6
P.A. Horne (NZ)	head	Waqar Younis	Faisalabad	1990–1
P.A. Emery (A)	bruised thumb	Mohsin Kamal	Lahore	1994–5

vs SOUTH AFRICA

| D. Gough (E) | bruised arm | A.A. Donald | Lord's | 1994 |

vs SRI LANKA

| J.G. Wright (NZ) | fractured nose | R.J. Ratnayake | Wellington | 1982–3 |
| C. Sharma (I) | | | Kandy | 1985–6 |

vs WEST INDIES

G.R. Viswanath (I)	broken finger	M.A. Holding	Kingston	1975–6
A.D. Gaekwad (I)	head	M.A. Holding	Kingston	1975–6
B.P. Patel (I)	mouth	V.A. Holder	Kingston	1975–6
C.M. Old (E)	wrist	A.M.E. Roberts	Trent Bridge	1976
B. Wood (E)	hand	A.M.E. Roberts	Lord's	1976
Sadiq Mohammad (P)	forearm	C.E.H. Croft	Port of Spain	1976–7
Sadiq Mohammad (P)	jaw	A.M.E. Roberts	Georgetown	1976–7
Wasim Bari (P)	face	C.E.H. Croft	Kingston	1976–7
P.M. Toohey (A)	face	A.M.E. Roberts	Port of Spain	1977–8
P.M. Toohey (A)	broken thumb	A.M.E. Roberts	Port of Spain	1977–8
C.P.S. Chauhan (I)	forearm	S.T. Clarke	Bombay	1978–9
B.A. Edgar (NZ)	elbow		Christchurch	1979–80
G. Boycott (E)	forehead	C.E.H. Croft	Oval	1980
Abdul Qadir (P)	shoulder	C.E.H. Croft	Lahore	1980–1
Taslim Arif (P)	broken finger	S.T. Clarke	Lahore	1980–1
Zaheer Abbas (P)	forehead	C.E.H. Croft	Karachi	1980–1
R.W. Marsh (A)	head	C.E.H. Croft	Adelaide	1981–2
Yashpal Sharma (I)	head	M.D. Marshall	Port of Spain	1982–3
M.B. Amarnath (I)	face	M.D. Marshall	Bridgetown	1982–3
G.M. Wood (A)	broken finger	J. Garner	Bridgetown	1983–4
S.B. Smith (A)	broken finger	J. Garner	Kingston	1983–4
T.A. Lloyd (E)	head	M.D. Marshall	Edgbaston	1984
V.P. Terry (E)	broken arm	W.W. Davis	Old Trafford	1984
G. Fowler (E)	forearm	M.D. Marshall	Oval	1984
T.M. Alderman (A)	bruised ribs		Brisbane	1984–5
K.C. Wessels (A)	forearm	C.A. Walsh	Adelaide	1984–5
G.M. Ritchie (A)	face	C.A. Walsh	Sydney	1984–5
I.D.S. Smith (NZ)	bruised forearm	M.D. Marshall	Bridgetown	1984–5
J.V. Coney (NZ)	broken arm	J. Garner	Kingston	1984–5
Salim Malik (P)	broken arm	C.A. Walsh	Faisalabad	1986–7
Qasim Omar (P)	face	C.A. Walsh	Lahore	1986–7

S.V. Manjrekar (I)	forehead	W.K.M. Benjamin	New Delhi	1987–8
D.B. Vengsarkar (I)	broken finger	W.W. Davis	Calcutta	1987–8
Salim Yousuf (P)	broken nose	M.D. Marshall	Bridgetown	1987–8
G.F. Lawson (A)	fractured jaw	C.E.L. Ambrose	Perth	1988–9
Arun Lal (I)	head	I.R. Bishop	Port of Spain	1988–9
N.S. Sidhu (I)	wrist	M.D. Marshall	Kingston	1988–9
G.A. Gooch (E)	broken finger	E.A. Moseley	Port of Spain	1989–90
R.A. Smith (E)	broken finger	C.A. Walsh	Antigua	1989–90
D.C. Boon (A)	forearm	C.E.L. Ambrose	Adelaide	1992–3
M. Prabhakar (I)	broken nose	C.A. Walsh	Chandigarh	1994–5

Marshall, with seven, caused more of these injuries than any other bowler. He is followed by Willis, Croft and Walsh, with six each, and Hadlee and Roberts, on five apiece.

Sources

Most of the cricket books and periodicals, plus many news-papers, published since 1974 have been of use in researching this book. The most valuable are listed below. I would also particularly like to thank Mike Brearley, Sir Colin Cowdrey, Mike Gatting, Alan Knott, Andy Lloyd, Micky Stewart, John Snow and Bob Willis for their assistance. Several quotations from Imran Khan were taken from a talk he gave at the National Theatre, London, on 8 November 1993.

BOOKS
Geoffrey Boycott, *Put to the Test* (1979); *In the Fast Lane* (1981)
Mike Brearley, *Phoenix From the Ashes* (1981); *The Art of Captaincy* (1985)
Greg Chappell, *Greg Chappell* (1986)
John Crace, *Wasim and Waqar: Imran's Inheritors* (1992)
Tony Francis, *The Zen of Cricket* (1992)
David Frith, *Thommo* (1980)
Mike Gatting, *Leading From the Front* (1988)
Graham Gooch, *Testing Times* (1991); *A Test of Fire* (1990)
David Gower, *A Right Ambition* (1986)
David Gower with Martin Johnson, *Gower: The Autobiography* (1992)
Richard Hadlee, *Rhythm and Swing* (1990)
Graeme Hick, *My Early Life* (1991)
Imran Khan, *All Round View* (1988)
Dennis Lillee, *Over and Out* (1984)
Craig McDermott, *Strike Bowler* (1992)
Trevor McDonald, *Clive Lloyd* (1985)
Malcolm Marshall, *Marshall Arts* (1987)
Patrick Murphy, *Declarations* (1992)
Pat Pocock, *Percy* (1987)
Viv Richards, *Cricket Master Class* (1988); *Hitting Across the Line* (1992)
Peter Roebuck, *Slices of Cricket* (1982)
Peter Roebuck and Ian Botham, *It Sort of Clicks* (1985)
Robin Smith and John Crace, *Quest for Number One* (1993)
Rob Steen, *Desmond Haynes: Lion of Barbados* (1993)

Index